D1562916

CORPORATE CAPITAL

Carol E. Hoffecker

CORPORATE
CAPITAL

Wilmington in the
Twentieth Century

Temple University Press   Philadelphia

Temple University Press, Philadelphia 19122
© 1983 by Temple University. All rights reserved
Published 1983
Printed in the United States of America

Library of Congress Cataloging in Publication Data

Hoffecker, Carol E.
Corporate capital.
Includes index.
1. Wilmington (Del.)—Politics and government.
2. Wilmington (Del.)—Economic conditions.   3. Wilmington
(Del.)—Social conditions.   4. Business and politics—
Delaware—Wilmington—History—20th century.   5. E.I.
du Pont de Nemours & Company.   I. Title.
JS1545.2.H63   1983   975.1′2   83-572
ISBN 0-87722-305-X

CONTENTS

Acknowledgments   vii

Introduction   3

CHAPTER 1
The Big Change Begins: 1912   11

CHAPTER 2
The Magic City: 1914–1932   60

CHAPTER 3
Mourning for an Old American City: 1933–1959   106

CHAPTER 4
When We Needed Unity the Most: 1960–1968   158

CHAPTER 5
Community in Conflict: 1969–1980   206

Appendix   263

Notes   267

Index   287

ACKNOWLEDGMENTS

To try to make sense of the history of modern Wilmington and to present my findings in a book that will communicate that sense to others has been both a personal and a collaborative effort. Many individuals and a few institutions have assisted me, as I worked to understand the city's history. I am particularly grateful to the University of Delaware and to Helen Gouldner, Dean of Arts and Sciences, for the sabbatical and financial support to complete my research. An invaluable grant from the National Endowment for the Humanities permitted me to devote an entire year to the project. It also provided for a research assistant. I was very fortunate to have the help of Scott Heberling, then a graduate student in history at the University of Delaware, who produced thoughtful, meticulous work of the highest quality. In addition, I am indebted to the Eleutherian Mills–Hagley Foundation for giving me office space in their excellent library during that year of intense work. The combination of these institutional benefactions eliminated distractions and difficulties that might have slowed the completion of the book by years.

A great many people helped me answer research questions. Like most historians, I often required the assistance of librarians. Since I did most of the research at the Eleutherian Mills Historical Library in Greenville, Delaware, I owe the greatest debts to Richmond D. Williams, Director of the EMHL and to his staff, particularly Betty-Bright Low and Daniel Muir, both of whom went out of their way to find relevant manuscripts and photographs. Barbara E. Benson, Director of Library, Historical Society of Delaware, likewise alerted me to items in her institution's collections that might otherwise have escaped my notice. I also received consistently friendly, professional help from various staff members of the University of Delaware's Morris Library and from Joann Mattern, Archives Branch Supervisor, State of Delaware, Division of Historical and Cultural Affairs in Dover.

Not all evidence of recent history is to be found in libraries, however. Much of it is still in the private hands and heads of those who have lived it.

One such person who was exceedingly helpful to me was Pearl Herlihy Daniels, who, in addition to supplying me with recollections gleaned from her extensive participation in the civic life of Wilmington, also made available to me her comprehensive manuscript and newspaper clipping files relating to several of the most important episodes in the city's recent history. This book would be poorer by far without the information that I gained by going through her carefully organized materials. The list of other people who agreed to be interviewed about their roles in Wilmington's history and welcomed me into their homes or offices includes former mayors and other public officials, civic group leaders, real-estate developers, and planners. Their names are listed in the bibliography and appear frequently in the notes, but their contributions to this book were so important that they deserve individual recognition here as well. In alphabetical order they are: John E. Babiarz, James Baker, Blair Both, the Rev. Mr. Lloyd Casson, Stephen Clark, William and Louise Conner, Muriel Crosby, Pearl Herlihy Daniels, Oliver Deehan, Donn Devine, Martha V. du Pont, Irénée du Pont, Jr., Dudley Finch, Arnold Goldsborough, Richard Haber, Harry Haskell, Peter A. Larson, Thomas F. Luce, Thomas Maloney, William Miller, Richard V. Pryor, Louis L. Redding, Philip G. Rhoads, Allan Rusten, Richard P. Sanger, Patricia Schramm, B. Gary Scott, H. Rodney Sharp, Jr., James H. Sills, Jr., Francis X. Tannian, John Webster, Jr., Leon N. Weiner, and James D. Wilson.

The preparation of this book depended on the abilities and expertise of many people. Notable among these were several typists, Debra Bowers, Betty Sherman, and Wanda Cook, and cartographer Marley Amstutz, whose clear, complex maps will surely contribute to readers' comprehension. Critics and editors who have helped me include Barbara E. Benson, who read the manuscript at every stage and provided wise counsel, and my colleague Raymond Wolters, who read the manuscript and gave me useful suggestions based on his own extensive research into race relations in Wilmington.

CORPORATE CAPITAL

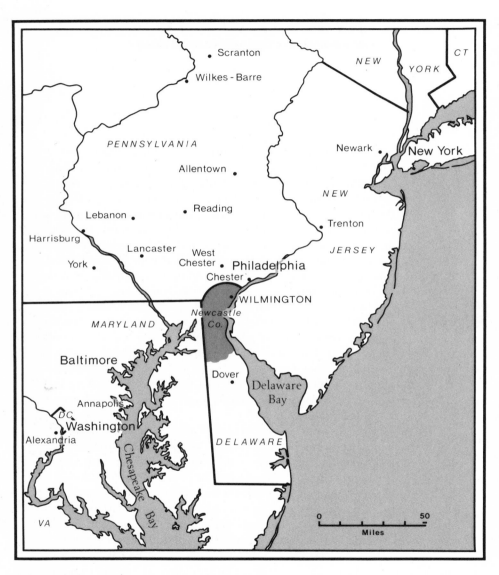

New Castle County and its principal city, Wilmington, in relation to other cities of the Middle Atlantic Region. *(Map by Marley Amstutz, Cartographer)*

INTRODUCTION

In 1900 Wilmington, Delaware, was an industrial city not unlike the other medium-sized cities of the Delaware River Valley: Trenton and Camden, New Jersey, and Chester, Pennsylvania. These cities, together with their much larger neighbor, Philadelphia, had grown to maturity as manufacturing centers during the previous century. Their most important industries were the founding and fabricating of iron and steel into boilers, industrial machinery, and ships. Subsidiary industries included tanning and textiles. The great river and the railroads were the arteries that bound the industrial cities to sources of raw material and to their customers, most of whom were either other manufacturers or transportation companies. "Trenton Makes—The World Takes," "What Chester Makes Makes Chester," the densely packed brick industrial cities proudly proclaimed to patrons traveling along the Pennsylvania Railroad's East Coast corridor line connecting New York, Philadelphia, Baltimore, and Washington. The development of an economy based on heavy industry in these Delaware Valley cities had produced an intensely blue-collar society that in 1900 was attracting immigrants from Europe, as later it was to bring black migrants from the rural Southeastern United States.

The fates of the four mid-sized Delaware Valley cities in the twentieth century have much in common. In every case heavy industrial production, after brief peak times during the two world wars, has declined almost to extinction. The hardest hit cities have been Chester and Camden. Both are so close to Philadelphia that their former hinterlands have become bedroom suburbs for the big city, leaving Chester and Camden with impoverished tax bases, high unemployment, and large populations of poorly skilled black residents whose fathers came north in flusher times in search of work in nearby port facilities and factories. Trenton and Wilmington, somewhat larger, further removed from Philadelphia, and more economically diversified have been less affected by these trends. The healthiest cities in the Philadelphia region are those most remote from the big city and the big river. Lancaster, Reading, and Allentown, located far inland from the tidal Delaware, continue to prosper with diverse industries, many of which require skilled workers. None of the inland cities has been stricken to the same degree by the cycle of urban decline that has nearly prostrated their sister communities in the Delaware River Valley.[1]

Wilmington, then, belongs to the middle group among the cities in its region with respect to its modern development and present prospects. That Wilmington has not succumbed so completely to the decay that has overtaken its upstream neighbor, Chester, is, however, due less to factors of location and size than to the chemical industries that make their home in northern Delaware, most particularly E. I. du Pont de Nemours & Company, the largest chemical producer in the United States. The juxtaposition of this multibillion-dollar, highly technical industry with the old industrial city in which its home offices and experimental laboratories are located has made Wilmington's history in the present century something of a paradigm for a more general transformation in American life. In the late nineteenth century, cities and their economies were characterized by locally owned, moderate-sized factories located in urban settings surrounded by the densely packed neighborhoods that housed their poorly educated, semiskilled workforce, which included many newcomers to America. The twentieth century has replaced this old society with one whose central characteristics include technically oriented big-business enterprises that employ highly educated workers who live in the suburbs of a city that, beyond its big business core, has become the last refuge for the poor, the old, the racial minorities. Among the mid-sized cities in the Philadelphia region, Wilmington has undergone this transformation most completely. It has lost the most population within its corporate limits and gained the largest suburban population relative to its total metropolitan size. This book is about how that change came about and what it has meant for the community as a whole.

The Du Pont Company had its beginnings in 1802 as a waterpowered black powder manufactory near Wilmington on the Brandywine River, a tributary of the Delaware, but Du Pont did not become the dominant influence on Wilmington's economy until one hundred years later, when the company undertook the aggressive growth strategy that made it a leader in American big business. In 1906 the company began construction of a large office building in downtown Wilmington that signaled the beginning of a new economic foundation for the community. Under the influence of Pierre S. du Pont, the Du Pont Company was among the first enterprises in America to rationalize fully its corporate organization under professional managers. According to the eminent business historian Alfred D. Chandler, by 1910 the Du Pont Company was already "employing nearly all the basic methods that are currently used in managing big business."[2] The decision of the leaders of this enterprise to retain its corporate offices in Wilmington rather than follow other large companies to New York City is the key to Wilmington's subsequent development. Not only did the Du Pont Company, and the other chemical companies that it spawned, bring new kinds of residents to the city—middle- and upper-income managers, scientists, and technicians—but the du Pont family, enriched by the almost incomparable success of their investment, became very influential with regard to the rest of the community.

One important aspect of the change that big business brought to Wilmington, then, was the emergence of a powerful elite, and this is one area where Wilmington differs from most American cities. Sociological literature includes many studies analyzing the importance of power structures in twentieth-century American cities. The first, and most famous, are *Middletown* and *Middletown in Transition*, the two books in which Robert S. and Helen M. Lynd dissected society in Muncie, Indiana, during the 1920s and 1930s. In the latter work, the Lynds devoted a chapter to the "X family"—actually the Balls—who were not only the dominant economic force in Middletown but also the major supporters of the city's newspaper, schools, hospitals, and the other cultural and philanthropic institutions. Like the du Ponts, the X family were economic dominants who elected to remain in the small city that had provided their wealth. Thus, they controlled not only the town's economy but its values as well. The Lynds commented on the unusualness of this situation, writing that "one can classify American small manufacuring cities into two groups: those in which the industrial pioneers or their sons still dominate the local business scene, and those in which 'new blood' has taken over the leadership; it is likely that a census would show today a numerical predominance of the second group among cities containing major industries. Middletown is, therefore, probably a minority city in this respect."[3] So is Wilmington.

In making this distinction between city power structures, the Lynds reflected a view that is shared by other sociologists, who have found that most industrial elite families no longer live in the minor cities where their industries are located. Especially since World War II, the more common phenomenon among small cities is an economy that depends upon a facility owned and managed by a large firm that maintains its headquarters in a distant metropolis. An example of such a place is Cibola—actually Ypsilanti—Michigan, which was the subject of an important study by Robert O. Schulze in the late 1950s. Schulze discovered that when Ypsilanti's economy shifted from one of small, locally owned and managed factory units to one dominated by a large, out-of-town firm, the city's power structure was dramatically altered. In the old days of local industry or "local capitalism," the power elite, like that in Middletown and Wilmington, was indigenous, and economic power and political power were exercised by the same industrial leaders. Under the changed conditions, however, the economic leaders who constituted the new elite were imported plant managers who reported to higher-ups elsewhere. These managers were reluctant to become involved in local politics. The community thus lost control over its own economy. Yet, even though the big out-of-town-led industries that now dominate Ypsilanti wield great potential power over the city, they do not exercise it, because "the local community has grown ever less important to the survival and prosperity of its dominant economic units."[4]

This altered relationship between business organizations and the communities they inhabit is one of the principal signs of what social scientists perceive as the shift from industrial society to advanced industrial society. But while the power structure that Schulze found in Ypsilanti may be a common one among smaller communities that are host to an element of a larger decentralized corporation, researchers have found different patterns of development in other kinds of cities. Floyd Hunter's classic study, *Community Power Structure*, based upon interviews conducted among residents of Atlanta, Georgia, in the early 1950s, indicated that the economic leaders of that large regional commercial city continued to exercise influence commensurate with their financial power, because they had a very significant stake in the community as a whole. Time and again Hunter's interviewees told him that the top executives and financial owners were the real movers and shakers in Atlanta and that smaller businessmen and lower-ranking executives, no matter how impressive their formal roles in civic organizations, were merely the messenger boys for the top men.[5]

A decade later Robert A. Dahl addressed the same question in his study of New Haven, Connecticut, appropriately titled *Who Governs?* Dahl's conclusions were very different from those of Hunter. He found that descendants of the old patrician families who had once controlled New Haven no longer had significant power. Instead, power was now diffused among a variety of groups, including industrial and commercial leaders and local politicians representing ethnic constituencies. The involvement and influence of any particular group depended largely on the nature of the public question at hand—that is, those who would be most affected took the greatest interest and wielded the greatest power. It was this shift from a single to a plural power structure that permitted the rise of Richard Lee, the dynamic mayor of New Haven, who was so spectacularly successful in controlling the city's urban renewal and redevelopment in the 1960s. Lee should not be perceived as being at the top of a pyramid, Dahl argued, but rather "at the center of intersecting circles," the broker whose ties to all the various groups were the source of his ability to get them to work together.[6]

The most recent study of the changing locus of community power is that of J. Rogers and Ellen J. Hollingsworth, who, in *Dimensions in Urban History*, have attempted to define a model of community history. In their view the typical American city began as a one-industry town in which a small elite exercised power over a large, unskilled work force. As the community grew, its middle class expanded and its economy diversified. By the late twentieth century, the cities that underwent this transformation have developed a broad power base of middle-income residents who demand that their local government be professionally administered to supply amenities as well as strictly utilitarian services.[7] Major theoretical hypotheses concerning community power have also been defined by sociologist Terry N. Clark, who writes that the larger a community is and the greater the variety of potentially powerful groups it contains, the less likely it is to develop a single power elite group such as Hunter found in Atlanta or the Lynds in Middletown. Likewise, "an economically diversified community is less likely to have economic actors important in politics than is a company town."[8]

This brief review of the best-known historical-sociological studies of community power demonstrates the anomaly of Wilmington's position. Unlike Ypsilanti, Wilmington's big business leadership is indigenous, yet the Delaware city is neither so large nor so economically diversified as Atlanta, with its strong local elite and commercial base, or New Haven, with its many power centers. Of them all, Wilmington resembles the Lynds' Middletown most closely, and if the Lynds found Muncie to be unusual in the 1930s because the X family retained their power base in their old home town through the second generation, how much more is this true of Wilmington, where the du Ponts have been involved in the community since 1802. But there is an important difference between Wilmington and Muncie, because in the latter the X family derived their wealth and power from a local jar factory that has made the city a light industrial, working-class town. Wilmington, however, is not primarily the site for Du Pont Company manufacturing, although the company does have three nearby plants, but is mainly an administrative and research center. If one were to apply the Hollingsworths' model, therefore, Wilmington would appear as something very strange indeed: a middle- to upper-income community of highly educated people with monolithic economic and elite structure. To make matters even more confusing, Wilmington's present socioeconomic form has been grafted onto a community that was once devoted to heavy industry. A strange set of circumstances indeed, that is not covered by existing models of urban development.

One can speculate that without the intervention of the du Ponts and the subsequent growth of the chemical industry, Wilmington today would be nothing more than a decayed husk of its former industrial self. In the years after 1906, the influence of the du Ponts on the city became virtually all-important. Wilmington quickly changed from being a manufacturing city with diversified, if rather ineffectual, leadership and equally matched political parties to a city identified with a single industry, ruled by one family and one political party. The du Ponts used their great influence to benefit the community, but only in the ways that they selected. The Du Pont Company's personnel needs reshaped the city's residential patterns and precipitated suburbanization, and the philanthropy of individual du Ponts built schools and highways and created an impressive new civic center for the city during the 1920s. These positive actions stopped short, however, of encouraging other needed reforms, such as charter reform— which was needed to energize a very weak city government—and housing reform in a city that still retained many inadequate structures from its industrial past. The du Ponts also took over control of the Delaware Republican party, which ruled state and city politics until the 1950s. Through the party the local elite controlled the branch of government most essential to them, the State Highway Department, and professionalized the other major branch of state government, public education. Even the Great Depression and the New Deal did not seriously disturb the power of the local elite; in fact, federal programs adopted the elite's own priorities. Change in the power structure came only after World War II, when a new generation of family members and company leaders proved less willing than their predecessors to take a commanding lead in civic affairs.

World War II was a turning point in other ways as well. The wartime revival of old heavy industries attracted newcomers to the area, including blacks who were relegated to the oldest, most deteriorated parts of the city. But the long-term winners in the wartime and postwar economy were the chemical companies, particularly Du Pont, which brought highly trained technical and managerial personnel to the Wilmington area in great numbers. The trickle of middle- and upper-income suburbanization during the 1920s and 1930s became a torrent after the war as these middle-income newcomers settled in the area, and the city quickly slid into serious decay. Neither the city, with its problems of decline, nor New Castle County, with its problems brought by rapid growth, possessed governmental structures or political leaders capable of dealing with these situations. Suburbanization took place in a virtual governmental power vacuum. The governmental organizations that shaped suburban development were the State Highway Department and the public school districts, both institutions that had been created by du Pont family civic action a generation before. Meanwhile, an absence of coordinated planning in the city during the 1950s produced a series of unfortunate decisions in the areas of urban renewal and the location of Wilmington's section of the interstate highway I-95. While some members of the local elite did participate in these decisions, their role was a restricted one. The Du Pont Company, which had always attempted to remain aloof from community affairs, was particularly so during these crucial years. There was no one in the du Pont family to come forward as a community leader, and an earlier generation of du Ponts had so structured government and politics as to discourage other citizens from gaining much power over events. It was not until the late 1950s that the Democratic party became strong enough to challenge the long-entrenched Republicans and restore competition to Wilmington's politics.

The failure to direct the federal bulldozer in the 1950s exacerbated the problems brought on by the continued migration of rural black people into an urban economy that had little to offer them. By 1960 Wilmington was a city in deep trouble in spite of the health of its chemical industry. Shocked by what they saw around them, the city's industrial leaders were finally galvanized into action. Led by H. B. du Pont, they formed the Greater Wilmington Development Council (GWDC), which undertook to revive the city's long-neglected central area and to encourage systematic city planning. The GWDC also made tentative efforts to solve Wilmington's serious social problems but quickly retreated from these endeavors when their efforts proved to be both ineffective and embarrassing.

In 1968 Wilmington experienced a short-lived but sharp riot following the death of Dr. Martin Luther King, Jr. The riot intensified suburban fears of the city and set the stage for the deep animosities that developed during the 1970s over interdistrict school desegregation and the relocation of the region's primary health care facility. In 1978, after several years of bitterly contested legal battles, a federal judge ordered the dissolution of the Wilmington and suburban school districts and the imposition of busing to overcome the area's pronounced racial imbalance. Simultaneously, another court battle raged over the decision of the Wilmington Medical Center to move its major facility from the city into the suburbs. Both of these issues produced far more diversified citizen involvement than had marked community life in earlier periods, and relatively speaking the old elite have become just another group—although a potentially powerful one—competing for control over decision making. Thus at a time when residents of Greater Wilmington perceive themselves to be further than ever apart on policy issues, they are also more on their own than at any time in living memory.

Suburban residents stubbornly resist the implications of the fact that the city is still the central core of their community; yet when one part of the whole suffers the other parts are affected also. The validity of this observation is only now becoming evident as some inner-ring suburbs begin to experience the cycle of deterioration that heretofore has been associated only with the city. This phenomenon demonstrates that the dividing line between the city and its suburbs, regardless of its present governmental and symbolic value, is nonetheless purely arbitrary, and the suburbs can ignore the interests of the city only at their own peril.

CHAPTER 1

The Big Change Begins: 1912

*In every town and small city of America an upper set of
families stands above the middle classes and towers over
the underlying population of clerks and wage workers.
The members of this set . . . hold the key to local decision.*
C. Wright Mills

In October 1912 Wilmington, Delaware, celebrated Old Home Week, a
public-relations extravaganza designed to advertise the city's industrial
advantages to the world and to welcome back old-time residents who had
moved away. The week of gala activities opened with the ringing of the fire
bell atop the venerable City Hall on Market Street between 5th and 6th
streets. Hotels, theaters, and restaurants had eagerly prepared for the
anticipated crowds. The Empire Vaudeville Theatre booked "Baby Zelda,"
the self-proclaimed "greatest child comedienne on the vaudeville stage
today," and Guy Daily, "the human fish," who could smoke, sing, and
sleep under water.[1] Each day brought some parade, concert, exhibition, or
reception. The city's German societies, the Sangerbund choral society, and
the Turnverein, an athletic club, performed. The local Italians staged a
Columbus Day parade; the city's fire companies marched to show off their
newly acquired motorized equipment. People came to gawk at the "mon-
ster parade" of locally owned automobiles rolling down Market Street. This
last event was followed by a masked carnival of mummers in the downtown
streets and the culminating grand finale of fireworks in Brandywine Park at
Washington Heights.[2]

What sort of city did the old-timers returning to Wilmington see? In
1912 Wilmington was a city of about 80,000 people. The *Official Souvenir
Program* for Old Home Week touted Wilmington as "unequalled as a
manufacturing city by any of its size in the United States."[3] Many
smokestacks belching bituminous ash attested to the city's industries,

which produced railroad cars, leather goods, ships, and other heavy industrial products. Since 1880 there had been a change in the mix of industries
that made up Wilmington's economy. The sharp decline in shipbuilding
and carriage making, the two most important in the mid-nineteenth century, had been offset by rapid expansion in tanning and railroad car
construction and maintenance. It remained a blue-collar town. Fifty-one
percent of Wilmington's workers were employed in manufacturing, the
highest percentage of industrial workers ever achieved in Wilmington.
Among industrial employees salaried office workers constituted only 12
percent; nonmanufacturing professionals and white-collar workers
accounted for only another 17 percent of Wilmington's workforce.[4]

In 1912 Wilmington was an old city, its antiquity symbolized by the
City Hall, a relic of the federal period built in 1798, when Wilmington had
been a small town of perhaps 3,000 people sustained by flour milling and
shipping. From the perspective of 1912, the City Hall was either a venerable relic or an antiquated eyesore, depending upon one's attitude towards
history. In either case, Wilmingtonians agreed that it was an embarrassment as the municipal symbol of an up-to-date, forward-thinking, twentieth-century city. Like the older sections of the city, it was too small, too
cramped, too dirty, and too old-fashioned.

Wilmington's roots go back to the early days of European exploration
and settlement along the coast of North America. Its location offered
colonists several important advantages: direct access to the sea, high,
healthy ground, and rich nearby farmlands. The first permanent settlers
were a small group sent by the Swedish government. The Swedish colony
had been a settlement of subsistence farmers strung out along the Delaware River for forty miles from modern-day Philadelphia in the north to
Smyrna Creek in the south. Because the colony failed to develop a strong
commercial base, there was no impetus for the Swedes, or the Dutch who
succeeded them, to create a town at the original Christina settlement. It
was not until the 1730s, a hundred years after the Swedes landed, that a
group of English Quaker merchants established the town on the Christina
that was to become Wilmington.

From the early 1680s until the Revolution, William Penn and his
descendants controlled the western bank of the Delaware River. During
this period of nearly a hundred years, the economic relationships and
political boundaries of the region took on their modern forms.[5] Delaware
and Pennsylvania, although under the same proprietary administration,
remained separate colonies. Philadelphia became the major Delaware
River city, while Trenton, New Jersey, and Wilmington, roughly the same
distance from the Quaker city in opposite directions, became the other
principal river towns. County and local government took form during these

years too, and the Penns distributed land and granted charters to markets, towns, and schools.

The geography of the Delaware River Valley—its hills, plains, streams, and marshes—was the principal factor controlling colonial settlement patterns. The fall line, which separates the hilly piedmont region to the west from the flat, sandy coastal plain, runs diagonally across New Jersey from New York City, crossing the Delaware River just above Trenton, and progresses in a southwesterly direction slightly northwest of Philadelphia and on through Wilmington into Maryland, toward Baltimore and Washington. Wilmington lies at the point immediately below the fall line where the drainage systems of northern New Castle County merge. The most successful colonial settlements were those located on navigable streams near the fall line, where a natural break in the types of transportation occurred and where waterpower could generate manufacturing and milling enterprises. Philadelphia, located near the confluence of the Delaware with its principal tributary, the Schuylkill, possessed the most favorable site within the river valley, as Penn's agents knew when they selected it to become the proprietor's "green country town" in 1681.

Wilmington's location at the meeting point of the Christina and Brandywine Rivers was second only to that of Philadelphia in the Delaware River Valley. Its Quaker founders, Thomas Willing and William Shipley, laid out the town along the Christina, a river that has its origins in several small streams and ponds in the plain southwest of the city. The Christina was navigable to small craft from the hamlet of Christiana, several miles west of the city. About two miles northeast of Christiana, near the town of Newport, the river joins the Red Clay and White Clay creeks, streams that have their beginnings in the hilly piedmont to the northwest. The expanded stream, now a minor river, passes through tidal marshes to Wilmington, where it meets the Brandywine, a rapidly falling stream from the hills north of the city. Thus enlarged by the last of its tributaries, the Christina flows past the marshes of Cherry Island into the Delaware River.

Over the years men expanded upon these natural transportation routes by building roads. Colonial farmers created overland routes along the crests between drainage basins to bring their crops down through the hills of Pennsylvania and northern Delaware to Wilmington. In the early nineteenth century, chartered turnpike companies improved those routes in an effort to expand the city as a market for farm produce, especially wheat. Those highways, or turnpikes as they were called because of the turnstile at the pay booth, remain the major axes of Wilmington's highway system. The Philadelphia Pike paralleled the Delaware River in the most eastern part of New Castle County. Moving westward, one next came to the Concord Pike, or Wilmington and Great Valley Turnpike, as it was

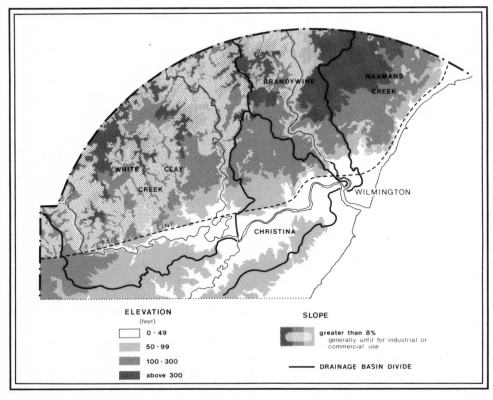

ELEVATION
(feet)

- 0 - 49
- 50 - 99
- 100 - 300
- above 300

SLOPE

greater than 8%
generally unfit for industrial or
commercial use

—— DRAINAGE BASIN DIVIDE

The physical features of New Castle County showing elevations and waterways. *(Map by Marley Amstutz, Cartographer)* sometimes called, which went to Concordville, Pennsylvania, along the ridge that separates the Brandywine and Delaware River valleys. Farther to the west, the Kennett Pike to Kennett Square, Pennsylvania, ran between the Brandywine and the Red Clay Creek, while the pike from Newport to Gap, Pennsylvania, which had an alternative terminus in Wilmington, called the Lancaster Pike, divided the country between the Red Clay and Mill creeks. In addition, smaller roads linked Wilmington with New Castle and Newport.

In the eighteenth century, the region around Philadelphia and Wilmington was the bread basket of North America. Wheat, the premier cash crop for the area's farmers, was ground at waterpowered mills located on streams at the fall line. Although Philadelphia's was by far the larger and more diversified port, Wilmington held its own as a milling and grain shipping center. Grain reached Wilmington from New Castle County and parts of southeastern Pennsylvania. Heavy wagons labored over uncertain roads from Chester County to Wilmington or from Lancaster through Gap to waiting riverboats at Newport. Hostelries lined the major routes at intervals of every few miles, ready to provide supper and a night's lodging to tired teamsters. At Wilmington the farmers sold their grain to the town's merchant millers at Brandywine Bridge. Here, at the point where the Brandywine's rapid flow was slowed as it entered the coastal plain, sixteen mills were built side by side on either side of the creek to take advantage of the waterpower above and the navigability below the fall line. The mills attracted related industries to the area, such as barrel making and ship-building. Although it was primarily associated with flour milling, the Brandywine also provided the power for a paper mill and six saw mills before the end of the eighteenth century.[6] Altogether these activities gave Wilmington a population in excess of 4,000 by 1810.

During the first half of the nineteenth century, the Brandywine and other streams in the region—the Red Clay, Mill, and White Clay creeks—declined as flour milling sites but expanded their importance as locations for other industries. A variety of factors doomed flour milling in the Wilmington-Philadelphia region, such as local soil exhaustion, the ravages of the Hessian fly, and the opening of more productive farms in the West. Meanwhile, two new waterpowered industrial enterprises proved to be of lasting importance to Wilmington: The E. I. du Pont de Nemours & Co. powder mills organized in 1802 by French émigré about two miles upstream from Wilmington, and Joseph Bancroft's textile mill located less than a mile upstream from Brandywine Bridge. By the 1830s the Du Pont powder mills were the largest of their kind in the United States, employing 140 workers, most of whom lived in company housing on the mill property.[7]

In that same decade, steam technology began to reshape New Castle County's economy. In 1837 the Philadelphia, Wilmington and Baltimore Railroad was constructed along a route running down the Delaware River Valley within the flat coastal plain. The railroad paralleled the Christina River through Wilmington then turned southwest toward the Chesapeake Bay. The railroad changed Wilmington's economy. It offered outlets for the industrial expertise and the capital accumulation spawned by the mills. The production of railroad cars and equipment became the city's leading industry, followed by steamboat construction and other related foundry work. Driven by steam engines instead of water-wheels, the new industries did not string out along the streams of the hilly regions north and west of the city, but rather clustered in the city to take advantage of good transportation and labor supply. These industries, mostly locally owned and managed and employing between 50 and 500 men, were drawn to the excellent transportation potential of the narrow strip of land between the railroad and the Christina. Other industries, principally carriage making and leather tanning, took up manufacturing sites nearby. By the end of the Civil War the industries that were to epitomize Wilmington's economy when the Old Home Week was celebrated in 1912 were already in place.[8]

In the years from 1830 to 1910, while Wilmington's population grew from just over 4,000 to nearly 70,000, the city's physical growth followed a path already well established in the colonial period. Wilmington was planned in the 1730s as a modest port town. Its founder, Thomas Willing, following the example of nearby Philadelphia, that compelling model for most American city planners, laid out the town as a grid. In early nineteenth-century maps of the Wilmington area, the city's straight lines, looking as if they were set up on a loom, contrast boldly with the surrounding area where roads and streams turn and twist with the contours imposed by nature.

The rectangular plots on straight streets has significant advantages. To the seventeenth and eighteenth centuries' neoclassical sensibilities straight lines suggested simplicity and proportion of design. Rectangular plots were easy to survey and when cut down to any size still offered frontage onto the street. English architectural styles in the eighteenth century emphasized rectangularity, which fit perfectly the shape of these plots. In addition, it was easy to find one's way in a town laid out in a regular fashion. To this geographic regularity, nineteenth-century Wilmingtonians added simplicity of nomenclature, partly patterned on that of Philadelphia. Beginning with Front Street, which runs east-west parallel to the Christina, the city's streets were numbered. Market Street was laid out as the major artery running perpendicular to the river. To the east of Market Street, most of the streets were named for trees; a few blocks to the west of

Market Street looking south from 8th Street about 1915. (*Courtesy of the Eleutherian Mills Historical Library*)

Market began a series of streets named consecutively for the presidents of the United States.

In the second half of the nineteenth century, horse cars and then electric trolleys expanded the geographic mobility of city dwellers, until by 1900 Wilmington was crisscrossed by trolley lines. The physical expansion of the city was very much influenced by the old turnpike routes, which became the major arteries for the trolleys. Those routes, together with topographical features and the needs of industry, defined the city's development in the era that preceded zoning regulations and planning.

Industrial Wilmington consisted of a number of regions with specialized functions. Industry was most highly concentrated along the Christina River, while commercial enterprises clustered on or near Market Street, especially between Front and 10th streets—the two zones making a sort of T-shaped nonresidential area. In the surrounding residential areas, the value of housing was closely tied to topography. Without exception, the low, flat plains near the Christina, so desirable for a railroad or industrial enterprise, were the sites of the city's cheapest, tiniest, least desirable houses. By contrast, on the higher ground of the piedmont region to the northwest the more expensive and commodious houses were erected.

Henry Seidel Canby, a literary critic reared in one of Wilmington's Quaker families at the turn of the century, captured the socioeconomic significance of the hills in his nostalgic reminiscence, *The Age of Confidence*:

> From the ballroom at the top of the Opera House where we went
> for dancing school there was a view of the whole town at once;
> and it always surprised me to see how deeply its crisscross of
> streets was buried in foliage. The factory districts below were
> grimy and bare, but to the north and west the roofs were hid in a
> forest with only a "mansion" here and there or a church steeple
> projecting. Beyond the business and shopping section, and toward
> the hill tops, were tight little streets, heavily shaded and walled
> with red-brick fronts built cheek to cheek, with decent chins of
> white marble steps, and alley archways for ears. Here the well-to-
> do had lived when the city was still a little town, and had been
> content to hide their arbored side porches and deep if narrow gar-
> dens from the street. The industrial prosperity of the eighties had
> ended the Quaker restraint. In my day those who could afford it
> lived further westward in houses that sprawled in ample yards,
> thickset with trees and shrubbery behind iron or wooden fences.
> Here was a God's plenty of architecture. Brick boxes of the seven-
> ties, with cupolas or mansard roofs, . . . beside new contraptions,
> some of green serpentine, but the latest of brick pseudo-Gothic,
> with turrets, pointed towers, and Egyptian ornaments of wood.

Architecture for the poor was less subject to fashion, Canby recalled:

> To the southward of the hilltops lived the "plain people" by
> thousands in rows of brick houses with identical windows and
> doors, no more differentiation in homes than in their lives; and
> below them again, reaching down into the factories were the
> slums, where congestion was painful, dirty water ran over broken
> pavements, and the yards behind were reduced to a dump heap.
> Here the decent order of our town broke down into shrill voices,
> fighting, smells, and drunkenness.[9]

In 1864 an enterprising land developer named Joshua T. Heald created Wilmington's first public transportation company, The Wilmington
City Railway Company. The company constructed a horse-car line from the
PW&B station on Front Street up Market to 10th and then westward out
Delaware Avenue along the crest of the watershed separating the Brandywine and Christina rivers. This region was then still semirural, filled with
cow pastures and farm fences. In the years that followed, the prosperous

The Du Pont Building as seen from 11th and Market Streets about 1915. *(Courtesy of the Eleutherian Mills Historical Library)*

factory owners, executives, and lawyers who constituted the cream of Wilmington society moved uptown to the avenue region. There they built large homes with ample, well-planted yards, self-consciously constructed in styles ranging from Mansard to Gothic to Queen Anne.

The introduction of electric trolley cars in the 1880s brought a flurry of middle-income housing construction north and west of the city. In the late eighties, the Wilmington City Railway Company built an electric trolley line from center city (colloquially referred to as "downtown" in Wilmington) out North Market Street to the city's edge where the street became the Philadelphia Pike. In 1901 the company opened an amusement park on the Shellpot Creek about on half mile north of the Brandywine Bridge. The park's function was to encourage ridership on the line, especially until its potential as a residential area was fully realized. Simultaneously, another transit company, the Peoples Railway, built a line westward to Brandywine Springs, an early nineteenth-century spa that the management converted into a rival amusement park.

Until the 1960s Wilmington was divided into councilmanic wards. In the years from 1880, just before electric trolleys were introduced, to 1920, the census year closest to the time when trolley ridership reached its peak, population distribution by wards changed radically. Although the city's total population increased by 150 percent during those forty years, the number of people living in the old downtown wards increased very little, and in the first ward actually declined. The big increases came in the more distant wards to the north and west, especially the 9th Ward, adjacent to North Market Street, and the 7th Ward, centering on Delaware Avenue. The 9th Ward grew from a little over 2,000 persons in 1890, when it was Wilmington's smallest ward, to become the largest, with nearly 19,000 people by 1920. Meanwhile, the population of the 7th Ward increased from 4,624 in 1890 to 18,726 three decades later.[10] Another rapidly growing section of the city was the southwest, including portions of the 5th, 10th, 11th, and 12th wards. A closer look at developments in those three sections as well as in the downtown area tells the story of what was happening to Wilmington in the years just prior to World War I.

The 9th Ward, the part of the city north of the Brandywine, enjoyed the most spectacular growth. Usually characterized as a middle-class residential district, the ward was in reality more varied. Indeed, in the early twentieth century the 9th Ward became a microcosm of the city's population as a whole. Unlike other wards, the 9th encompassed not one, but all of the city's topographical features. Its eastern portion, bisected by the Pennsylvania Railroad's PW&B line, was part of the coastal plain and included Cherry Island, a large undeveloped marshy area that fronted on the Delaware River east of the railroad. Cherry Island had been incorporated into the city during the nineteenth century as part of a promoter's dream that it could attract more heavy industry to the city. In spite of special tax benefits and Chamber of Commerce ballyhoo, it failed to bring in a single company because its transportation advantage was more than offset by the costliness of backfilling the marsh. After years of failure to sell the marsh to industrialists, the city finally gained a tenant in 1901 when the Pennsylvania Railroad announced plans to build extensive construction and maintenance shops on the marsh land at Todd's Cut.

This announcement was the best economic news that the city had had in years. Wilmington's railroad car production was already declining, and the only new industries coming into Wilmington were hosiery and underwear factories, which offered poor-paying jobs to women and did little to aid the city's overall growth. [11] Furthermore, the future of the city's largest industrial firm, the Harlan and Hollingsworth Company, manufacturers of steamboat and railroad equipment, was in doubt because that company had recently been absorbed by a giant new trust, the United States Ship Building Company.

The Pennsylvania's announcement of its new shops coincided with the railroad firm's decision to elevate its tracks through Wilmington and to build a commodious new passenger station there. Businessmen believed that these plans were sure to provide much local employment and to expand the city's economy in every way. Simultaneously, the federal government began work on a bulkhead along the western bank of the Delaware River from the Christina to Edgemoor. That project, which would give Cherry Island the potential to become a port, was expected to attract more new industry to the area. Soon after, there was another sign of industrial growth along the river when the Delaware Malleable Iron Company announced that it would construct a large factory just south of the Christina. [12]

Riding the tide of optimism generated by those plans, membership in the Board of Trade, precursor to the Chamber of Commerce, jumped from about 132 to 382 in 1903, [13] as board members envisioned not only an industrially revitalized city but a more beautiful and commercially prosperous one as well. The board's journal proposed that the sleazy rundown area around the railroad station be demolished and replaced by a handsome public square "around which hotels and business houses of dignity may be built" to give strangers arriving by train or merely passing through the station a more favorable impression of Wilmington. [14] Meanwhile, numerous plans were afoot to extend trolley service from Wilmington to surrounding towns such as West Chester, Kennett Square, and Media in Pennsylvania and to various points "downstate" in Delaware. Those transportation improvements augered well for expansion of the city's retail sector.

In this hopeful mood, housing construction picked up, especially in the 9th Ward. The Street and Sewer Department, for once building ahead of demand, converted Price's Run, a stream running through the eastern part of the ward, into a sewer in 1903. A Philadelphia construction firm bought land there and began what was by far the biggest homebuilding project in the city's history. [15] Within a year 248 homes designed to appeal to railroad workers were built in the vicinity of Vandever Avenue. The

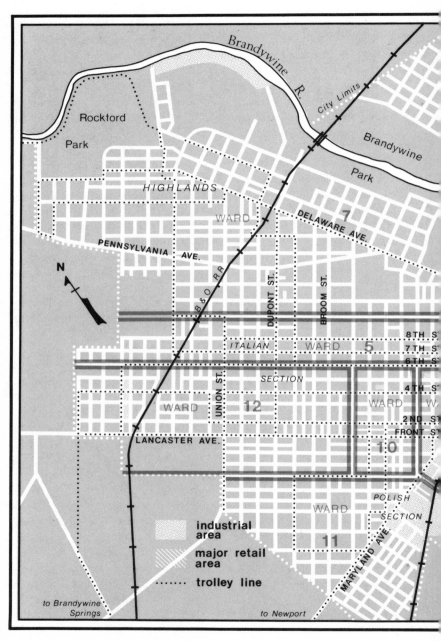

Wilmington in 1912, showing the city's wards, major streets, and trolley lines, as well as its industrial and retail centers. *(Map by Marley Amstutz, Cartographer)*

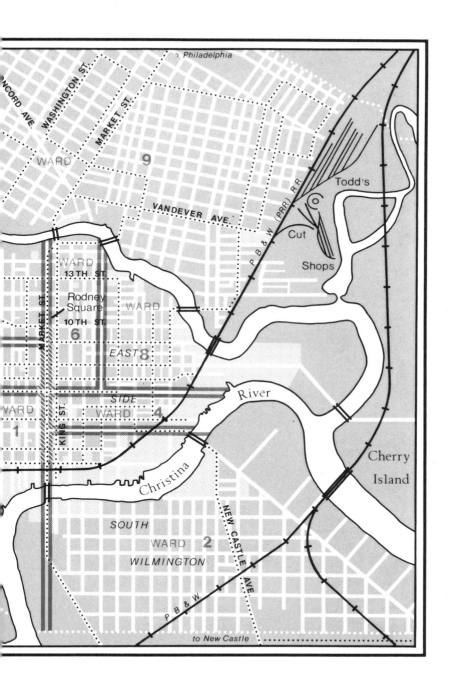

to Philadelphia

WASHINGTON ST.

CONCORD AVE.

MARKET ST.

WARD 9

VANDEVER AVE.

P. B. & W. (PRR) R.R.

Todd's
Cut
Shops

WARD
13 TH ST.

Rodney
Square

10 TH ST.

MARKET ST.

6

WARD

EAST 8

KING ST.

SIDE
WARD 4

WARD 1

River

Christina

Cherry
Island

SOUTH
WARD 2

NEW CASTLE AVE.

WILMINGTON

P B & W

to New Castle

homes were brick duplexes and rows with small yards both front and rear. Some had front porches and slate-covered oriel windows on the second floor front. There were provisions for small stores on the corner lots. Those houses were an improvement over the older working-class housing in the city. They were set back at least a few feet from the pavement and had such modern conveniences as indoor plumbing, hot running water, electrical wiring, and up-to-date design. They differed little, in fact, from contemporary housing designs for the white-collar market except for their location on low ground adjacent to a marsh and close to industrial plants and eyesores of various kinds. In that respect the new workers' neighborhood in the 9th Ward was similar to older workers' sections of the city.

As one went westward in the 9th Ward toward the Concord Pike, the land rose, nonresidential land uses became less common, and lot sizes increased. In this region land developers created distinct neighborhoods. Along the axis of Washington Street, builders constructed houses very similar in design to those near Vandever Avenue, only the mix favored duplexes over rows and the houses were a bit less densely placed. Here lived a variety of people, including skilled workers, clerks, and small-time merchants. Descendants of Irish, English, and Germans intermingled with second-generation Jewish immigrants in this respectable but unpretentious zone.

Farther to the west was Baynard Boulevard, the showplace of the 9th Ward. This section of the city had been farmland until the early 1890s, when a group of businessmen headed by Samuel H. Baynard, a Market Street store owner and local Republican politician, formed the North Side Improvement Company, which bought the land and planned a prestigious residential neighborhood, to be called Washington Heights. Although the city engineer's office laid out the new section in the same methodical grid that characterized the rest of Wilmington, Baynard Boulevard, the major artery of the new development, distinctively ran at an angle somewhat off the usual ninety degrees from Brandywine Park to the city limits, where it crossed the Concord Pike.[16] The North Side Improvement Company then began a successful campaign to have the county build a bridge across the Brandywine at Washington Street to link the boulevard directly with the downtown.

Baynard proved himself to be a dynamic, clever real-estate developer who combined public influence with philanthropy to promote Washington Heights. From his position on the City Park Commission, he pressed for improvements to the north side of Brandywine Park, adjacent to his land. He urged the commission to start a small zoo and donated some of the animals himself. In addition, he presented the city with its first sports stadium, complete with concrete bleachers. Also a member of the city

Hotel Du Pont lobby as it appeared in 1913. *(Courtesy of the Eleutherian Mills Historical Library)*

school board, he donated a piece of property located at the intersection of the boulevard and the Concord Pike to be used as the site of a public elementary school.[17] A Methodist, he also built a church called Washington Heights Methodist Church at the opposite end of his Boulevard. When Baynard's coreligionists proved unwilling to pay for the mortgage, he sold the building to a Presbyterian congregation that was just then seeking new quarters and became a Presbyterian himself.[18]

These shrewd philanthropies spurred the sale of lots. The Gothic church overlooking the park, the stone, castlelike school, the tree-lined boulevard, all pointed to a high-quality residential neighborhood. The *Sunday Star* called the area "a marvel of beauty," the city's most progressive section, demonstrating the aesthetic ideals of the "city beautiful" movement. "New homes by the hundreds have been recently erected [there]," the paper gushed, "homes modern in character, and yet within the reach of the average citizen."[19] Although some large, impressive homes were built there, the boulevard section did not attract Wilmington's old elite. They stayed on the other side of the Brandywine in the Delaware Avenue-Pennsylvania Avenue section. The people who came to the boulevard represented new money—higher-ranking white-collar employees of industrial firms, and successful merchants, some of them Irish or Jewish.

The new houses they bought were divided into relatively few large, light, and airy rooms instead of the many smaller ones that had characterized construction in the Victorian era. Builders were responding to the public's desire for greater simplicity and informality in design as well as for modern comforts and amenities. A writer for the *Star* noted that before the advent of central heating, people shut up the least-used room in the house, the parlor, during the winter. "The most crying fault in the American house of moderate dimensions," the *Star* lectured, "is still that the parlor is made too formal . . . a growing tendency to make the room more a part and parcel of the house is apparent, however. In the homes of those who are in moderate circumstances nothing more instantly reveals a vulgar taste than the attempt to differentiate the parlor from the rest of the house by rich and ornate furnishing. It should not be a museum of unrelated treasures, nor should it bristle with fragile bric-a-brac. It should proclaim a welcome to everyone who enters it. . . ."[20] Ninth Ward homes with their plain wooden doric porch pillars and rectangular brick forms proclaimed the new middle-income ideal. Only the oriel windows and an occasional turret added a fancy touch. Inside, the typical duplex was roomier than the old city rowhouse. Because the parlor had been eliminated, the sitting room could be expanded into a large living room. The new houses also eliminated the dark, confining corridor that in older houses led from the front door, past the parlor, to the staircase. Now the front door opened directly on to the living room with the staircase usually incorporated to one side.

In 1912 residential construction in Wilmington was undergoing financial as well as architectural changes. In the nineteenth century, investors would build a row of houses in the expectation of renting them, since the skilled and clerical workers, trolleymen, or other citizens of modest means could ill afford to buy. Banks offered little help to the would-be home buyer, because they chose not to mortgage small properties. Cooperative savings societies arose to meet this need in the 1870s, but they were often ill-managed and short lived. During the first decade of the twentieth century, Wilmington's bankers finally discovered the opportunities in residential real estate. At that time the major banks each started real-estate departments that acted as agents for landlords and for buyers and sellers of property. The banks also began to offer mortgages on terms that attracted purchasers of modest means. This change in banking policy made new middle-income residential sections like the 9th Ward possible. The banks

The City-County Building, constructed in 1916 on King Street between 10th and 11th Streets, facing Rodney Square and the Du Pont Building. (*Courtesy of the Historical Society of Delaware*)

did not, however, as yet extend large loans to builders. Consequently, contractors lacked the capital to construct more than a few houses at a time and were in no position to question the city engineer's imposition of the grid street plan.[21] The effects of this system of construction are everywhere visible in those residential sections of the city developed between 1900 and 1940. Uniform, narrow rectangular lots defined the buildings before they were built. Contractors, seeking to differentiate their properties and to keep current with the latest styles, made minor cosmetic adaptations in the basic house plan. By the end of World War I, the reign of the slate oriel window "Queen Anne" porch style yielded in favor of a wide choice of "colonial" facades in imitation of the style that was becoming the hallmark of more patrician neighborhoods.

People moved from houses in the center city to new ones along the trolley lines in a discernible pattern that reflected factors such as socioeconomic status, place of work, and ethnicity. Blacks, who accounted for just over ten percent of Wilmington's population during the city's industrial phase, were the least likely to leave the center city for the periphery. Poles and Italians clustered in the west and southwest. Germans, Irish, and Jews were more inclined to move northward into the 9th Ward, while native whites moved either to the 9th Ward or to the more fashionable Delaware Avenue depending upon their wealth and place of employment.

Blacks were the most invisible of the city's major ethnic groups. In this former slave state, they were subject to legal segregation and relegated to the least desirable jobs. The position of black people in Wilmington reflected the border state situation of Delaware. During the nineteenth century, the city's black residents were primarily employed as unskilled laborers and service workers, such as laundresses or servants. In common with the pattern of Southern cities, black servants usually resided in small rowhouses on alleyways behind the homes of their employers. The censuses of both 1910 and 1920 showed only two wards in the city with fewer than 200 black residents. But this preghettoization pattern was beginning to change, for as the well-to-do began moving to the edge of the city and immigrant whites began filling their old neighborhoods, blacks were pushed out into the back alleys of the center city area. In 1914 the *Sunday Star* reported on this phenomenon: "The negro population . . . of the city is huddled on back streets, narrow streets, in alleys. . . . In the heart of the city are to be found numbers of these 'shacks' called houses which are specially and carefully reserved for the exclusive use and occupancy of negroes. It is rather a custom in our city to have a house in front and an alley running at the side. Were you to venture cautiously down the alley into what you would expect to find as the backyard of the house, you will find two or more brick houses of one or two rooms inhabited by whole families, for which they are bound to pay a good high rent." These houses, the reporter found, were "unspeakably unsanitary, with open sewerage and very often with not any at all." In addition to these sorry downtown quarters, blacks lived in the soggy areas east of the Christina and Brandywine in neighborhoods that had no names except "over 3rd Street Bridge" and "over 11th Street Bridge." Here, in jerry-built "shacks floating on the stagnant water of the swamps," literally on dumping grounds, occupants were especially susceptible to rheumatism, typhoid, and that great killer of negroes, tuberculosis.[22] In 1914 the city's population was 90 percent white, yet one-third of all those who died of tuberculosis were black.[23]

In 1912 the United States had reached the climax of its greatest period of immigration from Europe. Between 1880 and 1914, millions of people came to America to escape from the consequences of overpopulation, abrupt economic changes, authoritarian governments, and religious persecution. In contrast to the immigrants of the mid-nineteenth century who had come mainly from the British Isles, Scandinavia, and Germany, these latter immigrants represented the nations of Southern and Eastern Europe, principally Italy, Russia, Poland, and the Austro-Hungarian Empire. Generally speaking, among cities on the midatlantic coast, proximity to New York City was the prime factor in the relative attractiveness to immigrants, just as proximity to the South was the key factor in the attraction of blacks. Wilmington, being midway between Washington and New York, represented a sort of equilibrium point in this demographic pattern. In 1910 about 16 percent of the residents of the Delaware city were immigrants, compared to nearly 40 percent in Trenton, New Jersey, and 35 percent in Philadelphia. By contrast, compare Wilmington's 10 percent black population to Philadelphia's 8 percent and the 4 percent in Trenton. Wilmington's newcomers represented the major ethnic groups of the new immigration: Russian Jews, Poles, and Italians.[24]

Few Jews came to Wilmington until the mass exodus from Russia began in the 1880s. By 1900 there were about 250 Jewish families living in the city. Most were employed in the wholesale and retail trades or in services such as barbering or tailoring.[25] Evidence is inadequate to say whether they shunned industrial employment out of choice or because employers' prejudice excluded them. It is clear, though, that self-employed Jews were successful in part because they developed mutual assistance agencies that provided some cushion against failure in these high-risk enterprises. Typically, Jewish merchants began on a small scale in little stores just off lower Market Street that catered to the city's industrial workers. Too few in number to constitute an exclusive ghetto, they clustered near their stores in multiethnic neighborhoods. The city's first synagogue, Adas Kodesch, was located in this area at 6th and French streets near City Hall.

The migration of Wilmington's Jews from their original area of settlement followed very much the pattern of Jewish migration in Philadelphia, where Jews quickly abandoned their initial areas of settlement to relocate in middle-class residential areas of predominantly native white composition.[26] As some Jews prospered, usually as merchants or professionals, they moved from the old downtown neighborhood into new housing on the city's periphery. Excluded from the most prestigious Delaware Avenue-Highlands section where the city's old industrial families resided, they moved to the 9th Ward. By the 1920s about half of Wilmington's 4,000 Jews lived in the 9th Ward, the richest Jews living interspersed among WASPs of similar socioeconomic status along Baynard Boulevard, while Jews who were not so well-to-do sought less expensive homes nearby.[27] In following this pattern, the Jews were maintaining their ethnic alliance while responding to the opportunity for upward mobility that America offered.

The immigration of Italians and Poles to Wilmington, like that of the Jews, occurred in the period from 1880 until the outbreak of World War I. But unlike the Jews, who have almost entirely abandoned their second-

T. Coleman du Pont, 1863–1930. (*Courtesy of the Eleutherian Mills Historical Library*)

generation urban neighborhoods in the 9th Ward for the suburbs, there are still discernible Italian and Polish communities in the city. The first Poles to settle in Wilmington came from the German-occupied section of Poland. Unable to speak English, they sought employment in industries where there were German-speaking foremen to hire them, particularly foundries and tanneries. Tanneries were spread out through much of the older section of Wilmington on both the east and west sides. By the turn of the century, however, the trend was for new tanneries to locate in the rapidly developing lower west side, in the vicinity of Maryland Avenue. Two of the largest were there: Ford's Morocco factory between 2nd and 5th streets on

Pierre S. du Pont, 1870–1954. *(Courtesy of the Eleutherian Mills Historical Library)*

Greenhill Avenue, and Blumenthal's, which then claimed to be the second largest morocco factory in the world.[28]

At first Poles found homes in the same downtown sections of the city that housed other poor workers. By 1890, however, they had developed distinct residential enclaves closely linked to the group's employment. There were two Polish neighborhoods. The smaller was on the east side near several foundries. There Poles shared their neighborhood with other ethnic groups. In 1913 they built their church, Saint Stanislaus Kostka, just a stone's throw from the venerable Old Swedes Church on 7th Street. A larger, more solidly Polish community took shape in the newer southwest-

John J. Raskob, 1879–1950. *(Courtesy of the Eleutherian Mills Historical Library)*

ern part of the city, close to Maryland Avenue. Saint Hedwigs, a Gothic church built in 1904 and one of the largest and most elaborate churches in Wilmington, was at the center of this community. Other Polish institutions—the Polish Turn Hall, the Falcons, and a library association—were located in the same area.[29] This neighborhood, roughly encompassed by a triangle formed by the Pennsylvania Railroad tracks, Lancaster Avenue, and Broom Street, lay along the axis of Maryland Avenue pointing toward Newport. The area was close to the new morocco factories and to railroad and foundry jobs, yet it was cut off from the rest of the city on two sides. The southwest section was newly opened and offered Polish factory workers the opportunity to buy small but new brick row homes priced within their budgets. The decade of greatest Polish migration to Wilmington was from 1900 to 1910, when the Polish population increased 131 percent, from 1,495 to 3,458.[30] It is undoubtedly no coincidence that this growth coincided with a wave of speculative housebuilding in the Maryland Avenue area.

The city's Italian community came of age in the same period and reached about the same size. Like the Poles, they, too, were attracted to the west side, but they settled a bit farther north in the vicinity of Union Street between Lancaster and Delaware avenues. The most significant factors in the choice of location were place of work and the opportunity to buy or rent new but inexpensive houses in a developing area where family groups could find lodging near one another. Initially, Italians came to Wilmington in the 1880s as construction workers for the Baltimore and Ohio Railroad. Coming from a country strewn with rocks, many were accomplished stone masons who found work in that trade. It was Italian workmen who built the massive stone block bridges for both the B&O and Pennsylvania railroads. Italians also built and repaired stone walls at the Du Pont Company's black powder yards at Hagley and laid city streets and sewers. By 1900 the Bancroft textile mills were employing many Italians as well. Although the 1910 census shows Italians living in every ward of the city, nearly half of them were concentrated in the city's 5th War, between 6th and 9th streets west of Market.[31]

In the late 1880s, Nicholas Fidanza, an Italian-born carpenter and grocery owner, began building houses and apartments in the Union Street area, which he rented to fellow countrymen.[32] Another factor in the expansion of this Italian colony was the construction of the "Bancroft Flats" at the western edge of the city. William P. Bancroft, son of the English-born textile manufacturer Joseph Bancroft, was a dedicated, frugal, civic-minded Quaker. While serving as an executive in the firm started by his father, Bancroft undertook a number of carefully thought out philanthropies. He is principally known for the substantial gift of land that marked the beginnings of Wilmington's park system and for his endowment that allowed the Wilmington Institute to become a free public library. In 1901 Bancroft formed a real-estate company called the Woodlawn Company, in part for the purpose improving housing conditions for workers. Inspired by English model housing and convinced that workers were better off renting than owning their own homes, Bancroft's company constructed 390 brick two-story row homes along Union Street, an area that was then on the verge of urban development. The monthly rent for the apartments, known as Bancroft Flats, was $10, which was about the weekly wage paid to Bancroft Mill workers. Although the flats were not restricted to Bancroft employees, many of the early tenants did work for the textile firm, and these people were often Italians.[33]

In common with many ethnic groups, Wilmington's Italians established groceries and bakeries that specialized in their native foods. They also developed a variety of fraternal, political, and mutual assistance societies. These lodges were for males only and were originally oriented around particular regions of Italy. In time, however, as the community grew and Italians from various parts of the homeland commingled, provincialism declined.[34] During the 1890s Miss Jennie Weaver, an energetic and strong-willed social worker, opened a settlement house in the Italian neighborhood where residents could take Americanization classes and participate in recreational activities. Although the Neighborhood House did not press for conversion to Protestantism, its success posed a threat to the Catholic Church. The Irish-dominated churches on Wilmington's west side initially offered the newcomers but a tepid reception.[35] It was not until 1924, when the Italian community numbered about 3,5000 that the Diocese of Wilmington established an Italian parish, Saint Anthony's. John Francis Tucker, the Wilmington-born priest assigned to the new church, has perfected his Italian while attending a seminary in Rome and, later, while serving as a chaplain in the U.S. Army during World War I. A dynamic, self-confident leader, Tucker organized numerous religious, recreational, and sports clubs at Saint Anthony's that made the church a powerful anchor for the community.[36]

The forces of change that were shaping the new parts of the city were also influencing the old downtown section. In 1912 Market Street between Front and 11th streets was the heart of the city's retail district, which extended roughly in a rectangle from Tatnall Street in the west to French Street in the east, and from Front to 8th streets. There were to be found the city's major retailers in clothing, dry goods, shoes, and household furnishings. The city's transportation hub was the Pennsylvania Railroad Station at Front and French streets. Built in 1906 by the well-known Philadelphia architect Frank Furness, the station translated Roman architecture into brick and steel. Its large waiting room featured a high ceiling supported by massive arches. Outside, a clock tower was the building's most prominent feature. Leaving the station, a visitor emerged onto Front Street, which, in spite of years of intermittent entreaties by the Board of Trade, still presented a tawdry appearance. Two second-class hotels—the Stoeckle, owned by a local brewery, and the Merritt—both featuring steam heat, electric lights, and cafe-style restaurants, confronted the visitor as he or she emerged from Pennsylvania Station.

Strolling on Market Street was a major recreational activity for most citizens in 1912, especially on Friday and Saturday nights,when the street was crowded with shoppers.[37] The ever-increasing army of young female sales clerks and office employees was particularly in evidence, promenading to show off their smart new clothes. "Smartness," as the society editor of *Delaware Life Magazine* explained condescendingly, "consists in wearing the very latest; in walking, in holding yourself in the most aristocratic manner, in using the latest and 'swellest slang' . . ."[38] Another writer in the same magazine defended working girls against the charge of "coarseness" imputed to them by "society" people, but, clearly, many of Wilmington's old monied families regarded the growing number of splashily dressed young women with distaste.[39]

In 1912 the retail center of the city extended from the vicinity around 4th and Market, site of Lippincott's, Wilmington's one department store, to about 8th Street. The original identity of most of the stores as century-old houses was disguised by new facades and a clutter of signs and billboards. There were several hotels along Market Street, none very distinguished. The largest, the Clayton House at 5th Street, had been a first-class hotel when it opened in 1871, but by 1912 it was looking rather seedy and was shortly thereafter converted into a movie theater called the Queen. Indeed, one of the signs of the times was the growing popularity of movie theaters. The movies had great power to create rising expectations and new material demands in the expanding mass culture. In 1912 there were six theaters on Market Street and more were being planned.

Above 8th Street, offices displaced retail establishments. In 1881 the county courthouse had been moved from the town of New Castle to a plot at the crest of the hill separating the Christina from the Brandywine bounded by 10th and 11th streets and Market and King streets. Since then, lawyers' offices had taken over much of that neighborhood. The city's banks were still scattered along Market Street, but the trend was for the financial establishments also to move uptown. The city's largest bank, The Equitable, built Wilmington's first skyscraper, a six-story office building at 9th and Market, in 1892. Other banks, the Wilmington Savings Fund Society and the Delaware Trust, stood on opposite corners at 9th and Market.

By 1912 a new, even more impressive center for the city's economic and political activities was being created at 10th and Market streets. Here, on the high ground surrounding the Court House Square, the best location for a center of prestige and power in the city, the Du Pont Company had just recently erected a twelve-story office building.

The modern history of the Du Pont Company has been told many times.[40] Suffice it to say here that the gunpowder company founded by Eleuthère Irénée du Pont on the banks of the Brandywine in 1802 underwent a modernization one hundred years later that completely and radi-

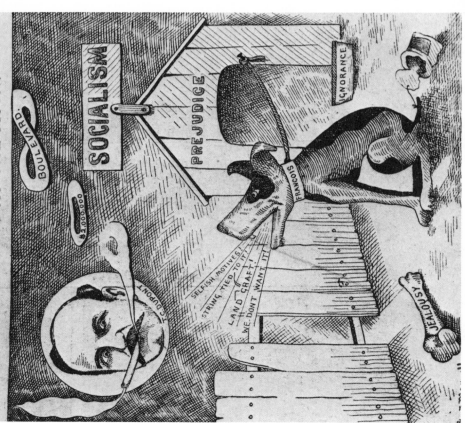

The du Pont Highway project as seen by a political cartoonist and by a department store. These pictures appeared in the Wilmington *Sunday Star* on December 10, 1911, and April 9, 1911, respectively. (*Courtesy of the Historical Society of Delaware*)

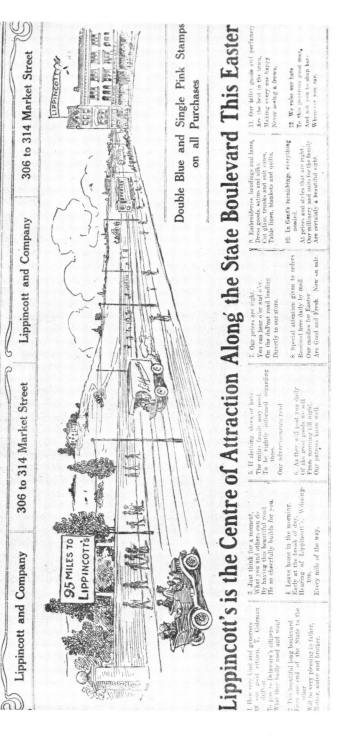

Double Blue and Single Pink Stamps on all Purchases

Lippincott's is the Centre of Attraction Along the State Boulevard This Easter

1 How very kind and generous
Of our good citizen, T. Coleman duPont
To give to Delaware's citizens
What they badly need and want.

2 This beautiful long boulevard
From one end of the State to the other
Will be very pleasing to father,
Mother, sister and brother.

3 Just think for a moment,
What you and others can do
By having this beautiful road
He so cheerfully builds for you.

4 Leave home in the morning,
Early at the break of day,
Hearing of Lippincott's, Wilmington,
Every mile of the way.

5 If clothing, shoes or hats
The entire family may need,
To be rightly informed regarding these,
Our advertisements read.

6 As they will post you daily
Of the good goods we sell
From morning till night,
Our patrons know well.

7 Our prices are right.
You can hear o'er and o'er,
On the duPont road leading
Directly to our store.

8 Special attention given to orders
Received here daily by mail
Our candies for Easter
Are Good and Fresh. Now on sale.

9 Embroideries, bandings and laces,
Dress goods, satins and silks,
Cut glass, trunks and suit cases,
Table linen, blankets and quilts.

10 In Gents furnishings, everything needed.
At prices and styles that are right:
Our millinery and suits for the family
Are certainly a beautiful sight.

11 Our toilet goods and perfumery
Are the best in the town,
Making every one happy
Never seeing a frown.

12 We raise our hats
To the generous good man,
And ask you to shop here
Whenever you can.

cally altered the company's direction of growth, the du Pont family's fortunes, and the twentieth-century development of Wilmington.

In 1902, after the death of company president Eugene du Pont, grandson of the founder, the surviving family elders decided to sell the firm, then the largest manufacturer of explosives in America. The company had grown in the late nineteenth century by acquiring controlling interests in numerous small powder companies and by building new factories in various parts of the United States where explosives were used for industrial, and particularly mining, purposes. In spite of its size and dominance in the explosives industry, as late as 1902 the Du Pont Company was still managed as a family enterprise. Corporate decisions were made by a committee of elder du Ponts who were impervious to outside suggestions for modernization, even when these came from younger men within their own family. The impact of the company on Wilmington was modest, because the du Ponts and most of their workers lived in their own insular world northwest of the city between the Kennett Pike and the Brandywine River, adjacent to the company's original mills at Hagley.

Among the men who gathered to decide the fate of the company, only one, Alfred I. du Pont, was young and vigorous enough to challenge his elders' decision to sell. A combative man steeped in family tradition and trained in the manufacture of powder, Alfred was determined not to lose the destiny that he regarded as his family birthright: the opportunity to own and manage the firm. In the most dramatic and significant moment in the company's history, the older du Ponts agreed to sell the company to Alfred for $12,000,000.00, provided that he brought into its management his cousins T. Coleman and Pierre S. du Pont, both of whom were more experienced executives and financiers.

T. Coleman du Pont was chosen president of the reorganized company. Tall, expansive, adventuresome, and highly ambitious, Coleman had grown up in Kentucky, where he managed a coal mine and a steel company before he found his true calling as a business promoter and financier. Cousin Pierre, the treasurer of the reorganized company, was the son of Lammot du Pont, the first du Pont to manufacture dynamite. The eldest of ten children, Pierre willingly accepted the heavy responsibility of becoming a substitute "Dad" for his younger brothers and sisters after his father's death in a plant explosion. Pierre's was a complex personality. He was a quiet but alert man, the least personally imposing of the three cousins, but ultimately the most important. Like Alfred, he had grown to manhood on the Brandywine and was powerfully tied to his family and its business tradition, yet in his deliberate, detached way he was as eager as Coleman to move the firm away from its antiquated moorings toward a major role among America's big business industries.

The houses lining Vandever Avenue were constructed during the first decade of the 20th century near the new Pennsylvania Railroad shops at Todd's Cut. *(Courtesy of the Eleutherian Mills Historical Library)*

At the turn of the century, American business was undergoing a profound and, at the time, highly controversial remodeling. Assisted by the financial power of a few large investment banks, many industries were reorganized on a colossal scale into nationwide monopolies or "trusts." In Wilmington, for example, the old Harlan and Hollingsworth Company was bought out by the United States Ship Company, a subsidiary of U.S. Steel, one of the largest of the new trusts. The Jackson and Sharp Company, another leading local industry, was absorbed into the St. Louis based American Car and Foundry Company. The immense economic power exercised by these business combinations was either frightening or exciting, depending on one's point of view. To Coleman and Pierre du Pont, the desire to create a powder trust was irresistible. For Coleman it represented his biggest opportunity yet in business promotion. For Pierre consolidation offered the means by which powder production could be brought to the highest level of efficiency and thus be made more profitable to his family without becoming more costly to the customer.

According to his biographers, Alfred D. Chandler and Stephen Salsbury, it was Pierre more than Coleman who directed the creation of the modern Du Pont company.[41] The first step in this process, gaining complete control over the smaller explosives firms, T. Coleman managed through a deal whereby little money changed hands but many stocks and bonds were exchanged. Once in control of these companies, Pierre systematically studied their operations with an eye toward a large-scale consolidation of functions in every step of the business from the purchasing of raw materials to the sale of the finished product. The Du Pont Company remained a family-owned business, but under Pierre's leadership it was no longer managed solely by members of the family. Capable men from the acquired powder firms were brought into the big new company and those du Ponts who were retained had to earn their positions. In Pierre's view it was more important to provide the family with dividends than with jobs.[42]

Consolidation greatly increased the company's need for management personnel and office space. The office building on the Hagley property from which Coleman's predecessor, Eugene, had directed the company was clearly inadequate. But where should new offices be located? Coleman's preference was for New York City, the mecca for big business, where he had other enterprises afloat. But both Pierre and Alfred argued that the company should remain near the Brandywine. The matter being of less importance to Coleman than to the others, he agreed but insisted that the headquarters be located in an urban setting close to banks, railroad connections, and hotel facilities. This compromise brought the Du Pont Company into the heart of Wilmington.

In 1904 the Du Pont Company bought land on the northwest corner of 10th and Market streets and began demolishing the structures there. A year later Pierre reported to the executive committee that the new building was being designed to accommodate 549 employees, most of whom would be employed in the Accounting Department (150) and in Sales (129).[43] The company proceeded to work out a complicated set of agreements for the construction and ownership of the building. In 1903 the du Ponts had chartered a bank, the Wilmington Trust Company, which handled the financing and construction of the building and shared its office space with the powder corporation.

During the construction a difference of opinion arose among the three cousins over the question of the building's name. The debate, which revealed their differing temperaments and attitudes toward business and family tradition, boded ill for their continued cooperation. Ever the practical businessman, Pierre suggested the name "Wilmington Trust Building," which, he said, would help advertise their new bank. When Alfred, then vacationing in Miami, heard of this he indignantly wrote to his cousin Coleman that the only name possible was "du Pont de Nemours . . . This building should stand as a monument to our ancestors, as it is their industry and frugality which is directly responsible for its construction."[44] The pragmatic T. Coleman suggested calling it simply the Du Pont Building, since, he said, that's what people would call it anyway. Alfred was only partially assuaged by this compromise, which he believed put utility ahead of filiopatristic duty. But T. Coleman was the president, and the stone cutter carved "Du Pont Building" into the main portal.

In 1912 the du Ponts built a large addition to their building to house a 200-room first-class hotel advertised as "Wilmington's Million Dollar Hotel."[45] It was an improvement that both the city and the company desperately needed. The hotel was as splendid as any that one might see in the most cosmopolitan metropolis. The ballroom, with its intricately gilded baroque appointments, vast mahogany doors, and curved marble staircase, was stunning beyond anything ever built in Wilmington before or since. The restaurant, lobby, and other public rooms were equally impressive in their rich design, quality of workmanship, and costliness of materials. Easily eclipsing every other hotel or meeting place in the city, the Hotel du Pont came to be known simply as *the* hotel among Wilmingtonians, just as the Du Pont building was *the* building and the Du Pont Company, *the* company.

The big new office building and hotel changed one face of the Court House Square in a way that made nearby structures appear puny and out of date. The county courthouse building, in particular, though only about thirty years old, looked like old-fashioned gingerbread next to its larger, more streamlined neighbor. The juxtaposition made Wilmington as a whole look like an unimpressive backwater town. John J. Raskob, Pierre S. du Pont's assistant, proposed to remedy that situation. A native of Cleveland and the son of poor Catholic Alsacian immigrants, Raskob was more comfortable dealing with city and county politicians than was Pierre. It was Raskob rather than one of the du Ponts who organized the campaign to tear down the old courthouse and build an imposing new city-county building on King Street facing the old Court House Square. The square would then become a public park separating the Du Pont Building on one side from the city-county building on the other. In time he expected that other monumental buildings could be constructed on 10th and 11th streets facing the square.

Raskob's vision for a more impressive Wilmington was part of a much larger national effort aimed at improving urban life. In 1912 many American urban leaders were zealously and optimistically committed to a variety of reforms that, taken together, made up a major part of what was called the Progressive Movement. In cities throughout the nation, young lawyers, journalists, and businessmen, and their female counterparts—social workers like Jane Addams of Chicago—were battling against corrupt "bosses" and supporting programs to make government more "businesslike," to educate the immigrants, to improve living conditions for the poor, and in general to bring Americans closer to fulfilling their dreams of a decent life.

This house near 30th and Washington Streets was typical of residences designed to appeal to middle-income buyers in 1912. *(Courtesy of the Historical Society of Delaware)*

The movement transcended political parties. Two presidents of the United States, Theodore Roosevelt, a Republican, and Woodrow Wilson, a Democrat, identified themselves as Progressives. In 1912, one of the most colorful and exciting presidential election years in American history, the Progressive Movement split the Republican party when the party renominated its incumbent president, William Howard Taft, over the former Republican president, Theodore Roosevelt, his more progressive rival. The Roosevelt wing of the party then formed a third party, the Progressives, with Roosevelt as their standard bearer. This split permitted Wilson's election. In Wilmington, for instance, where the Democratic candidate received nearly 8,000 votes, the GOP 4,500 and the Progressives 5,200, a combined vote of the latter two would have given the Republicans a substantial majority.

Viewed another way, the results testify to the popularity of the Progressives among the city's voters; a popularity that was especially evident in the more affluent wards in the newer parts of the city.[46] One manifestation of this diffuse social and political phenomenon was the urge to beautify cities. The City Beautiful Movement, as it was called, had its start at the Chicago World's Fair in 1893.[47] Visitors to the Columbian Exposition had been amazed and dazzled by the dramatic architectural and spatial effects created by Daniel Burnham's Great White City on Lake Michigan. The long mall, offset by fountains and heroic statuary and flanked by impressive Roman-style buildings, demonstrated what cities might become with proper planning.

During the years between the World's Fair and the entrance of the United States into World War I, enthusiasm for the City Beautiful swept American cities. Its greatest impact was, not surprisingly, in Washington, D.C., where the Capitol Mall underwent substantial development. In Philadelphia an old neighborhood was demolished to make way for the Benjamin Franklin Parkway, modeled on the Champs-Elysees. John J. Raskob and Pierre du Pont shared the ideals of the City Beautiful movement. They wanted Wilmington to become a progressive, forward-looking, attractive city not only for its own citizens but also to impress businessmen who came to the city to do business with their company. Furthermore, Raskob and du Pont had the wealth and power to give life to their dream.

It is difficult to reconstruct the chain of events that led to the creation of Rodney Square, because Raskob at first moved secretly, but the main outline of his action is visible. Everyone agreed that both the Wilmington City Hall, on Market Street below 6th, and the New Castle County Courthouse were inadequate structures. The city hall had been hopelessly unsatisfactory for decades and was dirty and decrepit from over 100 years of heavy use as the mayor's office, municipal court, police station, and city jail. The county courthouse also was too small, and although it housed irreplaceable records including deeds, wills, and tax data, it was not fireproof. Neither the city nor county had the money to build new facilities, nor would they have been likely to join ranks on a collaborative effort without outside mediation. In about 1912 Raskob quietly organized "a group of civic-minded citizens" who began to buy up properties along King Street between 10th and 11th streets.[48] His next step was to rally citizen support for a joint city-county building and to secure approval from city and county officials and from the state legislature to finance the structure. At this point Raskob had to go public. He, therefore, invited the public to come to his office in the Du Pont Building to sign petitions addressed to the various public authorities requesting a new city-county building. In December 1912 the newspapers published sketches of the proposed building and public square. A series of public meetings was held to further broaden the base of support. Two months later, in February 1913, both Republicans and Democrats in the state legislature voted overwhelmingly in favor of a bond issue to finance the project.[49] J. J. Raskob was appointed to head a commission composed of politicians and leading citizens to oversee the work. In 1917 the City-County Building was completed in the best City Beautiful classical style.

Taken as a whole, Raskob's success was a stunning demonstration of his talents. He knew when to be secretive and when to draw the public into his plans. He was helped in this endeavor not only by his close association with Pierre du Pont but also by his careful wooing of the city's lesser businessmen. Raskob created the conditions in which retail merchants and owners and managers of small factories felt themselves to be active participants in the city's development even after the big powder company had eclipsed their dominance. To this end he founded an organization called the City Club, which rented space at the Hotel du Pont for luncheons, cards, billiards, and meetings. The Club's roster included members of the du Pont family, but it also dipped below the highest social stratum to include those middle-level businessmen who ran stores, managed real estate, served on the school board, or got elected to city council.[50] A newcomer himself to the city and ultimately a very rich and famous man, Raskob served as a bridge between two socioeconomic worlds at this crucial moment in the city's adaptation to its recently acquired big-business economy.

In striking contrast to the City-County Building success story, however, was the failure of Wilmingtonians to agree on city charter reform. Like the old City Hall, the city's charter was an antique relic of an age when the town was small and the duties of government few. With the rise in urban population and the development of transportation, sanitation and power technologies in the latter years of the nineteenth century, Wilmington, like other cities, experienced an expansion in government. Schools had to be built and staffed, police hired, sewers dug, pavement laid, franchises granted, and reservoirs constructed. Wilmington's government, mired in petty political squabbling, seemed destined to prevent progress. The city's economic leaders, although unwilling to enter the political lists as candidates for public office, were determined to make the city competitive in the contest for new industry. They resolved their difficulty by pressing the state legislature to create bipartisan citizen commissions that operated independently of the mayor and city council to administer the water department, parks, streets and sewers, and other municipal services. The role of the mayor and city council was reduced to one of near-impotence.[51]

At the turn of the century, in cities through the country, Progressives were demanding charter reform to make government more "businesslike": that is, efficient and responsible, and more answerable to "the people." Reformers suggested various means to achieve those ends, the least radical of which was the restructuring of muddled urban governments to make them congruent with the U.S. Constitution's three branches: executive, legislative, and judicial. Wilmington's charter typified the problems that ensued when these three functions were commingled. Autonomous commissions managed the major city departments with no overarching executive leadership; lines of authority between the mayor and city council overlapped; and the city could undertake no project that could not be financed through current revenues without securing permission from the state legislature for a bond issue.

For years a band of dedicated businessmen pressed unavailingly for a new charter. Finally, in 1912 a blue-ribbon bipartisan committee was established to draft a new charter bill. The committee included Robert H. Richards, a leading Republican attorney who was close to the du Ponts, and Thomas F. Bayard, scion of Delaware's oldest, most distinguished Democratic family. The committee recommended a charter that would eliminate state interference in city affairs, reduce the number of political appointments to city offices, and divide the responsibilities of the mayor and council. It provided for a professional administrator to coordinate and superintend municipal services. The provisions of the proposed charter were published in newspapers and discussed at public meetings. The widely read *Sunday Star* spoke earnestly on its behalf and predicted that a large majority of voters would ratify the charter.[52] On election day, 1 June 1912, supporters of charter reform were disappointed. Eight out of every nine of the fewer than 9,000 ballots cast were against the charter.[53] The vote demonstrated the apathy of many citizens. Among those who bothered to

Upper-middle-class taste in housing at the turn of the century is typified by these Queen Anne style homes on Jefferson Street above 9th Street. *(Courtesy of the Historical Society of Delaware)*

vote were many party hacks who depended on political favors for city jobs. But, in the "strange bedfellow" tradition of American politics, the antis also included sincere reformers who objected to the proposal because it did not include provisions for initiative, referendum, and recall, three icons of popular control in the Progressive era. These people, organized as the Referendum League, could not bear to take a half a loaf of reform, so they scuttled the chance for change. Some opponents, among them the Socialist party, Labor Unionists, and blacks, believed that the new charter would

Upper-middle-class housing during World War I in the highlands section near Rockford Park shows the popularity of the colonial revival style. *(Courtesy of the Eleutherian Mills Historical Library)*

give city officials too much power, make them less answerable to popular sentiment, and lead to an increase in taxes without a comparable increase in services.[54] The thrust of these arguments reinforces the observation of Professor Samuel Hays that the main proponents of city charter reform during the Progressive Era were businessmen seeking efficient administration of urban affairs, not lower-income people or political radicals.[55] Throughout the United States, numerous cities, both large and small, adopted new home rule charters during the Progressive Era.[56] Wilmington was not among them. Charter reform in Wilmington died a death of disillusion that divided the ranks of the reformers and buried the charter issue for many years. Presumably the charter's supporters could have used J. J. Raskob's talents to reach a consensus between the new elite businessmen and the old local business community, but the du Pont group was conspicuously uninvolved in the reform movement.

The leading family's reticence perhaps stemmed from T. Coleman du Pont's position as the "boss" of the state Republican machine. Politics in Delaware at that time was unusually unsavory. In 1910 the *New York Evening Post* described the state uncharitably, but not entirely inaccurately, as a "degraded and debased little rotten borough with a polluted and debauched electorate."[57] Delaware had gained this unenviable reputation during the 1890s, when an unscrupulous political opportunist with the unforgettable name of John Edward O'Sullivan Addicks had mounted a

Wilmington's "Chateau Country" had its beginnings in these homes of du Pont family members located on the Kennett Pike adjacent to the Du Pont Company's earliest mills on the Brandywine. "St. Amour," the turreted house in front, was the boyhood home of Pierre S. du Pont. *(Courtesy of the Eleutherian Mills Historical Library)*

lavishly financed effort to bribe the state legislature into making him a U.S. Senator. Addicks, a native of Philadelphia, had acquired a fortune buying and manipulating gas company franchises in numerous American cities. He was known disparagingly as the "Napoleon of Gas" or "Gas Addicks." His political exertions changed the GOP in Delaware from a minority party with strength only in industrialized New Castle County into a party with statewide power but deeply divided loyalties. Addicks used his money to bribe voters and legislators alike in order to establish a block favorable to him. Wilmington's conservative businessmen, shocked to see their party falling into such disreputable hands, turned to the aging Henry Algernon du Pont as the genteel symbol and standard bearer of their opposition.

Colonel H. A. du Pont, a West Point graduate, had distinguished himself as an officer during the Civil War before turning to a career in business. He was active in the Du Pont Company in the late nineteenth century and was president of the Wilmington and Northern Railroad, which served the powder yards. The Colonel staved off an Addicks victory in the 1890s but could not get himself elected. Then in 1900 Coleman du Pont took up residence in Wilmington and entered the fray on his cousin's behalf. Coleman went on the offensive, using the tactics employed by the Gas King. After more than a decade of futile efforts by both sides to elect their favorites, Colonel Henry A. du Pont entered the U.S. Senate in 1906, where he served until his defeat in 1916, long after Addicks had run out of funds and left the scene.

1912 proved to be a year of embarrassment for the Colonel. In February of that year, a fellow senator from Missouri, Democrat James H. Reed, in a speech on the Senate floor, accused du Pont of corrupt political practices. Later that spring witnesses at a public hearing described a meeting in the Du Pont Building where H. A. du Pont and T. C. du Pont were present when $25,000 in cash was put on a table to be distributed in Delaware's Kent and Sussex counties on behalf of the machine.[58] Senator Reed's charges drew national attention to the sleazy nature of Delaware politics and pointed to the fact that Coleman du Pont had eclipsed Addicks in the state's GOP not by cleaning house but by outbribing him. But whatever his methods, Coleman had succeeded in doing what Addicks could not: he had united the party and made his political machine the dominant force in the state.

In 1912 T. Coleman du Pont was the most powerful and the best known figure in Delaware, not only because he was president of the state's largest corporation and leader of a well-oiled political machine, but because he was in the process of constructing in Delaware the first modern automobile highway in the United States. Coleman's interest in roads sprang from a number of sources. He had trained as a civil engineer at the Massachusetts Institute of Technology, where he learned the principles of road construction. Subsequently, his involvement in the financing and management of urban transit companies taught him a great deal more about transportation. He had also worked for a time with Tom Johnson, a steel company owner who, influenced by reading Henry George's popular economic treatise, *Progress and Poverty*, had become a famous reform mayor in Cleveland, Ohio. The ideas of Henry George and Tom Johnson strongly appealed to Coleman du Pont. In *Progress and Poverty* George attempted to explain the mysterious irony that amid America's rising material prosperity, poverty was also increasing. He concluded that the cause of this anomaly was that landowners were deriving unfair and economically unsound profits from the progress earned by society as a whole. His solution was to treat land as common property to be leased to individual owners, who would pay a "single tax" on the unearned increment they received from the land's increasing value.[59] As mayor of Cleveland, Johnson did not enact the single tax, but he did urge similarly socialistic schemes, such as public ownership of the city's transit facilities, which, like land, became more valuable as the population and economy expanded.

These various strands of training, career, and ideas influenced Coleman du Pont's innovative approach to highway building. His concept for the engineering of roadways was totally new, his philanthropy on a scale that appeared literally unbelievable. Boasting that he would "build a monument a hundred miles high and lay it down on the ground,"[60] he announced in 1908 his plan to personally finance and oversee the construction of a highway from Delaware's southern border to Wilmington. With the advent of the automobile, he later wrote, "I realized the wonderful development of which our little state is susceptible."[61] He envisaged the highway as a super road, a modern spinal column for the state, with a massive 200-foot-wide right of way adequate to allow separate lanes for automobiles, horse-drawn vehicles, trolley cars, and pedestrians. In addition there would be space on either side of the roadway to lease to utilities and for other concessions. In order to maintain this unprecedented width and to minimize interruptions to traffic flow, the highway would follow a then novel plan to skirt towns along the way rather than to pass directly through them.[62]

Coleman du Pont's breathtaking plan met with mixed reactions from Delawareans. Farmers, a naturally conservative group suspicious of big city financiers, were hostile to the project because du Pont planned to ask the legislature for powers of eminent domain. They were inclined to believe that the millionaire businessman had some ulterior motive for wanting their land. Most Wilmingtonians, by contrast, were gleeful at the prospect of getting a modern highway at no cost to the taxpayers. Typical of the reaction in the city was a 1911 advertisement for Lippincott's Department Store depicting motorists driving along a highway past a sign which read "95 miles to Lippincott's." Far on the horizon the store appeared as the centerpiece of the gleaming city.[63]

Opponents such as farmers and the Socialist party argued that Delaware should take care to look a gift horse in the mouth. They believed that du Pont was demanding a right of way of unprecedented breadth so that he could personally profit from leases to various concessions along the route.[64] Du Pont countered that he did indeed believe that the land adjacent to the highway would increase greatly in value, but since he planned to turn the entire roadway over to the state, it would be the public, not he, who would benefit. Indeed, it was his expectation that revenue from leases would fully defray the cost of the highway's maintenance. The *Sunday Star*, a staunch supporter of the du Pont road, published a cartoon that summed up the attitude of the highway's adherents. Coleman, depicted as the moon, was being attacked by a howling socialist dog who barked "selfish motives" and "string tied to it." The dog's house was labeled "prejudice," his bowl "ignorance," and his bone "jealousy."[65]

In speeches and pamphlets Coleman campaigned for his concepts. He was a founder of the National Highways Association, which lobbied for an interstate system to cover the nation with fifty thousand miles of modern roads designed for automotive travel. He argued that in the coming era of automobile and truck travel it would be the physically isolated Americans, farm folk especially, who would benefit most from good roads. With improved transportation the farmer could increase both his profits and the nation's food supply. The national economy would be quickened to the advantage of all.[66] In a speech to Wilmington-area engineers, du Pont suggested a scheme by which the city could finance its own expansion and simultaneously add to its housing supply by following the example of his principles. Wilmington, he said, should buy right of ways of 200 feet along all its major approach roads. The city could then lease roadside land at rates low enough to attract housing contractors. Later the developed land would produce tax revenues for the city.[67] How different the city's history might have been had government officials been daring enough to follow his advice.

In 1911, after several years of public debate, the state legislature authorized the Coleman du Pont Road, Inc., which was given the power of eminent domain. The company began construction in Sussex County, where it soon ran into various legal obstacles that convinced du Pont that he must scale down his boulevard plan from a 200-foot to a 100-foot right of way. Robbed of its original dimensions, the highway was reduced in some sections to a two-lane concrete road, but it heralded the automobile age in Delaware and became the backbone of a state highway system.

Meanwhile, highway construction had become a national priority. In 1916 Congress passed the Federal Aid Road Act, a law that established a grant-in-aid program to assist states in road construction. To qualify for aid, each state was required to have a highway administration agency. Consequently, in 1916 Delaware's legislature created the State Highway Department. The department, led by a chief engineer, was to report to a five-man bipartisan commission consisting of the governor plus one representative appointed by the governor from each of the three counties and Wilming-

These California bungalows in Elsmere typify the houses built in the trolley suburbs around Wilmington during the World War I era. *(Photograph by the author)*

ton. The incumbent governor, John G. Townsend, Jr., an advocate of good roads who had the support of T. Coleman du Pont's political organization, chose du Pont as the commissioner from Wilmington.

The enactment of this legislation cast the du Pont road project in a new light. To avoid claims of conflict of interest, du Pont resigned from the commission and entered into negotiations with the Highway Department to turn over the completed portion of his road to the new state authority. In 1917 Coleman du Pont and the Highway Department reached an agreement whereby the financier continued to provide funds for the completion of the road at the rate of $44,000 per mile.[68] When the highway was finally completed in 1923 T. Coleman du Pont had spent $3,917,004.00 to build his 100-mile monument.[69]

Cities shrink or grow on the basis of their economic functions and modes of transportation. In 1912 both of these major factors were undergoing profound alteration in Wilmington. The significance of the Du Pont Company's growth and of its owners' decision to move into the city have already been suggested; a bit more needs to be said about transportation.

In 1912 the automobile was still a plaything of the rich. As we have seen, during Old Home Week the promise of a parade of cars could draw a crowd. It was not until that year that the city council adopted an ordinance requiring that motor cars be driven on the right-hand side of the street. The drivers of vehicles had so much trouble adapting to the law that the police assigned mounted officers to keep traffic to the right on Market Street and King Street.[70] The city had adopted its first ordinance regulating automobiles in 1904, at the request of auto owners. That same year, Pierre S. du Pont presided over the meeting held at the Wilmington Country Club at which the Delaware Automobile Association was formed to lobby for loose government regulation. Members agreed "to place their automobiles at the disposal of members of city council and invite them to take a ride in order to demonstrate the importance and advisability of not placing too great a limit on the speed of automobiles."[71] Pierre personally took two street and sewer commissioners for a ride in his car and reported that "they seemed much surprised at the rate of speed which can be maintained with apparent safety."[72] Subsequently, city council raised the speed limit for cars from eight to twenty miles per hour, but, at the same time, they required auto owners to obtain a $2.00 license from the street and sewer department that the department could revoke for careless driving. As an additional safety precaution, motorists were to sound a horn or bell at each intersection.[73] Five years later a state law superseded the city's attempt to regulate automobile traffic.[74]

Before the State Highway Department was created in 1916, county roads outside the city of Wilmington were hardly better than they had been in colonial times. There was no coordinated road system. The Levy Court, New Castle County's five-man elected governing body, had charge over roadways and bridges. It, in turn, divided that responsibility among road supervisors for each of the county's subdivisions, called hundreds. As late as 1910 the Levy Court reported that only 63.56 miles of the nearly 1,000 miles of roadways in the county were "improved"—that is, macadamized.[75] Aside from these few old turnpikes that charged tolls for the privilege of bumping along their gravel-strewn surfaces, roads were merely mud paths.

For the great majority of city people, the trolley car was still the only substitute for walking. The pattern of trolley expansion thus shaped urban residential development. The Wilmington City Railway Company seldom extended its line beyond actual settlement. Its lethargy was upset in the late 1890s by competition from the more aggressive Peoples Railway Company. Thereafter the two companies met in head-on competition in some central city areas, but in general the W.C.R. Co. directed its main line northwest along Market Street into the 9th Ward, while the Peoples Railway Company seized upon the other major growth area, to the southwest, with its line to Elsmere and Brandywine Springs.

Trolley companies were the first major generators of electricity, and it was common for the same company that supplied transit service to sell electric power also. Utilities could be profitable, but involvement in them was risky, because they were heavily dependent on local politicians for franchises, and because they were subject to financial manipulation. Holding companies piled upon holding companies in the transit and power business. Two reasons for this pyramiding were the desire to create intraurban monopolies and the desire to build interurban connections. The Wilmington City Railway, for example, extended its track north toward Chester, where it joined the line of a Pennsylvania transit company that ran from Chester to Darby and then into Philadelphia. The urge to consolidate interlocking lines was overwhelming, as was the urge to control urban politicians in order to ensure that conditions remained favorable. The ordinary citizen had reason to fear the power of these privately owned monopolies, and arguments over the rights and responsibilities of the trolley companies were a stock-in-trade debate in every American city at the turn of the century. No wonder, then, that Mayor Tom Johnson of Cleveland made national news when he, himself a former transit owner, successfully instituted public ownership of that city's trolley lines.

In Wilmington one might have expected the outcome of the utility battles to have been absorption by Philadelphia traction interests. Indeed, there was rumor of such a takeover in 1893, when the very well financed Widener and Elkins interests in Philadelphia were said to be planning a mammoth trolley line to extend from the Quaker City to Washington, D.C., absorbing all in its path.[76] Nothing ever came of this scheme, but in 1898 the Wilmington City Railway Company was sold to Philadelphia capitalists.[77] By 1906 the W.C.R. Co. was part of the Interstate Railway Company, which included a number of lines in Pennsylvania and New Jersey.[78] These mergers culminated in 1910 with the creation of the Wilmington and Philadelphia Traction Company, which, in spite of its name, was a purely Wilmington-area concern that included among its other holdings the Old Wilmington City Railway Company, the Wilmington City Electric Company, and the Wilmington Light and Power Company. Five years later the syndicate completed its monopoly of the city's transit facilities with its purchase of the Peoples Railway Company and the New

"A street in Wilmington's Polish section." Low-income housing of the 1920s from Grace T. Brewer, "Report of the Americanization Bureau, 1924–1925," *Bulletin of the Service Citizens of Delaware* 7, no. 3 (January 1926). *(Courtesy of the Historical Society of Delaware)*

Castle and Delaware City companies.[79] Meanwhile, Wilmington's competing power companies were consolidated into the Wilmington Gas and Electric Company in 1901 and sold to a large Philadelphia-based syndicate eight years later.[80]

Pierre S. du Pont and Alfred I. du Pont were among the seven directors of the Wilmington Light, Power and Telephone Company, a consolidation of Delmarva Telephone and Wilmington Electric Light and Power, and a subsidiary of Wilmington and Philadelphia Traction. Pierre, like his cousin T. Coleman, had been involved in the traction business before his return to Wilmington in 1902. He had worked for Tom Johnson's Lorain Steel Company, which manufactured rails for trolleys. This job drew him into the management of several traction companies, most particularly those of Dallas, Texas. Pierre subscribed $50,000 to the new Wilmington power company in 1906. The total capital stock of the company was $1,250,000, of which the Wilmington Trust Company was trustee for the first mortgage. The power company's president, Charles C. Kurtz, was also a vice-president of the Wilmington Trust. The company owned a telephone plant in Wilmington and controlled the telephone trunk line between Philadelphia and Baltimore. Although all of its operations returned good profits (about ten percent on investment in 1906) the Wilmington City Railway was its biggest money-maker.[81]

In 1910 the company was reorganized and recapitalized minus the telephone business, which had competed feebly with the Bell Company, with Pierre, Alfred, and Coleman du Pont and J. J. Raskob as principal stockholders. Five months after the creation of the Wilmington and Philadelphia Traction Company, the WL&P Co. was leased to it, and the power companies' stockholders exchanged their shares for those of the traction company. Under its new leadership the traction company improved the quality of existing service but approached expansion conservatively. In 1911, for example, the company's president, in a letter to Pierre, expressed his caution on the question of extending service out of the Concord Pike from Wilmington to West Chester. "There is considerable pressure from several quarters that the extension on Concord Avenue should be made. I do not consider that a largely profitable business would be done but probably it would justify our investment out as far as Lombardy Cemetary [sic] [about one mile beyond the city limits] but we should recognize the necessity of patcence [sic] in regard to satisfactory returns." He continued, "Aside from the question in such cases as to a certain duty of occupying territory which is at least nearly ripe for street railway service, I have no doubt that the public should be able to look to a street railway company to go a little bit ahead, in its occupation of new territory, of immediately, profitable returns."[82] A more audacious policy might have proved foolhardy financially, but it would undoubtedly have speeded the suburbanization of the Concord Pike area.

Even with such careful management, the company did not prove to be as immediately profitable as its investors had hoped. The gas industry cut into the company's sales of electric power for lighting, and in 1912 sluggish business conditions retarded electric consumption. Wilmington had in that year 47 electricity customers per thousand people, which compared favorably with Baltimore's 30 and Philadelphia's 23 but looked poor compared to 71 in Allentown and 86 in Hartford, Connecticut. The manager of the company's power department accounted for this difference on the grounds that Wilmington's population included about 15,000 "colored" who "have no value as electric prospects."[83]

The du Ponts were surely in a position to control not only the development of traction lines and electric power in Wilmington but also to set the course for the city's government. In 1907 T. C. du Pont demonstrated his ascendency over the city's politics when his Republican machine succeeded in electing its candidate, Horace Wilson, as mayor. Almost immediately, however, Wilson attempted to gain independence from the party chairman by refusing to name a man chosen by du Pont to a vacancy on the board of street and sewer commissioners, the body that controlled traction franchises. The row within the GOP delighted the Democratic press and destroyed the mayor's chance for renomination.[54] In spite of the financial and political power that ownership of the traction company gave to the du Pont family, Pierre chose to sell his shares in the Wilmington and Philadelphia Traction Company in 1913.[55] One must assume that he was interested more in profits than in power—of either the electric or the political variety.

To the trolley-traveling public, the net result of all this wheeling and dealing had not amounted to much. Aside from a brief flurry of aggressive competition between the Wilmington City and the Peoples lines around 1900, the trolley companies in Wilmington were content to follow population trends rather than to lead them. A principal element in Wilmington and Philadelphia Tractions' conservatism was that, unlike trolley companies in some other cities, they did not speculate in suburban real estate.[56] In 1912 trolleys extended from the city in only three directions: up north Market Street toward Chester, through south Wilmington to New Castle, and west on the Capitol Trail through Prices Corner to Brandywine Springs. In each case these lines were responsible for the opening of suburbs. Elsmere, on Peoples Railway's Brandywine Springs line, and Montrose, later renamed Bellefonte, on the Wilmington City Railway's Philadelphia Pike route, were Wilmington's pioneer suburban communities.

Elsmere began in 1886 when real-estate promoter Joshua T. Heald saw an opportunity to attract working-class people to a suburb near the junction of the newly built Baltimore and Ohio Railroad and the Wilmington and Reading Railroad. Heald laid out small building lots that he sold for about $200 apiece. Buyers could erect their own homes or hire a contractor. Since Elsmere was outside the city limits, it was exempt from regulations concerning the use of fireproof building materials, and its residents were not assessed for city taxes. The suburb was within walking distance of railway yards and some factories, and the railroad fare to downtown Wilmington was only five cents. Advertising for Elsmere stressed both the cheapness of suburban living and the escape from city noises and fumes.[57]

In 1902 newspaper advertisements announced another workingman's suburb, Montrose, north of the city, where lots costing from $74 to $149 were offered for sale. A lot in the new "village of homes" could be had for $10 down plus $1 a week, and transportation via the trolley line was available to downtown Wilmington and to the Pennsylvania Railroad's new shops at Todd's Cut.[88] In the decade that followed, other tracts were offered for settlement close by these original sites, each with its appealing name suggestive of a snug retreat and its claim of offering more house and more fresh air for less money than could be had in the city. A 1905 advertisement for Richardson Park, adjacent to Elsmere, screamed at the newspaper reader, "Stop paying rent; you must stop it; it will ruin you. Just think of it, no rent, no taxes, no interest, no assessment, everything as free as the air you breathe . . . These beautiful lots are away from the noise and bustle of the city, no smoke, no dust, no fever, plenty of good water. . . ."[89] Another technique developers used was the appeal to the conscience of parents. "Get your children into the country," urged an advertisement for Montrose. "The cities murder children. The hot pavements, the dust, the noise, are fatal in many cases, and harmful always. The history of successful men is nearly always the history of country boys."[90]

When Old Home Week took place in 1912, trolley suburbs were still small and rare in the Wilmington region. Eighty-four percent of New Castle County was still farmland, tied to the city by a systemless hodge-podge of muddy roads. According to the 1910 census there were over 2,000 farms in the county, one-half of them farmed by their owners. The chief products were livestock and the grains to feed them.[91] Fully 70 percent of New Castle County's 123,188 people lived in the city of Wilmington. Elsmere had only 374 inhabitants. Montrose, by then renamed Bellefonte, was not even listed, but Brandywine Hundred, in which it was located, had a total population of 4,440, fewer than all but two of the individual wards in Wilmington. New Castle, with 3,351 inhabitants, and Newark, with 1,913, were the only towns north of the Chesapeake and Delaware Canal with populations over 1,000.[92]

By 1912, forces that would change this highly centralized demographic pattern were already at work. The whole American economy was being remade by big business corporations, and the automobile was on the verge of becoming a mass-produced vehicle within the means of millions of middle-income city dwellers and farmfolk. In Wilmington these dramatic changes were epitomized by the ·new-found importance of the du Pont family and of their reorganized explosives company. Within the course of a decade the three du Pont cousins had begun fashioning a new Wilmington with a new job structure, a new civic center, a new mode of transportation, and a new political and financial power base. Yet those who came to see their former home town during Old Home Week in the fall of 1912 saw only a hint of the great changes to come. They may have marveled at the new Du Pont Building, but, on the whole, Market Street was much as it had been in the 1890s, and the remembered foundries, tanneries, and railroad-related industries were still paramount in the city's economy. Not a trace of the Coleman du Pont Highway was yet to be seen in New Castle County. No one could have known that within two years Europe would be at war and that the expansion of the explosives industry would transform Wilmington into the "Magic City."

CHAPTER 2

The Magic City: 1914–1932

Whenever Wilmington is mentioned outside of Wilming-
ton this thought occurs to the mind of the person to whom
this city is mentioned: "Oh, yes, that's the 'powder town'
which has more wealth per capita than any city of its size
in the country."

Sunday Star, *18 March 1917*

In immediate retrospect 1914 had been a bad year for Wilmington's powder makers. The Du Pont Company's dividend on its common stock was only 8 percent, half of what it had been just two years before. In its annual report, the company laid the blame for lower profits on two conditions: the federal government's successful prosecution of the "powder trust," which had divided the company's assets in 1913, and "depressed conditions" in the national economy caused by the outbreak of war in Europe.[1] No one at the time knew how long the war was to last, how gigantic would be its demands for resources, and how the war would bring dramatic changes to the American powder industry and to the city where that industry was concentrated.

The federal government's antitrust suit against Du Pont, like so many of the famous "trust-busting" efforts of that era, was far less damaging to the company's position in industry than would appear at first glance. The suit grew from the bitter denunciations of a small powder company owner who had once been associated with the Du Pont-dominated Gun Powder Trade Association. His words struck a responsive chord at a time when the Justice Department was eager to take on the giant trusts in order to restore competition to the American economy. After several years of tedious argument, the case was settled by a judicial decree that required the Du Pont Company to create two new powder companies to manufacture dynamite and black powder in competition with itself. Du Pont called these firms Hercules and Atlas, both well-known as trade names in the gunpowder business. The big company was required to provide its new rivals with manufacturing facilities equal to roughly one-half of its own production capacity, for which Du Pont was to be recompensed in securities.

Although the settlement appeared to weaken the Du Pont Company and did reduce the company's sales from $36.5 million in 1912 to $26.7 million in 1913, Du Pont was still the giant in the field. Since the decree dealt with production capacity, not assets, Du Pont was able to foist off its oldest plants on the Hercules and Atlas powder companies.[2] Furthermore, the American military establishment had intervened in the case to urge upon the court the desirability of maintaining one supplier for military powder. Consequently, contrary to the presumed goal of restoring competition, the court permitted Du Pont to maintain its monopoly in at least one line of the powder business—military powder, which, being the most erratic branch of powder making, was considered the least desirable. In peacetime the demand for military powder was low, but in wartime when demand soared the producer had to construct new facilities only to see expensive plants go to waste when orders were promptly canceled at the restoration of peace. Who could have foreseen in 1913, when the court's decree went into effect, what extraordinary times lay ahead?

The busting of the gunpowder trust had little effect on Wilmington, since it became the corporate headquarters for all three powder makers. Both the Hercules and Atlas companies began business in the city in offices they rented in the Du Pont Building. The bulk of their business was in the manufacture of dynamite for mining, road building, and other industrial uses, by far the most important products of the powder industry. At the end of 1913, the first year of competition among the three companies, Atlas had assets of $7.7 million, Hercules of $14.7 million, and Du Pont of $74.8 million.[3]

Germany invaded Belgium in August 1914. Within days Europe was thrust into a war that was to prove the most devastating in history. By the early twentieth century, the Western nations were capable of more complete mobilization for war than had ever been possible before. State bureaucracies efficiently managed conscription laws that brought seemingly endless streams of young men under arms, while factories spewed forth the weapons of war—rifles, artillery, uniforms, items for logistical support—all as expendable and replaceable as the men who used them. The governments of the major combatants—France, Germany, Austria-Hungary, England, and Russia—were willing to make any sacrifice in order to prevent victory by the other side. No resource was left untapped; no potential advantage left untried.

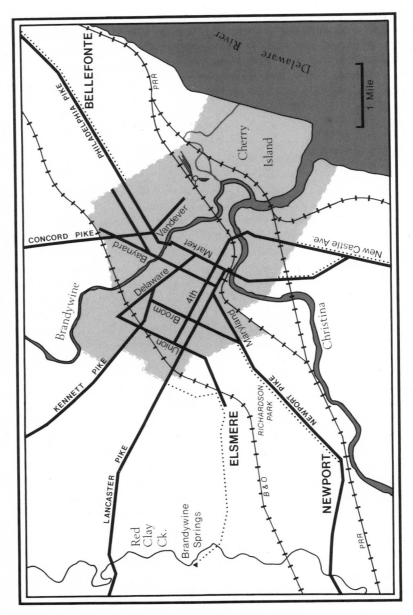

The Wilmington Area in the 1920s. (*Map by Marley Amstutz, Cartographer*)

For the initial three years of the war the United States was not a combatant. Yet, despite President Woodrow Wilson's declarations of neutrality, America's huge industrial capacity was used in support of England and her principal ally, France. Britain alone among the nations at war had the surface fleet necessary to protect transatlantic cargoes. The Allied Powers bought vast amounts of war material from the industrial giant of the western hemisphere, most particularly gunpowder for the thousands of cannons and millions of rifles that boomed ceaselessly along hundreds of miles of trenches. As the sole manufacturer of military powder in the United States, the Du Pont Company became inevitably the major supplier of the powder used by the Allies.

Pierre S. du Pont, who in 1915 succeeded T. Coleman du Pont as president of the company, drove a hard bargain with the Allied governments. Powder that the company had sold to the U.S. government at $0.70 a pound before the war cost the French and British over $1.00 a pound. Pierre justified the high price on the grounds that the enormous orders forced him to expand the company's production facilities with no guarantee that this huge capital investment would be redeemed when the war ended. By early 1916 Du Pont had built $60 million worth of new facilities, while the number of employees had risen from just over 5,000 to more than 60,000.[4] Gross sales for 1916 were 1,130 percent above sales in the immediate prewar period. In just three years Du Pont's assets had climbed from $74.8 million to $217.8 million.[5]

In the midst of skyrocketing orders, unheard-of profits, and frantic pace of operations, bitter controversy split the du Pont cousins. Differences in approach to company affairs between Pierre and Alfred had already been apparent in the contretemps over the naming of the Du Pont Building. While Pierre quietly concerned himself with ways to maximize the value of his family's investment by modernizing operations, Alfred, a flamboyant personality and an old-fashioned powder maker who loved playing the role of friendly superior to his men, was more concerned with maintaining the family's business traditions. These dissimilarities were severely aggravated by two additional factors: Alfred's divorce and remarriage to a du Pont relative in 1907, and T. Coleman's decision in 1915 to give up the presidency of the company and sell his Du Pont stock. The divorce isolated Alfred socially from his large and closely bound family. The stock sale precipitated a law suit that broadened the split and exposed the company's leadership to the critical judgment of the public at large.

In 1914 T. Coleman du Pont relinquished the day-to-day management of the powder firm in order to pursue fresh investments in New York City real estate and offered to sell his stock in the powder company back to the company itself. Alfred agreed to this plan but objected to Coleman's price.

Aerial view of downtown Wilmington about 1930 looking northeast. *(Courtesy of the Eleuthe-rian Mills Historical Library)*

Pierre, who as company treasurer was empowered to carry on the negotiations, instead created a syndicate composed of his immediate family members, which bought the stock. Alfred, together with other family members who had not been included in the syndicate, accused Pierre of bad faith and brought suit in federal court to seek restitution.[6]

The case came to trial in the hot humid days of July 1915. Before gaping crowds of Wilmingtonians, the limousines of the local aristocracy daily arrived at the Federal building at 9th and Shipley streets. Inside the courtroom Pierre's friends and family sat on one side and Alfred's on the other. Reporters for the city's newspapers filed lengthy stories describing the proceedings in detail, especially the dramatic moment when John G. Johnson, the distinguished attorney for the prosecution, at the climax of his summation turned toward Pierre du Pont and John J. Raskob and declared that those two men must be taught that "it is better to be right than to make money."[7] The judge ruled that Pierre's stock purchase plan had technically been within the law. As a result, Pierre was able to channel control of the company and the lion's share of its enormous wartime profits into the hands of his brothers, Irénée and Lammot, and brothers-in-law, R. R. M. Carpenter, H. R. Sharp, and Charles Copeland. The two vehicles for his control were the Delaware Realty and Investment Company, a holding company for Pierre's stock that permitted him to distribute shares within his family without the inconvenience of paying inheritance taxes, and Christiana Securities, a broader-based holding company, controlled by the same group, that was destined to play a major role in Wilmington's history.

While Wilmingtonians witnessed this battle of titans, their city was undergoing changes that would soon transform it into a "Magic City."[8] The war brought unprecedented prosperity to Wilmington, expanding not only its munitions industry, but shipbuilding and general foundry production as well. The Pennsylvania Railroad, which employed 2,500 Wilmingtonians in its shops, switchyards, and regular train service, had never been busier. Between 1914 and 1919, the number of persons in Wilmington engaged in the leather industry nearly doubled. The number employed building and maintaining railroad cars rose from 2,000 to over 3,200, and the total wage-earning workforce of the city jumped from 22,000 to 29,000.[9] Orders strained the capacities of Wilmington's major shipbuilders, Pusey and Jones and Bethlehem Steel's Harlan plant. By 1916 a newspaper claimed that the three powder companies, Du Pont, Hercules, and Atlas, had 20,000 employees in Wilmington and vicinity, including those at Carney's Point, New Jersey, where Du Pont had enlarged its munitions factory.[10] Other new industries in the area included the steel plant built by the Worth Brothers in Claymont in 1916 and the Pyrites Company, which located its chemical facility in south Wilmington.

In 1918 readers of the *Every Evening* could take pride and hope in a full-page advertisement placed by leading local businesses that heralded "Wilmington, the Wealthiest City per Capita in America."[11] The editors of the *Sunday Star*, writing in a similar vein in 1917, declared "Whenever Wilmington is mentioned outside of Wilmington, this thought occurs to the mind of the person to whom this city is mentioned: 'Oh, yes, that's the "powder town" which has more wealth per capita than any city of its size in the country.'"[12] Yet this and similar articles went on to point out that the "Magic City" had many unpaved streets, antiquated public schools, an inadequate stock of housing, and a reputation for civic lethargy—all problems that had to be addressed and overcome if the city was to maintain its current momentum after the war.

The war boom gave an impetus to attempts to meet the city's transportation needs, most particularly to long-neglected plans to construct a modern port at the mouth of the Christina River. Wilmington's old port facilities, which were upstream on the Christina between Church Street and Market Street, were virtually unusuable except for a few wharves where barges landed bulk commodities such as coal, sand, oil, gravel, and wood. Foreign commerce on the Delaware River invariably went to Philadelphia. Above its mouth, the Christina was too shallow for most ocean-going ships, and its banks were largely taken over by industrial plants. Until the war, however, there was insufficient reason to follow the advice of Wilmington's boosters, who had long pleaded the cause of a deep-water port. It was not until 1917 that the Chamber of Commerce began a concerted effort to organize support for the idea. It took four years, however, to advance the project to the point where the city council committed itself to a rather cautious $600,000 bond issue. Not until 1922 did construction get under way. In that year, the same in which the city adopted its motto, "First City of the First State," some Wilmington businessmen looked optimistically toward the day when the whole coastline of the Delaware River from the Christina to New Castle would be taken up by industrial production. "Wilmington is entering upon its greatest era of industrial, civic and community development since the landing of the Swedes" trumpeted the *Sunday Star*.[13]

In 1923 the Marine Terminal was completed at a cost to the city of over three million dollars. The contractor for the project was the Du Pont Construction Company, a subsidiary of the Du Pont Company. During the war Du Pont Construction had built 14 square miles of munitions factories, 10,790 workers' houses, and several automobile assembly plants. The Marine Terminal, which extended 5,000 feet along the Christina River and 2,000 feet along the Delaware, had four storage sheds and room to unload three ships of 7,500 tons simultaneously. Once built, it receded to the background of Wilmington's civic consciousness. The terminal was no longer the object of press boosterism, nor was it any longer perceived as the first step toward the hoped-for industrial boom in south Wilmington. Instead, the city's attention focused all the more intently upon the question of highway development and the increasing problems of traffic control.

Another pressing problem was the housing shortage caused by the war boom. Rents went up, but no one seemed willing to invest in new construction. In October 1916 an official of Wilmington's Chamber of Commerce declared that although the city needed one thousand new homes, contractors were finding it difficult to finance building construction. The war production boom had inflated the prices for building materials and labor and raised interest rates, while capital investments gravitated toward high-return industrial development.[14]

The problem of too-rapid growth was afflicting many industrial areas of the United States. In some places large employers constructed housing for their workers. The Du Pont Company, with its tradition—going back to

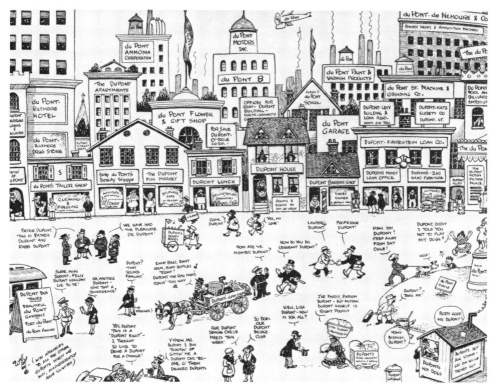

A 1933 satire of Wilmington's economic and social life from a local publication entitled "Bilmington." *(Courtesy of the Historical Society of Delaware)*

the company's beginnings in 1802—of providing workers with housing, was in the forefront of this approach. In the early 1890s, the company had built a guncotton factory at Carney's Point, New Jersey, on the Delaware River. Since it was engaged in making military powder, the factory was intentionally located in a remote area to render it "sufficiently inaccessible to visits from unauthorized persons."[15] Enterprising residents of nearby Penns Grove had rushed to build cheap housing for the workers. A Du Pont official recalled that these were "flimsy, jerry-built structures with the barest conveniences" that gave the village a "boom-town atmosphere reminiscent of goldrush days."[16] Hastily built boardinghouses rented the same beds to men on all three shifts, while some workers were reduced to living in tents. In 1914, faced with expanding the factory to meet war orders, the Du Pont Company decided to build its own village of workers' houses. The village, which ultimately contained 2,200 houses and service structures, resembled a military outpost with its neat rows of two-story houses, bungalows, dormitories, and apartment buildings constructed in varying sizes corresponding to the ranks that their inhabitants held in the plant. As the war orders increased, the company expanded its housing to include temporary barracks, many built on fields of growing crops, so urgent was the need. Assignments of residences were made on the basis of salary or wage level and length of service.

The ship and car building shops in Wilmington had no tradition of providing housing for their workers, however, nor did they alter their practice during the war years, even though, according to the newspapers, the housing shortage was costing them contracts.[17] It was not until 1917, the year in which the United States entered the war, that both public and private efforts were made to deal with the city's housing crisis. In that year a company called the New York-Delaware Realty Construction Company announced plans to build over 1,000 workingmen's houses in south Wilmington at Eden Park, near the Pyrites company, Eastern Malleable Iron, and the proposed new city port. This, the largest housing development ever undertaken in Delaware, was brought to a halt with little accomplished when the armistice was announced a year later.[18]

By far the most important, long-lived, and successful wartime housing project in Wilmington was Union Park Gardens, constructed under the auspices of the U.S. Shipping Board. The project, located on a 50-acre plot at the southwest edge of the city, at the intersection of Lancaster Avenue and Union Street, was adjacent to two trolley lines. It grew out of a meeting in May 1918 where local shipbuilders, officials of the city's Chamber of Commerce, and a representative of the U.S. Shipping Board discussed the effect of the housing squeeze on Wilmington's ship production. In the wartime emergency, events moved with unprecedented haste. Ballinger and Perrot, a nationally known architectural and engineering firm, was employed to design the community, and ground was broken in June 1918. Surprisingly, considering the pervading atmosphere of emergency, the architects were encouraged to use the most enlightened principles of the time in planning the community. Instead of erecting rows of simple brick houses of the kind that already predominated in Wilmington, the architects, assisted by John Nolen, a town planner from Cambridge, Massachusetts, constructed a model community of great variety, complete with serpentine street-plans and quaint English-style houses.[19] When completed, Union Park Gardens consisted of 506 private dwellings, mostly built in groups of four, although about 100 were semidetached or duplex homes. To create visual interest, the houses were located at varying distances from the curb and included twenty different house styles featuring an assortment of roof-lines.[20]

One measure of Union Park Gardens' enormous success was the ease with which the federal government sold off the houses to private owners at good prices in 1922. Union Park Gardens stands as a monument to the possibilities inherent in federal intervention in urban housing. But although some aspects of the project, such as the steeply pitched roofs and similar quaint and romantic features, were copied by private builders in Wilmington during the 1920s, the landscape design, including winding streets, staggered setbacks, and variation among house styles, completely eluded the construction industry. The city's grid plan frustrated some of these planning goals, but a major factor in the failure to maintain the level of construction of workers' housing reached in Union Park Gardens was the small scale of operations among local construction companies even as late as the 1920s. Typically, builders lacked the capital to construct more than a row of four to six houses at a time. Consequently, they did not concern themselves with questions about the overall effects of the blocks they were creating, except to ensure that their structures would sell within the price range already established by previous construction in the vicinity.

Whereas Union Park Gardens was designed for workers and their immediate supervisors, Wawaset, the other planned community built in Wilmington during the war years, was primarily intended for executive-level employees. Wawaset was built by the Du Pont Company at the intersection of Greenhill Avenue and Pennsylvania Avenue on land that had formerly been a fairground. Located at the edge of the city, midway between the du Pont family homes near Hagley and the Du Pont Building downtown, Wawaset was in an ideal location to satisfy the wants of the socioeconomic group for whom it was designed. As in the case of Union Park Gardens, the architects' layout broke with Wilmington's grid tradition to make the roadways conform to the natural contours of the land. Wawaset was a smaller version of Roland Park, Frederick Law Olmsted's parklike development in Baltimore, Maryland. About 100 houses were planned, representing a variety of styles and prices between middle and upper-middle income levels. The company sold its smallest houses, which were clustered in rows of four, for $5,000, while the largest free-stranding homes cost up to $14,000. Employees could purchase them on liberal terms of 10 percent down and a ten-year, 5 percent mortgage. The two dominant home styles in Wawaset were the steeply pitched roof, gabled English style, which also prevailed at Union Park Gardens, and the "colonial," a very generalized style that has dominated residential construction in Wilmington and in the eastern United States generally during the twentieth century. The plan produced an enclave of architecturally diverse houses, all set upon small but well-planned lots along narrow winding streets.[21]

During the period that Wawaset was being built, an important transi-

"Commencement at Wilmington" from Helen Hart, "Americanization in Delaware, 1921–1922," *Bulletin of the Service Citizens of Delaware* 4, no. 3 (Sept. 1922). *(Courtesy of the Historical Society of Delaware)*

tion was taking place in residential construction. Wawaset was, in effect, a suburb set within the city. Yet it was more closely linked to the trolley car era than to the emerging era of the automobile. The Du Pont Company's pamphlet describing Wawaset took pains to point out that the area was within walking distance of existing services, such as churches, schools, and stores, and was served by three trolley lines. The house plans, even for the more expensive houses, did not include garages, although owners could build them if they wished. The roadways were so narrow as to almost preclude the parking of cars. In all of these ways Wawaset represented not the beginning of a new era of construction, but rather the end of an old one; for by World War I, Wilmington, like the rest of America, had gone automobile-mad.

"All Wilmington keenly awaits the opening of the second annual Automobile Show at the Hotel du Pont tomorrow. To every nook and corner in the city word has gone forth that this will be a wonderful show, a strikingly beautiful exhibition, an assemblage of all that is marvelous in 'motordom.'"[22] Who could resist enthusiasm such as this? Few, it seems, for over 100,000 people reportedly visited the show in a city of only 110,000.[23] The city's leading newspapers, quick to join the bandwagon, began regular columns devoted to "motor topics." By the end of 1916, there were already fourteen automobile dealerships in the city.[24]

The explosion of automobile sales during the war years resulted from the confluence of local and national factors. Just at the time when Henry Ford's mass production techniques were bringing the price of cars within the reach of middle-income Americans, T. C. du Pont inaugurated his highway program for Delaware. Subsequently, wartime prosperity permitted the public to fulfill its growing desire for the motor car. According to the president of the city's Chamber of Commerce, there were already 4,000 automobiles in Wilmington in 1917, or one for every 28 city residents.[25]

The climb in automobile ownership went relentlessly forward. After 1912 the increase in the number of cars registered in Delaware averaged over 2,000 each year. A newspaper check of registration statistics in 1919 showed that car owners were concentrated not in the city but in the area immediately surrounding it.[26] As the 1920s began, the city's traction company was justifying its demand to raise fares from 6¢ to 8¢ on the grounds that although rush-hour passengers had reached an all-time high, cars had begun to cut into slack-hour riding. The company estimated that Wilmington's 15,000 car owners were all former trolley riders.[27] The railroads were also being affected. In 1922 the Du Pont Company switched from trains to trucks in moving chemical products from its Philadelphia plant to the tanneries that were its major customers in Wilmington.[28]

Another sign of the new era was the growing pressure to institutionalize a highway construction program. When the State Highway Department was created in 1916, the newspapers gave significant attention to a report by local highway engineers that revealed that divided authority between state and county government was responsible for the backwardness and inefficiency that characterized New Castle County's highway administration.[29] Since 1913 a concerted effort to improve New Castle County roads had produced fewer than 200 miles of paved road surface. The report emphasized the need for the centralization of funding and control so that a comprehensive plan could be established for deciding which were to become trunk and which were to become branch roads. Pressure in this direction came from out-of-state sources as well. In 1914 a group of engineers, highway officials, automobile manufacturers, concrete fabricators, and other interested parties founded the American Association of State Highway Officials, which joined forces with the Lincoln Highway Association, a group dedicated to the construction of a national transcontinental motor highway, to lobby for federal assistance for road building. In 1916 the lobbyists won their first big victory with the passage of the Federal Aid Act. Skirting the delicate constitutional problem of federal-state relations, the law provided that states that complied by adopting a state-wide highway department could qualify for federal funds to match those budgeted by the states themselves.[30]

In his first report to the governor, in 1917, the chief engineer, Charles M. Upham, outlined and justified the department's policies. Noting the important role that good roadways had played in France in the defense of Paris in 1914 and the position of Delaware in the congested northeast corridor of the United States, he argued the importance of building highways in Delaware as a national defense measure. "Already," he said, "the railroads are urging that whenever possible all freight should be shipped by motor truck" because the railroads were incapable of bearing the entire load. In light of this need, he assigned first priority to improving the radial roads reaching out from Wilmington that had been created 100 years earlier, during the turnpike era. The Philadelphia Pike, later to be incorporated into the Lincoln Highway, received his primary attention as the busiest road in the state. It should be resurfaced in brick, Upham said, as a war measure. He also urged the state to buy the Kennett Pike, then still a privately owned toll road, and Delaware's next most heavily traveled roadway. The other vestiges of the turnpike system—Concord Pike, Lancaster Pike, Newport Pike, and the New Castle Road—then being maintained, if one can call it that, by the New Castle County Levy Court, received less travel and could be safely ignored at least for a time. The chief engineer believed that the most significant aspect of modern highways was their impact on commercial development. "In the near future," he predicted, "truck companies will be formed to transport freight over the inter-city highways and the demand of freight traffic will be manifold."[31]

Among those commuters most anxious to improve the highways in and around Wilmington was Pierre S. du Pont. Following his mother's death in 1913, du Pont moved from his childhood home at the edge of the city to "Longwood," his estate near Kennett Square, Pennsylvania. Although he kept an apartment in the Hotel du Pont in order to maintain his Delaware residency, Pierre frequently drove between Longwood and his office in Wilmington. The trip from Wilmington took him out Delaware Avenue to Pennsylvania Avenue, which at the city border became the Kennett Pike, a privately owned, narrow, rutted lane that the State Highway Department had listed as its second priority in 1917.

Everything in Pierre du Pont's nature and environment, his faith that order and efficiency were the key to greater economic benefits, his belief in public service, his embrace of the motor car, coalesced to push him into highway reform. In 1916, acting through his attorney, du Pont offered the city $200,000 for the purpose of widening and repaving Delaware Avenue from 10th Street to its junction with Pennsylvania Avenue at Van Buren Street.[32] Later he extended the project to include Pennsylvania Avenue.

The Wilmington Institute Free Library, completed in 1923. *(Courtesy of the Historical Society of Delaware)*

Ironically, this man who at that very moment was spending millions to plant an arboretum together with exotic bushes and flowers on his estate at Longwood, was simultaneously engaged in destroying the trees that had once made Delaware Avenue the most beautiful and fashionable boulevard in Wilmington. To a resident who complained of the loss of trees along the avenue du Pont replied that the preservation of trees must not stand in the way of the city's welfare, which clearly, in his mind, lay in widening the street to accommodate two lanes of traffic in each direction.[33] Fashion was, of course, already fleeing Delaware Avenue for the northwest suburbs. The city must be practical so that the suburbs could afford not to be. In 1919 Pierre du Pont undertook the widening of his own commuter route when he purchased the Kennett Pike for $70,000.[34] Immediately, the Du Pont Engineering Company began modernizing the old road, and the following year turned it over to the state on condition that it prohibit the laying of trolley rails or the erection of billboards.

Pierre S. du Pont involved himself in a variety of civic enterprise and charities throughout his life, but it was in the period immediately following

World War I that his ideas and money were most significantly felt throughout Delaware. In public affairs, Pierre du Pont was always circumspect, detached, and even shy, but he knew very well what he wanted and how to get it. In his philanthropy as in his business career, du Pont's keen mind searched out the most efficient means to achieve explicitly stated ends. He set great store by professionalism and research, both aspects of his scientific outlook. It is not surprising, therefore, that his most famous philanthropic endeavors lay in the field of education.

Du Pont's first large-scale philanthropic effort in Wilmington was the construction of a new public library, to replace the mid-nineteenth-century Institute building at 8th and Market streets. In 1915 the civic square, flanked by the Du Pont Building and the City-County Building, was nearing completion, leaving two sides of the square to be brought into the harmonious whole. On 10th Street was the property of the First Presbyterian Church, which included a graveyard and a small eighteenth-century church building. The Wilmington Institute Free Library had its eye on that lot, and John P. Nields, an attorney who was president of the Library Board of Managers, privately asked Pierre du Pont to donate the funds necessary to buy the church's lands. The board hoped that a public subscription would provide the funds to construct an impressive classical edifice in keeping with the plan for Rodney Square.

The Wilmington Institute project reveals a great deal about Pierre du Pont's goals and methods as a philanthropist. Du Pont was sufficiently impressed by the idea to make the church an offer of $225,000 to acquire the lot.[35] At the same time, he suggested to the Library Board of Managers that they turn over their building plans to the building commission headed by John J. Raskob that had constructed the City-County Building, on the grounds that the commissioners had shown their mettle by ensuring that inefficient and graft-seeking politicians had not controlled that project. The Institute's board, composed as it was of consequential citizens, was a bit offended at this idea and was unwilling to lose control over the most important decision they were ever likely to undertake on behalf of the city. They therefore rejected the suggestion but tactfully told du Pont that, "It is, of course, necessary that the persons giving the money for the construction of a library building shall know that the money is properly spent."[36] Soon after, du Pont accepted the board's invitation to serve on its building committee along with the librarian, the city engineer, and a member of the board. Du Pont's response to the board's building plans reveals his intensely practical approach to the project. Instead of commenting on the aesthetics of the structure or its adaptability to its general purpose, his only critical remark was, "I should hardly think that adequate provision has been made in these plans for toilet rooms, the janitors' and scrubwomens' closets."[37]

Once assured of du Pont's contribution, the board published a brochure soliciting the public's support. "Today a great opportunity has come . . . A magnificent site on the Court House Square . . . has been donated by a public-spirited citizen. Plans have been drawn up for an adequate and imposing Library building."[38] Nields told du Pont that the campaign was designed "to make the people realize that the Library is theirs."[39] According to the library's records, he said, nearly two-thirds of its patrons came from the working-class neighborhoods on the south and east sides of the city and the board was eager to solicit contributions from this group to insure their respect for the institution. Pierre donated $45,000 to the public fund but charged the board to keep secret his contribution for land acquisition.[40]

As is so often the case in such transactions, legal difficulties arose regarding the disposition of the land. By the terms of its 1737 deed, the church was restricted in its use of the property. In addition, it became evident that the relocation of the graves and of the historic church building would be more costly than originally anticipated. At one point it appeared that the library would have to lease the property rather than buy it outright. When presented with these various difficulties, du Pont did not budge from his original intention to limit his gift for land acquisition to $250,000. Additional funds had to be sought elsewhere.[41]

By 1920 the lot had finally been prepared for building, but prices were very high because of the wartime inflation, and the Library Board discovered that the $300,000 building fund that they had raised three years before was now grossly inadequate. They therefore sponsored a bill in the state legislature to permit the city to bond itself for an additional $200,000. The bill passed in Dover, but some city councilmen were leery of committing the city's funds to a privately controlled enterprise, especially since the bond market was very volatile. Nields hastened to write to Pierre, who was in New York in connection with his work as president of the General Motors Corporation. "If it were possible to go to council and state that friends of the Library would underwrite the issue and pay par for the bonds, Council would immediately pass the resolution and the Board would immediately advertise for bids."[42] P. S. replied, "While I agree with you that the library project should be pushed to completion, I am disinclined to step in to remedy the deficiencies of a public contribution . . ." He suggested that the city offer a more attractive interest rate and concluded, "I do not care to do anything to help out this situation."[43] Subsequently, city council agreed to take whatever steps might be necessary to

Westover Hills, Wilmington's most carefully planned and expensive suburb of the 1920s, photographed June 23, 1930. *(Courtesy of the Eleutherian Mills Historical Library)*

sell the library bonds, yet without demanding control over the Library Board as Nields had feared they might do.[44]

In May 1923 Pierre S. du Pont stood in the lecture hall of the new building together with board president John P. Nields, architects A. M. Githens and E. L. Tilton, and Mayor LeRoy Harvey, for the opening exercises of the Wilmington Institute Free Library. In his remarks, Nields for the first time publicly acknowledged that du Pont's financial contribution had been a prerequisite to the success of his enterprise. In his own brief remarks, Mr. du Pont compared the "mortal remains" under the cemetery monuments that had once stood in that place to the "immortal remains" to be housed in the beautiful monument behind him and expressed his hope that Wilmingtonians would make use of the opportunities for education and self-improvement that the library could provide.[45]

Certain idiosyncrasies in Pierre du Pont's philanthropy were evident in his dealings with the Wilmington Institute: his insistence on the maximum public donation to the enterprise; his focus on the most concrete and practical details of the building plans; his desire to circumvent local politics, which he perceived as self-serving and sordid; his desire to personally remain in the background; and his faith in experts capable of making an objective analysis of needs. Pierre du Pont mistrusted unbridled democracy, believed that economic success was the inevitable outcome of effort, and was convinced that improved opportunities for public education would produce a more orderly, productive nation, to the advantage of all levels of society. He expressed these views most directly in a letter to his cousin, Zara du Pont, dated 22 August 1912. Zara, T. Coleman's sister, was a life-long campaigner on behalf of women's rights and the rights of labor; she had written to Pierre to request his support for women's suffrage. In his reply, Pierre declined to aid the cause—not because he did not believe in equal suffrage "as a principle," he said, but because most people of either sex were, as yet, unfitted for the vote and easily misled by demagogic politicians. "A cure for this is education," he thought, but not the education that might lead people to believe scandalous stories about the evils of American business and political institutions. Rather, he proposed "an education that will make men and women think—and think correctly; to fit them to do good and useful work, to train them in the ways of working hard and earnestly." This type of education would undermine the politicians, who practiced the art of "causing the unworthy to believe that they are entitled to everything without effort." He advised his cousin to stop allying herself with "the fault-finders and demagogues. You will make ten times more progress by improving people under our present system than by attempting to effect changes which are wrongly believed to cure all troubles without true effort."[46]

These are the attitudes and beliefs that du Pont brought to the Service Citizens of Delaware, the reform organization that he generously financed from 1918 until 1927. The initial idea for the Service Citizens belonged to du Pont's associate, John J. Raskob. From the first, the organization was characterized by meticulous organization and a will to succeed that was the hallmark of the du Pont-Raskob team's success in the business world. On 9 July 1918, Raskob invited distinguished citizens, mostly Republican leaders representing the state's three counties, to meet in his office in the Du Pont Building. He told the group that Delaware's population was educationally ill-prepared for modern life. He had become aware of the need for social reform in Delaware through the involvement with the state's war emergency Council of Defence, which had uncovered many cases of illiteracy among native Delawareans and the widespread inability to speak English among immigrants—all factors hurting Delaware's defense effort in the current war. Pierre then read a prepared address outlining his expectations for the Service Citizens. The group would not, he cautioned, use the word "reform" in the "odious sense . . . through destruction of all existing practices." "We shall," he promised, "proceed quietly and carefully" to support public officials by providing funds to hire experts and to gather the data necessary to reach decisions on the proper course of action. The Service Citizens, Raskob reiterated, was to be based on careful study and continuity of effort, and would be "conducted along strictly modern business lines."[47]

Although the diffident Pierre insisted that "one individual must not be allowed to conduct" the policy of Service Citizens,[48] his was the leading spirit of this organization called into being at his request to disseminate a trust fund, yielding $90,000 annually, that he had established. The Reverend Joseph H. Odell, a Presbyterian clergyman from New York who had officiated at Pierre's wedding in 1915, was named Managing Director. Odell had already served du Pont as the conduit for a benefaction of $5,000 to French orphans and wounded American servicemen. From the letters that accompanied these checks, it appears that the clergyman viewed du Pont with a sense of deference amounting to awe.[49]

Under Odell's leadership the Service Citizens engaged in two long range endeavors: Americanization and public education. Service Citizens took over the Americanization work among Wilmington's immigrant population already begun by the Council of Defence. Infused with generous funding, the program expanded its classes among Italians, Poles, and other foreign-born people. According to a Service Citizens report, nearly 1,000 immigrants received instruction in English and American life during 1919, and 124 of them were prepared to become American citizens. Service Citizens paid for the training of their teachers and supplied the impetus for teaching approaches especially designed to fit into immigrant life styles. Classes for Italian women, for example, were conducted in the familiar surroundings of their own homes rather than in a schoolroom. The organization also opened an "American House" in the industrial section of the city where workmen could take classes between shifts. In June 1919, and for several years thereafter, Service Citizens sponsored an elaborate graduation ceremony for the imigrants at Wilmington High School. Each group among the 17 countries represented carried its national flag and sang songs of its homeland. The evening culminated with the displaying of the American flag and singing of the Star-Spangled Banner. When experience showed that many of the immigrants were unable to carry on the most elementary activities because of the language barrier or ignorance of American customs, Service Citizens opened an advice agency called the Trouble Bureau. In its first year the Bureau staff conducted over 2,000 office interviews and made 1,300 house calls, mostly aimed at helping immigrants to bring relatives to America or at extricating them from legal difficulties.[50]

By far the most important and expensive work of the Service Citizens lay in the total reorganization and upgrading of Delaware's hiterto highly fragmented, grossly underfinanced public schools. By 1924 P. S. du Pont had spent over three million dollars through Service Citizens to build new consolidated schools throughout the state. His commitment was more than financial. Breaking with his habitual shyness, he spoke at public meetings and willingly suffered as the target of slanderous misrepresentation of his intentions in the newspapers owned by his estranged cousin, Alfred I. du Pont. As Pierre perceived it, school reform required not only money but the total reorganization of the state's 424 separate school districts into one efficiently managed whole, much as the Du Pont Company had reorganized the American powder industry twenty years before. At the urging of Service Citizens, the Delaware legislature adopted a highly controversial school code in 1919 that raised school taxes throughout the state. According to a recent study of Delaware's schools, the code also transformed "control and funding of education from a democratic and locally controlled system to a centralized and professionalized state system."[51]

School reform loomed so large that it completely absorbed the efforts and funds of Service Citizens. The organization hardly touched other important areas for social welfare, such as desperately needed housing reform and the reform of Wilmington's city charter. Service Citizens shied away from supporting middle-ranking business groups like the Rotary Club and Kiwanis in their unsuccessful efforts to secure more efficient, more powerful civic government. Perhaps Pierre du Pont did not wish to take on the Republican city machine on this matter, but it is equally probable that du Pont discouraged strong independent city government for fear that it would fall into the hands of politicians he would consider disreputable. As for housing reform, the Service Citizens showed some initial interest but never followed through. In 1918 the organization financed a study of health and housing conditions in Wilmington by the Bureau of Municipal Research of New York. The survey described the city's housing conditions as "desperate" and singled out bad housing on the east side, the city's poorest, most densely inhabited section. The survey noted that these conditions had exacerbated the death toll from the recent Spanish influenza epidemic in that part of the city. More shocking still was the discovery that infant mortality in the overpriced, overcrowded east side was higher than in New York City's notorious tenement district. The report claimed that Wilmington's wartime housing crisis had not abated. Over 7,000 people were still without adequate lodging, and high building costs discouraged builders' loans for the construction of houses for industrial workers. The report also warned that Wilmington must replace its "hit or miss" approach to development with logical planning that could prevent the growth of slums.[52] After commissioning the study, however, the Service Citizens chose to drop the issue.

After its initial period of organization, Service Citizens was essentially Pierre du Pont and Joseph Odell. When personnel problems arose, staff members had nowhere to turn beyond these two individuals, and du Pont demonstrated unalterable confidence in the judgment of his hand-picked director in the face of evidence that Odell could be quite tactless in his dealings with downstate Delawareans,[53] and unpopular with the office staff.[54] Nor was du Pont willing to entertain criticisms of Service Citizens' policies, even from outside experts such as the professor from Columbia University's prestigious Teachers College who dared to suggest that du Pont's philanthropic school program might be too paternalistic.

When he received an unsolicited report of the Service Citizens' activities on behalf of school reform in 1922, Columbia professor William H. Kilpatrick wrote to Odell with a well-intentioned warning that on his own recent trip to Delaware Kilpatrick had heard many critical remarks concerning Service Citizens' ramrod tactics. Queried further by Odell, Kilpatrick cautioned prophetically: "It may indeed do a distinct harm to accustom the people to have things done for them which they would not do for themselves."[55] Odell sent the correspondence to P. S. du Pont, who demanded that Kilpatrick supply him with a list of Service Citizens' critics. The annoyed philanthropist went on to say that "Service Citizens are spending a good deal of money in Delaware, which we would be glad to divert to other purposes if anything is being wasted."[56] Kilpatrick refused to supply names but suggested that du Pont undertake his own private investigation, to be led by someone who would not be known as du Pont's man. The professor further pointed out that "the strength of the Service Citizens seems to be such that there is real fear to oppose them."[57] The financier replied that he had no time for an investigation and ended the matter with a note to Odell that read, "Enclosed find copies of the last letters exchanged with Dr. Kilpatrick, who makes a very bad impression upon me. I shall let the matter drop."[58]

At first glance it might appear that du Pont's revolution in Delaware's public education had little effect upon Wilmington, since the city was specifically excluded from the most significant changes in the law. Under the School Code of 1919, the State Department of Public Instruction had jurisdiction over all public schools in Delaware except those in the city of Wilmington. Yet, by reorganizing the school districts around the city, the school code had a considerable influence over the development of Wilmington's suburbs. The immediate effects of the new school laws were in

Before and after photographs illustrate the State Highway Department's improvements to the Philadelphia Pike just north of the city, the first in about 1915, the second during the 1920s. *(Courtesy of the Division of Historical and Cultural Affairs, State of Delaware)*

direct proportion to how poor the rural schools had been. Thus, schools in northern New Castle County underwent less spectacular changes than those in rural areas more remote from urban influences. Nonetheless, the new law's emphasis on the consolidation of rural districts, its creation of a dependable tax-based income for education, and its acceptance of the concept of "special districts," in which citizens could vote to tax themselves to provide additional revenue for school purposes, were all influential factors assisting the process of suburbanization. In addition, the new school law significantly increased the amount of money from state revenues available to the city schools.

In the early 1920s, when these reforms were first being tested, the Wilmington public schools, although the best in the state by any standard, were backward in comparison to those of many other American cities. The Board of Education, which presided over Wilmington's school system, was an unwieldy elected body with representatives from each of the city's 14 wards. The School Board inclined to practices that were anathematic to professional educators. For instance, while the Board readily spent money to ensure that each ward would have its own school, Board members were extremely reluctant to vote tax increases to pay for improvements to, or replacement of, existing schools. The impetus to reform the city's schools coincided with America's entry into the World War I. In 1917 a citizen's committee surveyed Wilmington's schools and reported that, contrary to complacent popular belief, there was much that needed improvement. The teachers were ill-paid, the majority of the buildings were old, overcrowded, and lacked indoor plumbing, and the curriculum was inflexible. While Wilmington was spending $30 per child each year, the average among American cities was $45 per child. Whereas Wilmington's investment in school buildings was $85 per child, the national average was $200.[59] Three years later, in 1920, the Federal Bureau of Education found that "the school buildings in Wilmington are by far the worst that the survey commission has yet seen."[60] The out-of-state survey team could not refrain from comparing these decrepit edifices with the luxurious Hotel du Pont and with the generally thriving nature of the city's industries.

In the decade from 1910 to 1920, while the city's school population had grown by 20 percent, only one new school building had been opened: Number 30 in the fast-growing 9th Ward. Meanwhile, the city continued to use five schools that predated the Civil War. As late as 1925, only four of the city's 30 school buildings had been constructed during the twentieth century. Those in the older parts of the city had no play areas and lacked indoor plumbing. Such extra features as libraries, gymnasiums, auditoriums, and laboratories were rare or nonexistent. Even the High School, built in 1899, had no library.[61] Conditions in schools for blacks were particularly deplorable. The superintendent described conditions at the Howard School, the county's only high school for blacks, as being so overcrowded and unhealthy as to be "vicious."[62]

The decade between 1925 and 1935 witnessed the upgrading of the entire city school system, thanks to the new school code, which provided state aid supplemented by the direct largess of P. S. du Pont. In 1923 du Pont goaded the city into action when he offered $600,000 to build one large modern school for the city, on condition that the school board would match his gift by building two additional schools. Du Pont's gift built the Thomas F. Bayard School in southwest Wilmington. By 1930 the city had erected several other new schools, all for white children: Emalea P. Warner Junior High School, the William P. Bancroft School, and George Gray Elementary School. Each was capable of handling upwards of 1,000 students. Following P. S. du Pont's rigorous standards, the new buildings incorporated the best design features of the time. Architects strove to make their buildings imposing on the outside and cheerful on the inside. Classrooms were bright and airy, corridors well-lit, bathrooms, drinking fountains, and cafeterias hygenic, and the schools had specialized rooms for physical education, vocational training, home economics, and assemblies. As each new school was completed, several old ones were closed down. Nor were the segregated black schools completely forgotten, for in one of his final gifts to public education Pierre du Pont in 1928 furnished the $900,000 necessary to build a new Howard High School.[63]

In the meantime, during the 1920s the Wilmington High School had become hopelessly overcrowded, not so much because of increased population in the city and the suburban region from which it drew, but because nearly twice as many students were choosing to remain in school until graduation as in the decade before. Designed for 1,700 students, the High School's enrollment reached 2,700 in 1928 and 3,290 in 1931.[64]

The philosopher John Dewey's doctrine that placed the school at the center of society was popular among educators in those years. The school was no longer simply perceived as an academic institution, but rather as a mirror projecting back upon society myriad images of its best, most pure attributes. Dewey gave credence to the notion that education was a profession, a high calling demanding years of careful study. The notion that there should be a special science of education harmonized with the hopes and expectations of Pierre S. du Pont's educational reforms in Delaware. In Wilmington the culmination of these efforts was the erection of the Pierre S. du Pont High School in 1935, named for the philanthropist against his will. The school epitomized faith in the promise of professional, comprehensive public school education. Its massive yet elegant colonial architecture dominated a 22-acre plot in a growing middle-income residential neighborhood in the 9th Ward. The self-consciously monumental high school cost $1,800,000, all raised from public sources: $1,500,000 from a state bond issue and $435,000 from the Federal Public Works Administration, a New Deal agency. The three-story building contained a wide variety of well-equipped rooms, including an auditorium capable of seating 1,110 people, boys' and girls' gymnasiums, science laboratories, industrial arts shops, and various other specialized rooms. The high school was hailed in the local press as a fitting symbol of pride for the entire city, while Wilmington's superintendent of schools, writing in a national school administrators' journal, described it as "a worthy monument to the victory of the State over the forces of ignorance."[65]

There is an interesting postscript to the completion of P. S. du Pont High School to be found among its namesake's papers. Shortly after the school had opened, Pierre du Pont wrote a confidential letter to the superintendent informing him that it had come to du Pont's attention that one of the students in the new high school claimed to be a socialist and refused to study American History. As proof, du Pont said that he had been given socialist literature allegedly belonging to the boy in question. The superintendent promptly replied that his investigations showed the boy to be borderline retarded. The student had not refused to study American History but admitted that he had belonged to a socialist group, which he had quit after a teacher cautioned him about his philosophical views. Relieved, Pierre responded that he was glad to discover that the boy "is not quite the undesirable that has been represented."[66] This exchange might possibly have happened in any part of the United States during the Depression years, but it also recalls Pierre's cautionary letter to his cousin Zara thirty-three years before, in which he had said, "It is public school education that we need; an education that will make men and women think—and think correctly."[67] Apparently, questioning inherited truths was not "thinking correctly" in this concept of education.

Pierre du Pont's many benefactions to the people of his native state and city depended upon the continued profitability of both the Du Pont Company and the General Motors Corporation. After World War I, the Du Pont Company's profits might have fallen drastically had it not been that as president of the company Pierre wisely diversified Du Pont's product line into nonexplosive chemicals. When the war ended, the powder company possessed excess production capacity coupled with a large amount of liquid capital and considerable experience in the application of chemistry to market-oriented production. Given these factors it is not surprising that the company moved to diversify its product lines beyond explosives into other chemically based lines. This was not an entirely new move for the Du Pont Company where diversification had begun modestly in 1910, when

Du Pont acquired Fabrikoid, a small company in Newburgh, New York, that made artificial leather for automobile seats. After the war, however, the company moved aggressively to acquire other companies' production techniques and formulae on an international scale. Du Pont bought confiscated German dye patents, American chemical plants and pigments firms, and French cellophane and rayon technology. In addition, the company increased its own experimental station from a relatively simple explosive-testing facility to a much larger series of laboratories capable of improving upon the broad array of available products and discovering new ones. By the 1920s Du Pont had become the largest, most diversified chemical producer in the United States, but the enlarged company retained its corporate headquarters and laboratories in Wilmington.

The acquisition of a commanding share in General Motors Corporation presented additional opportunities for the du Ponts in the early 1920s. Irénée du Pont, Pierre's younger brother, and his successor as president of the Du Pont Company, saw GM primarily as a consumer for Du Pont products and argued that Pierre, GM's president, should move the automotive company's headquarters to Wilmington. Pierre and Raskob disagreed. Pierre viewed the motor company as an investment of his family and for the Du Pont Company as a whole. He therefore wanted to make it as profitable as possible on its own terms. This meant that GM should stand on its own, buy materials where the best deals could be made, and develop its own corporate personality away from heavy Du Pont Company influence.[68] As a result of this reasoning, Wilmington did not acquire a major new industry.

While the Du Pont Company was prosperous and expanding in the 1920s and bringing new management and scientifically based employment to the city, other sectors of Wilmington's economy did not fare so well in the postwar era. Much of Wilmington's industrial capital was tied to old, declining industries. The war had given the East Coast ship builders only a brief respite from their downhill slide. In the 1920s Wilmington's shipyards subsisted on repair work, and in January 1927 the largest, the Harlan plant, closed its ship facilities completely.[69] Few new railraod cars were being manufactured and the introduction of artificial leather, combined with the falling popularity of kid gloves, the lowering of men's shoe uppers to below the ankle, the reduction in of U.S. tariffs on imported leather goods, and the declining use of other leather products, created a crisis in the tanning industry. In 1921 Wilmington's tanneries reported that they were operating at only one-half capacity.[70] A U.S. Labor Department official estimated that 15,000 jobs had disappeared in Wilmington between 1919 and 1921. A few years later, there was another sign of Wilmington's decline as an industrial center when the Ford Motor Company, ignoring

A line of jobless men await assistance from Salvation Army headquarters at 4th and Shipley Streets during the Depression, from Mayor's Work and Relief Committee, *Work and Relief in Wilmington, Delaware in 1931–1932. (Courtesy of the Historical Society of Delaware)*

the wooing of the Wilmington Chamber of Commerce, built its East Coast
assembly plant in nearby Chester, Pennsylvania, where riverfront land was
more solid than Wilmington's marshy, but otherwise comparable, Cherry
Island. Retailers as well as industrial workers suffered. The all-time sales
high of 1919 was not reached again until 1925.

The shift from local industrial production to corporate management as
the dynamic force in the city's economy created the conditions for a
downward spiral in the fortunes of Wilmington's traditional economy. The
new business leadership did, of course, assist in providing a support system
that was beneficial to all businesses. The Du Pont Highway and the
improved public schools fall into this category. But in other ways the new
business leaders easily influenced the shape of things to come merely by
remaining aloof from activities that would have improved Wilmington's
potential to attract new industries. Executives of the Du Pont Company
were absent from leadership roles in the city's Chamber of Commerce, and
that in turn explains the failure to pour fill into Cherry Island, the city's
most conspicuously unused industrial space. Instead the Chamber of Commerce devoted itself to the relatively minor kinds of activities suitable to its
members' powerlessness. For example, in its short-lived magazine, *Wilmington*, published during the mid-twenties, the Chamber emphasized a
campaign to encourage downtown retailers to park off the streets so that
their customers could have access to on-street parking.[71] This ineffectual
campaign was hardly the kind of effort that justified the expense of printing
a glossy magazine, but it does illustrate the weakness among the retailers, factory owners, and transportation companies that supported the
Chamber.

Thus, even during the period of national business euphoria in the mid
to late 1920s, unemployment remained a lingering problem for Wilmington's industrial workers. In January 1929 a spokesman for the Central
Labor Council complained that companies that had their corporate headquarters in the city did not build plants there. "Labor feels that a full and
conscientious endeavor has not been made to induce the right kind of
plants to locate here. It is smoke and activity we want—as this smoke and
activity will advance every community interest."[72] But Wilmington's economy was now served by typewriters, adding machines, and test tubes
rather than by industrial smoke.

Wilmington was losing blue-collar jobs as it gained white-collar jobs,
but it took a long time before residents noticed the transformation. In 1936
the *Sunday Star* asked the question "Is Wilmington well on its way to
becoming a white collar town?" According to the newspaper, the answer
was a resounding "Yes." Statistics bore them out. In 1914, at the beginning
of the European war, there had been 319 manufacturing plants in the city,

Pierre S. du Pont and William du Pont are fourth and fifth from the left among this group viewing the women's sewing unit created by the Mayor's Work and Relief Committee, from *Work and Relief in Wilmington, Delaware in 1931–1932. (Courtesy of the Historical Society of Delaware)*

which employed a total of 15,048 workers. By 1919 wartime orders had expanded the work force to 21,420, but the number of plants, then 262, already showed signs of decline. At the height of the prosperous 1920s, Wilmington's factories were down to 193 and employed 14,410. The Depression speeded the decline to 151 plants and 9,820 workers by 1933.[73] Meanwhile, however, the expanding chemical and explosive companies, Du Pont, Hercules, and Atlas, not only increased their own payrolls, but also produced tertiary growth in banking, insurance, and brokerage houses in the city. The existence of the du Pont-owned Wilmington Trust and Delaware Trust, the two largest banks in the city, also quite possibly negatively influenced the access of the city's old industrial firms to fresh capital.

The shift from blue-collar to white-collar employment, the rapid increase in the number of automobiles, and the trend in favor of larger residential lots and detached houses, were all powerful factors operating on the real-estate market. In the course of the 1920s, the city's population declined by a modest 3.2 percent, but this statistic must be read in light of the county's population gain of 8.6 percent and, most particularly, of the astonishing increase of nearly 85 percent in the surrounding incorporated towns of Bellefonte, Elsmere, Newport, and Newark.[74] Although the city as a whole was beginning to lose residents, all parts of the city did not lose people uniformly; indeed, some areas were still growing. But the trend was clear. The oldest section of the city, near the Christina River, where rows of worker's homes stood adjacent to warehouses, factories, and rail lines, lost most heavily, while the more recently settled residential regions to the north and west were still growing. By 1930 the 9th Ward had a population of over 22,000 people, more than one-fifth of the city's total and an increase of 16 percent over the decade before. By contrast, the 1st, 3rd, 4th, and 6th wards, where wartime industrial workers had been crowded into slum housing ten years before, had lost nearly one-quarter of their 1920 population by 1930.

Home construction in Wilmington and vicinity during the 1920s reflected these economic and demographic developments. After the brief wartime emergency there were no more government programs directed at building housing for low- to middle-income groups, and since jobs for working-class people were declining in Wilmington anyway, private builders were disinclined to build for this group. Instead, the private market supplied homes for the increasing numbers of middle- and upper-income people who worked in management and technical positions. According to the Internal Revenue Service, in 1927 Wilmington was the richest city in the United States per capita. Only the much larger metropolises of New York, Chicago, Philadelphia, and Detroit claimed more millionaires.[75] Builders were quick to cater to this new affluent market. In 1924 Wilmington's Sunday newspaper readers saw a local architectural firm's advertisement entitled "Living in the Country," which was accompanied by a picture of a 12-room Tudor-style home. The text read:

> The motor car has given increased facilities for covering distances. The entire practicability of the business man, with little effort on his part, of finding himself amidst an environment totally different from that in which he has worked and accomplished his task, has made the little place in the suburbs an assured fact. Away from the hustle and grind of the city to a place of lawns, trees, flowers, and above all, a wide view across rich fields to some of the most beautiful rolling country, with perhaps a glimpse of one of this country's mightiest rivers—many such places exist within easy distance of Wilmington's business centers.[76]

Wilmington's best-known suburban development of the decade, Westover Hills, reflected the ideals expressed in this architectural advertisement. A carefully planned community located on the Kennett Pike just outside the city limits, Westover Hills, with its large lots, winding tree-lined streets, and gracious architecturally varied houses, each including an ample driveway and garage, demonstrated the best of suburban life. Architects and planners praised the development for its generous open spaces, aesthetic arrangements, and convenience to a major highway.[77] Yet Westover Hills, expensive as its properties were, was by no means the highest standard to which some Wilmingtonians could aspire. Farther out the Kennett Pike, between the original Du Pont powder yards and Pierre du Pont's estate at Longwood, "chateau country" was taking on its modern form. Christiana Hundred farmers saw the value of their lands skyrocket as members of the du Pont family and the highest executives in the company, some of whom were related by marriage to du Ponts, gobbled up land for their estates. The architecture they called into being varied from replicas of colonial Virginia mansions to French provincial farm houses and seventeenth-century chateaux, but always the settings were as expansive as in Jane Austen's England—one gentry estate after another. Roads were paved to accomodate the automobile age, but since the population density was very low, they remained narrow and winding to preserve the bucolic flavor.

The great majority of Wilmingtonians, the white-collar clerks, skilled artisans, and small retailers, still depended upon public transportation, and new residential construction for this market continued to follow the trolley routes out major arteries—North Market Street, Maryland Avenue, and Union Street. The trolleys led past pockets of new construction within the city to the new six-room colonials and bungalows in suburban regions. Mortgages for these modest houses could be obtained through building and loan associations, which reappeared in the 1920s in the wake of a state regulatory law of 1921 that restored public confidence in their soundness. And people were buying—especially new houses with the most up-to-date features, wired for all-electric living. As mentioned before, the 1920s were the first decade in which suburban growth outdistanced that of the cities nationally. In the case of Wilmington this pattern was particularly marked, because the city was losing population in absolute terms while the suburbs were gaining. True, the city's loss was a small one, 3,500 people, and easily explained by the loss of war work, but nonetheless it was the first time that Wilmington had ever experienced population loss, and it came at a time when its suburbs had added over 14,000 new residents, mostly in the lower-middle-income bungalow communities of Elsmere, Richardson Park and Bellefonte.

Although no one fully appreciated it at the time, the 1920s was a critical decade for Wilmington. New affluence gave the city a rare opportunity to plan for the future. The direction of change was clear. A new residential pattern was developing as the motor car began replacing the trolley car. Wilmingtonians had seen, during the wartime emergency, what good residential planning had accomplished at Union Park Gardens. They could see the effects of decay in the oldest parts of town. But aside from the completion of Rodney Square and the updating of its public school system, both prompted and partially financed by private funds, the community proved unable to turn its opportunity to creative use. At the end of the 1920s, Wilmington was a city of much unfulfilled promise. In retrospect four failures stand out: the failure to adopt an improved city charter; the failure to annex the growing suburbs; the failure to provide decent housing for the city's growing black population; and the failure to begin serious overall urban planning. In combination these failures exacerbated the effects of the Depression that followed and laid the groundwork for the "discovery" of serious urban decay in the post-World War II period.

Defeat of city charter reform in the early 1920s provided an unpropitious beginning for community action following the war and left Wilmington with a cumbersome, ineffectual, weak government. The reformers argued that a more professional, cost-effective civic government might help lure new people and industry to the city.[78] But, as in 1912, the politicians of both parties ganged up to defeat the measure. The Republicans, who enjoyed a consistent majority in city council, were opposed because they stood to lose control over patronage if there should be civil service reform; the Democrats were opposed because the proposed charter called for at-large elections, which, in a city with a Republican majority, would deprive them of their few seats on city council.

The question of annexation first became an issue in the 1920s. In 1925 there was a great stir when the mayor and city council proposed annexing the near suburbs, including the incorporated towns of Elsemere and Newport. Having moved out of Wilmington to escape city taxes and housing code regulations, the people in the suburbs adamantly opposed being absorbed by the city. During the decade the per capita cost of city government rose from less than $18 to nearly $25 per year, while the rurally controlled state and county governments severely overtaxed Wilmingtonians to pay for schools and highways in other parts of Delaware.[79]

For a long time, suburbanites acted as if services such as street paving, sewerage, and water supply could be had for little or nothing. The trolley companies were required by their franchises to maintain the major access roads into the city, water came from private wells, cesspools and septic tanks took care of wastes. By the mid-twenties, however, these makeshift utilities were no longer adequate or safe in densely built-up towns such as Elsmere and Richardson Park. In 1925, in response to a rather frightening report by the state sanitary engineer showing that the waters of its cess-

Union Park Gardens, a housing development created by the United States Shipping Board in 1918. (*Photographs by the author*)

pools and wells were intermingling, Elsmere's city fathers asked the state legislature for authority to bond the town in order to create a water and sewage system that would be linked to Wilmington's utility system.[80] The legislature passed the enabling bill, but the voters of Elsmere turned down the bond issue. The majority of voters not only feared higher local taxes, but also saw the measure as the first step toward annexation.[81]

Richardson Park faced similar problems. Its residential development was both rapid and planless. In 1927 the state sanitary engineer reported that 2,500 people had moved to the new suburb in its first ten years. Water, supplied by the Richardson Park Water Company, came from seven local wells and springs, some of which were so located as to become quickly polluted by cesspools. To safeguard the supply, the company added chlorine to the water in a haphazard, unscientific way.[82] By 1930 the Elsmere-Richardson Park area faced an additional problem—the possibility that the wells would go dry. To the danger of typhoid fever had been added that of fire.[83]

The suburb's dilatory solutions to these problems were couched in terms designed to preclude annexation. But the city government also acted in ways to discourage the need for annexation. Apparently without considering the long-range consequences, the city water department agreed to supply water to some suburban areas north of the city reachable by gravity flow from existing city reservoirs. The department charged customers in the suburbs at a higher rate than customers in the city but did not demand annexations as a price for its water. Two independent companies, Suburban, north of the city, and Artesian, the successor to the Richardson Park Water Company, developed the resources to supply other areas in the suburbs. In public education as well, the city was supplying cut-rate services to suburbanites. In 1927 nearly 400 suburban youngsters were attending Wilmington High School, while a similar number were enrolled in the city's elementary schools. Since the bulk of the funds used to support these schools came from city, not state, taxes, suburbanites were clearly getting a bargain at the expense of city taxpayers.[84]

By resisting annexation residents of the near suburbs saved themselves some money, but only at the cost of unplanned development and poor utility service. Their attitude condemned the city to stagnation. Already, in the 1920s, there was little undeveloped land remaining within its boundaries, and given the public's preference for new houses and for suburban living, residential values in the city were bound to decline. Wilmington's tax base was therefore becoming less elastic, less able to meet the needs of the future. Greater Wilmington might grow indefinitely, but Wilmington had reached its limits.

Another problem that was ignored during the 1920s was that of housing for the city's poor, especially those who were poor and black. Unlike some other American industrial cities, especially in the Midwest, Wilmington had not experienced a dramatic growth in its black population during World War I. There were about 9,000 blacks living in Wilmington in both 1900 and 1910, and only 1,000 more in 1920.

A history of strong racial prejudice had "kept Negroes in their place" in Wilmington. Although they were a relatively well educated group compared, for example, to immigrants, blacks were consistently overrepresented among day laborers, domestic servants, and laundresses. They had been traditionally employed in only the lowest, least desirable industrial jobs and were completely excluded from employment in clerical work, not to mention managerial or technical positions, which were available to whites only in the city's growing chemical industry. In the nineteenth century, a few blacks had risen above these severe limitations to become successful in service jobs such as barbering and catering. But in the early twentieth century, Italian and Greek immigrants coopted these positions. A few blacks had once been independent draymen, but since the cost of a motor truck far exceeded that of the old-fashioned horse and cart, they lost ground in that field as well. One result of these artificial limitations on black aspirations was that better-educated or vocationally skilled black people left Wilmington in greater numbers than did less skilled members of their race. Perhaps because of the city's small size and relatively small black population, Wilmington had few black retailers. The few black-owned businesses were primarily service-oriented ones such as beauty shops and funeral parlors. Businessmen, therefore, played a less significant role in Wilmington's black leadership groups than they did in other cities, such as Chicago and New York, and few blacks could secure jobs with black-owned establishments.

Young blacks were aware of these vocational barriers. Those who had the ability and good fortune to go to college seldom returned to Wilmington. A survey among students at Howard High School in 1925 revealed that none of the boys planned careers in office work, which was then by far the most common job for graduates of all-white Wilmington High School. The most popular job choices among black high-school males were chauffeur and auto mechanic, followed by musician, businessman, physician, and dentist. Among the girls at Howard High School, teaching ranked far above all other career choices.[85] Vocational training for black students trailed behind that offered to whites. Until the new Howard High School opened in 1929, with its special rooms for shop, hairdressing and home economics, Howard had been described by the city school superintendent as "the most classical school in the state for black or white, public or private."[86] Admirable though this emphasis on the tried and true curriculum of the past might be in training the mind, it also reflected the fact that Wilmington's employers refused to hire vocationally trained blacks.

Howard High School was the central institution for Wilmington's small but unusually able black intelligentsia. Its first principal, Edwina Kruse, who was of mixed Caribbean and German parentage, had carefully selected a faculty of outstanding merit. Her prize teacher, Alice Dunbar-Nelson, came to Howard in 1902 to escape problems with her husband, the famous poet Paul Laurence Dunbar. She, too, was a writer of poetry, short stories and nonfiction pieces, some of which appeared in national magazines. She headed the English department at Howard for nearly two decades. After Dunbar's death she married Robert J. Nelson with whom she edited a Wilmington-based newspaper aimed at blacks, called the *Advocate*. Dunbar-Nelson, who once referred to her adopted state as "a jewel of inconsistencies," embodied that theme in her own life. It was in large part because Wilmington was the most northerly city in its region to require segregated education that the city could attract teachers such as Dunbar-Nelson who were dedicated to improving the situation of their own race through education. Education and politics were two areas where Wilmington's white leadership did not ignore blacks. Mrs. Dunbar-Nelson, for example, became the first black woman in the United States to serve on the state committee of a major political party when she was selected a Republican committeewoman.[87]

Such narrow concessions to blacks did nothing to alleviate the consequences of segregation, which were becoming ever more severe, especially in the area of housing. As well-to-do people moved from their former residences on the periphery of the center of town to new locations farther out, they did not take their black servants with them. In part this was because modern conveniences such as central heating and automobiles made the near twenty-four-hour cycle of servant care less necessary. No one had to be present at dawn to light the fires or late at night to care for a just-returned horse and carriage. It was now more convenient to employ servants who lived some distance away and traveled between their own quarters, never seen by their employer, and "the house" by trolley car. Consequently, during the 1920s, as blacks were concentrating more than ever in the least desirable urban areas, whites came to feel that living in proximity to blacks was a sign of personal failure.

In 1926 a rumor to the effect that a black family had moved into one of the city's "better" residential neighborhoods "caused something of a panic." Real estate men, reflecting the fear, estimated that even an "inoffensive" black family could lower surrounding home values by 20 to 30 percent. Eager to maintain their commissions, some brokers reportedly went from door to door in some neighborhoods getting residents to agree not to sell to blacks.[88] The incident provoked concern in the press for the plight of blacks in the local housing market. An unnamed businessman commented that the city should undertake to build new houses for blacks within the price range they could afford. He also claimed that it had been a mistake to move Howard High School from its old location at 12th and Orange streets, just one block from the Du Pont Building, to the edge of a marsh adjacent to the Brandywine on the east side. As the community center for the city's blacks, he pointed out, the new Howard School was bound to push the group even more firmly into the city's oldest, unhealthiest neighborhood. He further noted that, contrary to public opinion, blacks paid more, not less, than whites for their paltry housing. If the city government or a group of philanthropic whites were to provide blacks with decent homes, the builders could charge fair rates to cover their costs and still bring down rents in the Negro areas because the housing market for blacks would no longer be so tight, and profiteering landlords would be forced to be competitive.[89] A group of blacks including clergymen and NAACP leaders took up this suggestion and organized a "Better Home Movement," but their appeals to contractors and philanthropists fell on deaf ears.[90] No one in the city administration or among the city's millionaires was interested in wrestling with the problem of housing for black Wilmingtonians, even within the context of strict segregation.

The fourth failure of the city lay in a general area that relates to the first three—planning. Like the other failures, planning seemed like an idea whose time had come, but events proved that it had not. The concept received a great deal of favorable publicity. Important people declared its necessity, but the results of all the talk, newspaper articles, meetings, and reports were pitifully meager.

By the 1920s city planning was no longer a new idea in America. Its practitioners were expanding their activities beyond the ornamental projects associated with the City Beautiful Movement to include zoning and the creation of efficiently organized highway and utilities systems. Zoning, first introduced in New York in 1916, was the most popular planning tool of the twenties. Wilmington was in line with most American cities when it adopted its first zoning code in 1924. The city map was divided into a series of regions marked off into categories ranging from a heavy industrial zone through commercial and light industrial zones to densely packed residential and, finally, detached, single-family residential zones. The plotting corresponded not to someone's plan for a future, better Wilmington, but to existing land use. The idea was to preserve residential land values by preventing the alteration of the existing neighborhoods.

Pierre S. du Pont High School, completed in 1935, capstone of the growing middle-income area in north Wilmington. *(Courtesy of the Eleutherian Mills Historical Library)*

Planning for a dynamic future-oriented community development, by contrast, aimed to do much more than even the best-drawn zoning law. The war emergency had provided the first opportunity for developmental planning concepts to gain an audience in Wilmington. In 1918 officials representing the city's Chamber of Commerce and the New Castle County Levy Court attended a conference in Philadelphia at which they discussed the need for a comprehensive plan to control development of the west bank of the Delaware River from Philadelphia to Wilmington. At the conference an engineer for New Castle County decried the haphazard, illogical, unconnected realty development along the river close to Wilmington. "It

seems to me that some comprehensive plan of development should reg-
ulate these activities so that when the time comes for extending the city
boundaries the new section will be logically connected."[91] But the Levy
Court was ill equipped to take on a positive role in planning. When the war
emergency ended, the construction boom petered out, and so, too, did talk
about comprehensive planning, not to be heard again for another decade.

In the meantime, the most pressing need for planning was in the area
of traffic control. "Wilmington's streets were made without a wise contem-
plation, even of wagon traffic," complained an editorial writer in the
Sunday Star, "and we have not yet any plan . . . that is looking toward the
future."[92] In 1920, when those words were published, the future was
already upon the city. With auto registrations in and around Wilmington
growing at a rate of 2,000 per year the city's streets had become highly
congested and dangerous.[93] People were free to park their cars on both
sides of even the most narrow city streets. There were no traffic controls at
intersections, nor were pedestrians safe in crossing the streets. While
these problems affected everybody, they were especially annoying to the
more well-to-do, who had begun motoring before cars had become a
ubiquitous menace.

Little by little, as the decade progressed, the city government and
police employed what means they could to cope with these difficulties. In
1922 police first assigned men to traffic duty.[94] Later, traffic lights were
installed at major intersections, streets were widened, ordinances restricted parking, and, in 1930, narrow streets that carried trolley traffic
were made one-way.[95]

Important though it was, traffic regulation could go no further in
improving transportation flow than the inherited street layout would allow.
Like zoning, it could only make the best of an imperfect system. By the
mid-twenties, residents on important arterial streets like Washington
Street and North Market Street were complaining about the rumble of the
heavy trucks that constantly traveled through their streets to get from the
Du Pont Highway south of the city to the Philadelphia Pike north of it.
Everyone recognized the need for an "industrial highway," to route trucks
along the edge of the city, paralleling the Pennsylvania Railroad to the east
from Wilmington to Philadelphia. In 1923 the Pennsylvania legislature
authorized construction of such a highway to the Delaware border.

Delaware had much to do before it could supplement the effort of its
sister state. In the mid-twenties, the State Highway Department was still
working on the completion of the approach of the Du Pont Highway into
Wilmington, which necessitated the construction of a new bridge over the
Christina River at Market Street and improvements to the unsightly
causeway that ran through swampy riverside lands linking the new bridge

to the state highway. Nowhere in the entire state road system, reported the state's highway engineer, was there "a section of road whose surroundings are less attractive, more disreputable, ill-kept and thoroughly disgusting than the South Market Street Causeway." The State Highway Department suggested that the construction of lighted sidewalks along the route might somehow replace the many dump heaps, delapidated shacks, and hovels "by encouraging the construction of stores, show rooms, garages, and other presentable places of business."[96]

Congested traffic, unplanned housing development, and slums such as those along the causeway cried out for action on a scale far larger than Wilmington could undertake alone, and in 1928 leaders from business and government joined with planners to create the Regional Planning Federation of the Philadelphia Tri-State District. With such top-level men as Pierre S. du Pont and John J. Raskob on its board of directors, the Federation was well funded and professionally staffed. In 1932 it published a handsome volume, well-illustrated with maps and photographs, entitled *The Regional Plan of the Philadelphia Tri-State District*.[97] The plan proposed a comprehensive, well-balanced, orderly development design for the entire region, especially in the area of transportation. Yet its authors attempted to fit their plans for future highways, port facilities, and airports into a broader pattern that included the creation of new parklands and well-conceived residential developments.

The planners projected into the future a pattern of demographic and economic growth based upon their study of the recent past. They noted that in 1900 the thirteen cities in the region had reached the peak of their proportion of the total number of regional inhabitants. Since then additional population growth had been in the suburbs. Yet population had not as yet spread out very far from the cities; according to the 1930 census, nearly 90 percent of the region's people lived within ten miles of either the Delaware or Schuylkill rivers. The authors also noted the effects of the automobile on transportation during the preceding decade. Rail passenger service had reached an all-time high in the region in 1920, but since that date had declined by an astonishing 40 percent, while automobile travel increased by 200 percent. They also found that far more people in the mid-sized cities of Wilmington and Trenton were using their automobiles to get to and from work than were doing so in Philadelphia, where public transportation was still predominant. Statistics showed that whereas 71 percent of Wilmington's 25,000 commuters traveled to work by car, only 47 percent of those in the entire region drove to work.[98]

The plan's most significant recommendation was for a system of major high-speed highways. The planners strongly endorsed the Industrial Highway already under construction in Pennsylvania parallel to the Delaware

River. In addition, their plan called for a series of circumferential routes to speed through-traffic around cities on well-landscaped parkways. Reacting to the transportation section of the report, John J. Raskob, whose ties to General Motors made him particularly interested in these recommendations, envisioned highways and cars designed for future speeds of 60 miles an hour and more. "We must have broad express highways, over which streams of cars may shoot untrammeled . . ."[99]

Less well publicized were the report's recommendations regarding future residential development, even though this was a subject to which the planners gave a great deal of attention. Anticipating a substantial increase in the population of the region and recognizing the trend toward suburbanization, the planners pointed to a number of housing developments that might serve as models for the future. Included in their list were Union Park Gardens and Westover Hills in Wilmington, which, although designed for different income groups, each demonstrated good planning techniques. Both communities were self-contained, yet fit well into their surroundings and had direct access to major highways. Both broke with the grid pattern in favor of following the natural contours of the land, and both integrated houses into a parklike setting. The authors of the report cautioned, however, that good planning such as this could be had only if there were some group, at either the county or local level, empowered to enforce it.[100] Unfortunately, the integration of highway construction, water resources, zoning, and residential development was far beyond the powers of either New Castle County or the city of Wilmington, and no one seemed eager to make it otherwise. Only the State Highway Department had the means to impose planning of sorts. The dictates of the marketplace, limited only by technology and topography, had sufficed heretofore, and might continue to do so indefinitely.

Thus, as Wilmington entered the troubled decade of the 1930s, the community could exert little influence over its own future. The city could boast of some achievements during the prosperous twenties—the public schools had been modernized and the city had built an impressive public square—but beyond these progressive steps, Wilmington's leaders had failed to come to terms with serious problems. Faced with falling urban population, degenerating slums, and an inability to coopt its growing suburbs, Wilmington could not battle back, especially under a city charter that ensured ineffectual government.

"Billions Lost in Big Bear Raid," the headline screamed at worried Sunday morning newspaper readers in October 1929.[101] In the week that followed, Wilmington's stockbrokers were so besieged by panicked clients that brokerage clerks had to labor all night to keep up with orders to sell. John J. Raskob, who enjoyed a reputation as a wizard of Wall Street, announced that he was buying stocks at bargain prices. Secretly, however, he, too, was selling.[102] The president of Wilmington's Chamber of Commerce also had reassuring words. Business conditions in Wilmington were still good, he said, and not likely to be affected by a downturn in stocks, which could only hurt the luxury goods market.[103] Pierre du Pont's brother, Lammot, claimed that since the collapse had been caused by the federal government's capital gains tax, a tax cut would soon restore the economy. As month followed month the Depression deepened, however, with no end in sight.

Wilmington was completely unprepared to face the Depression. After the initial period, in which the economic leaders had attempted to stave off collapse with reassurances, the downturn began feeding on itself. Workers were laid off first in industries that had never fully recovered from the war, such as shipbuilding, but soon the general lessening of industrial production affected the major chemical producers as well. The Du Pont Company's volume of business declined 18 percent from 1929 to 1930 and plummeted another 14.5 percent the following year. The city's largest employer laid off many of its home office workers and cut hours and salaries for those who remained on its payroll.[104] The economic downturn was especially severe for the city's black workers, since many employers replaced unskilled black workers with skilled whites.

When the Depression began, Wilmington did not have a central community chest to finance its welfare agencies. The city's major charitable organization, The Associated Charities (soon to be renamed the Family Society), depended on private contributions to fund its tiny professional staff. Associated Charities functioned as a clearinghouse to help people facing all manner of problems, from joblessness and family difficulties to mental illness. Staff workers interviewed applicants in their homes to guide them in choosing the appropriate form of aid, which might be assistance in getting a job, vocational training, medical help, or institutional care. Philosophically committed to the doctrine of self-help, the organization made outright gifts only when all other means were unavailing. In 1929, the last year before the Depression, the Associated Charities provided some sort of aid to 584 families; those who needed cash received an average sum of $30.00.[105]

Ethelda Mullen, the director of the association, saw her agency's major function as helping family units to cope with a wide variety of problems, including, but not limited to, unemployment. When the Depression began, she, like most people at the time, regarded it as a temporary condition. In her 1930 annual report, she stressed that low wages, not joblessness, was the primary economic problem facing working-class families, and in 1931 she was instrumental in having the name of the organization changed to the Family Society to emphasize its intended focus. But as the Depression deepened, the Family Society was forced to devote ever more of its resources to the jobless at the expense of its intended clients— the sick and unemployable. In 1931 the Family Society assisted 1,140 families, 807 of them capable of work but unemployed, some of them white collar. Typically, the unemployed had sold their homes and furniture and had used up all their credit with grocers and other retailers before they came to the society for help.[106]

As late as 1929, the state of Delaware had nothing worthy of the name of public welfare. Each county maintained its own almshouse for the destitute, just as in colonial days. A survey of public welfare in Delaware during the 1930s found that despite its small size and relatively high per-capita income, the state ranked with much poorer states in the South with regard to its standards of public assistance. During the late 1920s, the various uncoordinated agencies of the state and local governments charged with welfare activities spent a total of less than $5,000 a year to assist distressed people.[107]

For a number of years, Alfred I. du Pont had urged the state legislature without success to provide assistance to the many elderly people in the state who were without either pensions or relatives to care for them. He was appalled by the treatment of old people in the New Castle County almshouse. He found them to be "uncared for, not decently clothed, not fed, not properly buried."[108] Finally, du Pont took it upon himself to support the state's needy elderly in 1929, when he started mailing monthly checks to poverty-stricken old people throughout the state. During the next two years du Pont sent some $350,000 to 1,600 families and individuals.[109] In the meantime he continued to impress upon the legislators the necessity of improved institutional care for the indigent. In 1931 the legislature finally passed a law acknowledging the state's responsibility. Du Pont provided funds to erect a state welfare home to replace the county almshouses. The need for such a facility was so great that it was soon overcrowded with chronically ill people, mostly elderly, and had no space to spare for the merely indigent.[110]

When the Depression began, both the city and state governments were controlled by the Republicans, which made for cooperation among the branches of government and between government and the local elite. The governor, C. Douglass Buck, an engineer whose earlier experience in public service had been with the State Highway Department, was T. Coleman du Pont's son-in-law. By the spring of 1930, unemployment had become a critical problem beyond the financial resources of the Associated Charities. Yet it was not until the second winter of the Depression that government officials tentatively intervened. At that time Wilmington's mayor, Frank C. Sparks, created the Mayor's Employment and Relief Committee to assist the city's many jobless men, some of whom were living in wretched squalor along the causeway south of the city in makeshift shacks that looked like something out of the writings of Victor Hugo.[111] The mayor chose Frank A. McHugh, a secretary to Pierre S. du Pont, to chair the committee, which McHugh operated from a tenth-floor office in the Du Pont Building. The Mayor's Committee raised $275,758.74 in 1930–31, not from taxes but from a public appeal to the employed to contribute one percent of their earnings. In addition, the city raised $400,000 through a bond issue. Since McHugh was already on P. S. du Pont's payroll, none of the money went to overhead. In addition to paying McHugh's salary, Pierre du Pont provided the largest single contribution to the committee's work and also helped by hiring additional men, both blacks and whites, to work on his grounds at Longwood.

Working closely with existing welfare-dispensing agencies such as the Salvation Army and the Family Society, McHugh spent some of his funds to buy groceries for jobless families and to provide single jobless people with meal tickets redeemable at local restaurants. In this way Wilmington avoided what McHugh called the "morally debilitating displays" of soup kitchen lines. His committee also published a weekly employment bulletin "based on the positive angle that Wilmington Can and Will Care for Its Own."[112] In May 1931 the Society told newspaper reporters that it was spending $18,000 a month.[113] In that year the Mayor's Committee assisted 1,098 black families and 1,274 white families until its money ran out at mid-year, leaving the Family Society as the only agency between many poverty-stricken families and starvation. As winter came on, the committee conducted another canvass that raised over $100,000, much of which came from members of the du Pont family. The relief committee's appeal emphasized that its aid was directed to Wilmington's own unemployed, not to "floaters" and that the aid would be used solely for basic necessities.

In addition to its direct aid, the Mayor's Committee either found or created jobs. It compensated some State Highway Department workers and employed maintenance workers for hospitals. Other jobless men were put to work grading parkland, hospital yards, and similar noncommercial properties. According to Mayor's Committee statistics, 70 percent of the men were white, 30 percent black. It also opened a sewing room in an abandoned downtown office building that employed 200 women; mostly former servants, laundresses, seamstresses, and factory workers. The women were paid $14 a week to make hospital supplies and to alter donated garments for resale. To employ jobless white-collar people, the committee sponsored a traffic survey that studied traffic patterns, parking problems, and accidents as the first step toward improving highway safety and convenience. The secretary of the city's Central Labor Union credited the mayor's committee with keeping many families together and praised McHugh for his nonpartisan, nonsectarian, and nonracial approach to assistance.[114]

Judging from the tone of the report issued by McHugh's office, the Mayor's Committee was at least as concerned to create the impression that Wilmingtonians were not in distress as to make this so in fact. "The most striking accomplishment of the program," he wrote, "was the avoidance of flagrant and calculated displays of poverty. There were no depressing scenes such as long struggling breadlines and dingy soup houses. Apple merchants, peddlers, and like exploiters of hard times were conspicuous by their absence." The committee took pride in the hard-nosed attitude of the city authorities toward panhandlers. "The word got around" that Wilmington would not tolerate such behavior.[115] Once again, however, because the relief effort was considered only temporary, funds ran out and the Family Society director cautioned that her agency faced "a situation where it cannot take care of all the dependents who are referred to it." Not only was the Family Society strapped, but the state's Old Age Pension Commission and Welfare Home could not even begin to meet the many urgent demands placed upon them.[116]

The social, political, and economic problems left unresolved in two decades of prosperity were magnified as city leaders groped ineffectually to cope with the disaster that fell upon them in 1929. It was typical of Wilmington that the city government's response to crisis was to turn the problem of relief over to a committee funded and directed by Pierre du Pont. Even local labor leaders acknowledged in du Pont the ideal leader to assist the poor through the economic collapse.[117] Consequently, the interests and attitudes of the du Ponts dictated the nature of the relief program, especially its emphasis on the themes of keeping up appearances, discouraging aid to short-term residents, and concentrating employment for the jobless on highway and traffic-related projects. This policy, which was continued under belated state relief efforts from 1934 through 1937, was not without its critics. Some observers noted, for instance, that solving Wilmington's slum problem might be as useful a goal as improving automobile transportation, especially since many of the jobless had experience in the building trades. But the rehabilitation of blighted areas was not a priority goal of the city's leaders.[118]

As we have seen, during the first third of the twentieth century Wilmington's development was in the hands of a small group of extremely wealthy, civic-minded businessmen, each of whom had his own priority programs for improving the community. Reliance upon their private initiative to bring about community betterment resulted in excellent progress in some areas but neglect in others. Generally speaking, transportation and education were favored while the renewal of the city itself, especially of its growing areas of blight, was ignored. The standard of living for middle- and upper-income people was improved and suburbanization advanced, while the problems of the poor and the unskilled received only tangential attention. The first steps toward changing this orientation came with the introduction of fresh views and greater power and wealth from the federal government during the New Deal.

CHAPTER 3

Mourning for an Old

American City: 1933–1959

In the nine years I have lived in our City as it becomes denuded of its trees, uglier and hotter and filthier by the minute, I have mourned for what was one of the last really old American cities on the East Coast.
Clark Maynard, to Maurice du Pont Lee, 15 March 1954

With the inauguration of Franklin D. Roosevelt in March 1933, during the blackest days of the Depression, the United States entered a new era. In his campaign Roosevelt had promised the American people a "New Deal"—an amorphous term that suggested some degree of national economic reorganization. In the years that followed, the Roosevelt administration's policies expanded the role of the federal government in every aspect of American life. The New Deal's host of federal agencies and programs reached into communities like Wilmington in various ways. Designed to restore buying power and to achieve social welfare, the New Deal energized local government to put people to work, infusing funds into states and cities for public works. By the end of 1934, the Public Works Administration, the Roosevelt administration's first major make-work program, was assisting the financing of several job-creating projects in and around Wilmington. The PWA helped finance the construction of sanitary sewers in Elsmere, the building of a new school in Claymont and the P. S. du Pont High School in Wilmington, the improvements to the state hospital at Farnhurst, and the expansion of the city's waterworks, harbor, and parks.[1] The federal government also chose this time to construct a new federal courthouse-post office building opposite the Wilmington Institute Free Library, thus completing Rodney Square.

It is important to recognize that the make-work projects undertaken by New Deal agencies differed from those of the earlier Mayor's Employment and Relief Committee more in size and scope than in aims or priorities. Both were primarily concerned with providing jobs and stabilizing the economy, and neither was designed to become a permanent fixture in the job market. Furthermore, both the Democratic New Deal and the Republican, du Pont-controlled Mayor's Committee emphasized the same kinds of projects—highways and schools continued to take precedence over housing rehabilitation. But where the Mayor's Committee had funded only short-term projects, federal agencies funded long-term ones. For example, instead of improving the shoulders of an existing roadway, as the Mayor's Committee might have done, the Public Works Administration could afford to offer the State Highway Department the opportunity to construct a whole highway.

Indeed, highway construction was especially favored with federal funds during the Roosevelt administration, in part because highways were perceived as a general public benefit, but also because highway construction was labor intensive: there were many unskilled jobs to be done in road-building, so wages, rather than materials, made up the largest part of the total cost. In Delaware federal aid to highway construction further strengthened the already powerful State Highway Department. The department used the aid to pursue the transportation goals that had earlier interested T. Coleman and Pierre du Pont and to realize long-contemplated projects. During the Depression decade, federal policies encouraged the State Highway Department to expand its power over what were formerly city and county roads. In Wilmington the state highway department relieved the city street and sewer department of responsibility for the maintenance of the most important city streets. In addition, on 1 July 1935, the state highway men took control of all roads formerly under county authority, thus finally ending an awkward transition period of shared power that had persisted since the creation of the state department in 1917.[2] Swollen by extra federally funded workers and by its increased scope and power, the department built a series of new roadways in and around Wilmington that reshaped the city's transportation system.

The most important new highways of the period constituted an early form of circumferential construction; they hugged the edges of the city but were not limited-access roadways. One such was the long-awaited extension of Pennsylvania's Industrial Highway, U.S. Route 13. Prior to the mid-1930s, heavy car and truck traffic along the Baltimore-Philadelphia corridor passed through the center of Wilmington on Market Street and its northern extension, the Philadelphia Pike. The Industrial Highway created a bypass that skirted the eastern edge of the city along Heald Street and Church Street—old, slightly widened city streets—to the Governor Printz Boulevard, a new dual-lane road that paralleled the Pennsylvania Railroad tracks from Wilmington to the Pennsylvania border. The Church Street-Governor Printz route reconcentrated heavy interstate traffic away from Market Street into a densely populated section of the city's old east side working-class residential district. The route was designed to help ensure that future industries would continue to locate on the east side of the city, where trucking facilities could complement rail transportation. It was a common practice to incorporate working-class residential neighborhood streets into industrial highway plans in American cities in the 1920s and 1930s. There lay the path of least expense and least resistance. But in the long run such decisions were costly, because the heavy traffic only added to other factors that were reducing such neighborhoods to slums; the Wilmington case was no exception.

Other major highway building projects of the 1930s were the construction of the Lea Boulevard and Washington Street Extension parkways and the nearby Augustine Cut-Off, all relatively short, scenic roadways built at the north and west edges of the city. These new roads, designed according to the best planning standards, had the effect of sealing off the city's gridiron street pattern from the curvilinear county roads and suburban developments beyond. Thus, in subtle ways the federally financed but locally planned highway programs of the 1930s assisted the suburban movement and militated against urban annexations.

The New Deal's housing policy was a yet greater inducement to suburbanization. Housing policy emerged slowly and tentatively from Washington because the Roosevelt administration and its allies in Congress disagreed on the question of the federal government's proper role in the field of housing. The president took the view that the government's involvement should be limited to preserving the mortgage structure and to restoring jobs in the building trades. Some of his supporters, however, notably Senator Robert Wagner of New York, argued for a more interventionist policy, including the construction of permanent public housing to replace deteriorated urban tenements.[3] Ultimately both positions were written into separate laws that did very different things. Responding to the president's concerns, Congress created the Federal Housing Administration in 1934 to insure borrowers' mortgage loans. The FHA was a conservatively conceived and conservatively managed agency that took care to restrict its mortgage guarantees to houses and neighborhoods that were built and located so as to maintain their value. Generally speaking, therefore, this meant that the FHA preferred new suburban housing to old city housing. In 1937 Senator Robert Wagner succeeded in convincing a reluctant president to support public housing as well. The result was the

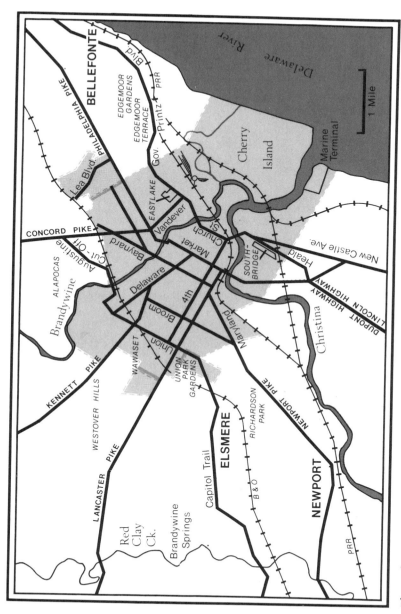

The Wilmington Area during World War II. (Map by Marley Amstutz, Cartographer)

Wagner-Steagall Housing Act, which created the U.S. Housing Authority for the purpose of providing decent housing for poor people.

The city's building trades, which had been in the doldrums early in the 1930s, revived during the second half of the decade because parts of Wilmington's economy improved, creating a market for middle- to upper-priced houses. By the mid-1930s, Du Pont, Hercules, and Atlas had all recovered their pre-Depression momentum, because manufacturers of consumer goods, especially in the automobile industry, replaced natural products such as leather and silk with cheaper synthetics made by the chemical industry. Du Pont, in particular, was on the verge of its greatest research and financial triumph with the introduction of nylon, the world's first successful fully synthetic fiber. The company's expansion required the construction of a large new office building adjacent to the Du Pont Building. Hercules, meanwhile, was busily developing its own new research laboratories, on a site west of the city along the Lancaster Pike. Responding to this economic growth, real-estate developers concentrated on building houses to appeal to white-collar workers, executives, and technical research personnel. In the city the last large area of open land was in the area around P.S. du Pont High School, a neighborhood that appealed to middle-income white-collar workers who could afford the six-room duplex houses in the five- to six-thousand-dollar range being built there. Not far away, in the near northern suburbs, the emphasis was on small developments of houses costing twelve thousand dollars and up, often situated adjacent to the new circumferential parkways. Bellevue Manor, Edgewood Hills, and Lindamere, all located between the Philadelphia Pike and the Governor Printz Boulevard, Alapocas on the Augustine Cut-Off, and Brandywine Hills on Lea Boulevard were typical of suburbs for more affluent administrators and scientists.

While the FHA insured mortgages in some of these and other suburban developments, the full impact of what federal mortgage insurance could mean for Wilmington's housing industry was not felt until 1939, when the Wilmington Construction Company announced plans to build Edgemoor Terrace, a development just north of the city, adjacent to the new Governor Printz Boulevard. The project, backed by FHA financing, was designed eventually to include 400 six-room, free-standing houses to be sold at prices below those of new city duplexes of comparable size. In earlier moderately priced suburban developments such as Bellefonte and Elsmere, the purchaser had bought a lot and then contracted for a house in the style of his choice, or he chose from a half-dozen or so look-alike bungalows. In Edgemoor Terrace, by contrast, the builder offered a fully integrated, mass-produced package. Would-be buyers were encouraged to visit the "brides' houses"—furnished models illustrating the two brick and wood colonial-style houses available. Each house was set on a quarter-acre lot and included an attached garage and full basement. All that was required to obtain a mortgage on the $5,150 house was a minimum of $550 down, plus a $29.61 monthly payment.[4] Edgemoor Terrace was the first suburban development in Delaware to use the tract techniques that were to become so common following World War II—a limited number of styles, furnished models, standardized lot sizes and materials, builders' promises of a community park and swimming pool (which never materialized) and a package-deal mortgage backed by the FHA. The mass production concepts of the automobile industry had been brought to the construction industry. Advertisements for Edgemoor Terrace were not lying when they declared that it cost less to buy a house there than to rent a house or apartment of comparable size in the city.[5] And the houses sold rapidly. The new community was a portent of future suburbanization, part of what one reporter called the "drift toward smaller, more open communities." In addition to neighborliness, Edgemoor Terrace offered "lower taxes, lenient purchase plans, extension of utilities, and improved transportation. . . ."[6]

The housing revival of the late 1930s, spurred by the FHA and growth in the chemical industry, had no impact upon urban slum neighborhoods, which disintegrated further during the Depression. From Edgemoor Terrace it was only about a mile along the Governor Printz Boulevard through the city to the Christina River Bridge that led to South Wilmington, an isolated part of the city whose residents complained that they lived in "the city that council forgot."[7] The city could offer few places worse than South Wilmington, a place where most houses were without running water or indoor plumbing. Because its residents had little political power and because the area was devoid of natural drainage, its sewer system was totally inadequate. Nearby, the rat-infested city dump was a reservoir of contagion and stench; social workers found that disease was rampant.[8] Conditions were not a great deal better on the east side, north of the Christina. In the early 1930s, housing surveys found that nearly one-half of Wilmington's 20,000 residential structures had no indoor toilets, and almost as many had no bathtub or shower; nearly three-quarters lacked central heating. Three thousand one hundred and seventy housing units had no running water, and over 1,000 families were doubled up in these inadequate dwellings. Most of these structures were in the city's oldest wards. In 1932 the State Housing Commission had called them "blighted areas" in need of "extensive rebuilding and rehabilitation," where development had ceased and real-estate values had climbed very little. The commission found that although those with incomes below $2,000 a year made up 80 percent of the city's people, the housing market was not supplying homes for them. Those earning less than $1,500 had to devote a high percentage of their scanty wages to pay for even the unsatisfactory housing that then existed. "It is imperative," the state commissioner urged, "that a sizable program for the construction of homes for the 80 percent of the people having incomes below $2,000 be undertaken." They advocated the rehabilitation of salvageable housing and the demolition of slums, but offered little guidance as to how this could be achieved, since they rejected the European practice of government-subsidized housing yet recognized that private developers would be disinclined to shoulder the cost of slum removal. Their only solutions were to call for greater efficiency in the housing industry to lower the cost of new construction for low-income families and a strengthening of the city's health code to permit the Board of Health to condemn deteriorated buildings.[9]

These supposed solutions offered little hope of reversing a serious problem. Why should real-estate developers demolish and rebuild in slum neighborhoods when suburban land was not only cheaper, but easier to sell to customers and to the FHA? There was also the race issue to be considered. Since the turn of the century, blacks had been concentrating on the east side while whites moved elsewhere. The strongest black churches were there, as were Howard High School and black social institutions such as lodges and political clubs. Their cultural and social organizations did not, however, save blacks from the social problems associated with poverty and segregation. Although they made up only 11 percent of the city's population, blacks accounted for 35 percent of those convicted of crimes. But since most of the victims were black, too, whites were apathetic.[10] The same prejudice and lack of concern dominated the thinking of most whites about the east side as a whole. As long as its problems remained within it, the rest of the city felt free to ignore them.

Against this background of community apathy and a housing industry that ignored the poor, the Wagner-Steagall Act of 1937 offered the promise of federally funded public housing. The law required each participating city to create a housing authority to be made up of private citizens and local government officials. The local authority could then apply for federal funds to finance the construction of public housing projects. The Wilmington Housing Authority was organized in 1938 to tear down slums and replace them with public housing. The bipartisan group of businessmen who made up the WHA board had barely established itself, however, when war broke out in Europe. Once again, Wilmington's economy responded to war's tempo. Industrial production mounted, and the local housing market felt the strain of increased demand. Because of the influx of people to work in war production, the WHA decided its first priority must be not slum clearance but rather the construction of new homes that could be con-

The newly completed Governor Printz Boulevard at Edgemoor in the late 1930s. *(Courtesy of the Division of Historical and Cultural Affairs, State of Delaware)*

verted into permanent low-income housing at the end of the war. Slum dwellers would have to wait until after the war for better housing.

The WHA faced a problem in selecting sites for public housing. After rejecting several sites because they were either too distant from industries or too close to expensive homes, the authority chose for its major project, intended for white residents, a 15-acre property adjacent to the intersection of the Governor Printz Boulevard with Vandever Avenue, a neighborhood of working-class houses originally built for employees of the nearby Pennsylvania Railroad maintenance shops. The residents there feared a decline in property values and objected strenuously to the project, but in vain. The WHA's director assured them that the 200 houses in the project, to be called Eastlake, would be as good as the houses already in the area.[11] Wilmington needed the additional housing and, besides, in war time it was unpatriotic to protest.

Eastlake was built in circumstances similar to those that had produced Union Park Gardens, Wilmington's World War I workers' housing project, a fact that makes the contrasts between the two all the more striking. Both developments offered carefully designed rental housing located near park land at the edge of the city. Yet the ultimate purpose, appearance, and subsequent history of the projects were very different. Union Park Gardens, planned as "an American Garden Suburb of exceptional merit,"[12] consisted of row and duplex houses, stylishly designed, but otherwise similar to moderately priced houses already available in Wilmington. The project was constructed solely as a war measure, and at war's end was sold off to individual home buyers. Now, over 60 years later, Union Park Gardens is still an attractive, well-maintained community of houses that sell quickly and at a premium.

Eastlake, by contrast, was constructed under the rules of the Federal Public Housing Authority to be transformed into low-income housing; more than half of its 200 units consisted of four-room apartments, and the entire project looked like apartment houses, rather than rowhouses. More significantly, Eastlake was one among hundreds of projects that the Federal Public Housing Authority was constructing simultaneously all over the country. Because of wartime shortages, the authority had a limited choice of building materials. Quality was sacrificed to utility; for instance, concrete floors rather than wooden ones were installed in Eastlake apartments and concrete play areas were used in place of asphalt.[13] Restrictions on building designs further reduced building and maintenance costs. The result was the monotone "project" look that one can see all over the United States in similar World War II government housing.

The only other type of war-related permanent housing project in Wilmington, Edgemoor Gardens, was never meant to be public housing. Financed by the FHA and located immediately north of Edgemoor Terrace on the Governor Printz Boulevard, the development was one of rowhouses designed for sale rather than for rent.[14] But unvaried design and unimaginative landscaping made Edgemoor Gardens more like its contemporary, Eastlake, than like the earlier Union Park Gardens. Edgemoor Gardens consisted of a series of short, narrow look-alike streets running at right angles to a straight central thoroughfare. Where Union Park Gardens gave a feeling of spaciousness, Edgemoor Gardens represented the same cookie-cutter building techniques as its neighbor, Edgemoor Terrace, only carried several steps further to achieve maximum economy.

Just three weeks after the Japanese attack on Pearl Harbor, the *Sunday Star* ran a headline that read, "This is What We're Fighting For!" Below was a large aerial view of Edgemoor Terrace captioned, "The United States is the country where people have the right to work, the right to a home and property, the right to a fair and understanding government, and the right to prosperity."[15] After the bitter Depression years, these were indeed the things that Americans were fighting for and working for in World War II. As had been the case in the Great War 25 years before, World War II brought many new jobs to Wilmington. The Du Pont Company's sales volume nearly tripled between 1939 and 1944, while Hercules' net sale climbed even more spectacularly.[16] Hercules, Atlas, and Du Pont all operated government-owned munitions plants in various parts of the country in addition to their own facilities. All three had gone well beyond explosives in developing other chemical products. In addition to powder, Atlas manufactured coated fabrics useful for ponchos, tents, and other military paraphernalia, as well as ingredients for the drug industry. Hercules made a variety of war-related products from tree pulp and rosin, while Du Pont manufactured nylon for parachutes and D.D.T. to protect jungle fighters, and worked secretly on the development of the atomic bomb. Although nearly all of the production facilities associated with these activities were outside Wilmington, the management and research efforts centered here expanded appreciably. Furthermore, unlike war production work, which might shut down when the fighting stopped, the jobs created in management and research were expected to continue into peacetime as the chemical companies converted their war profits and war-related research into consumer production.

The war did not change the components of Wilmington's economy, but it did lead to the expansion of plants, production and personnel. Many of the city's factories made materials such as sheet metals, rubber-lined tubing, and waterproof textiles that were used by other manufacturers in making finished articles. Since both wartime and peacetime production used these same articles, the factories that made them did not require conversion or reconversion. The biggest local plant producing directly for wartime use was the Dravo Company, which built landing craft and sub chasers. Landing craft made on the Christina carried U.S. Army and Marine units onto the beaches of North Africa, France, and Pacific islands. The war increased Wilmington's workforce by about 10,000 people from 54,741 at the end of 1940 to a peak of 64,000 two years later.[17]

As the war went on, the number of female workers employed in essential industries increased to compensate for men called into the service. Not only did women work in traditional female occupations, as nurses and office personnel, but they also were trained to be electricians at the Pennsylvania Railroad shops and, at Dravo, to be riveters. One of the most unusual assignments undertaken by women in the Wilmington area during World War II was working as WASP pilots, which they did for a time at the New Castle Air Base. The base was created from scratch in 1942 to play a major role in ferrying planes and supplies to war theaters in Europe and North Africa. Although the women pilots were not permitted to fly into combat areas, they did ferry planes about the United States.

The migration of families, the absence of fathers, and the increased numbers of working women contributed to the city's one serious social problem of the war years: juvenile delinquency. During the war more children than usual came home to empty houses after school. Some young people hung around bars frequented by servicemen or, ignoring the prohibition on pleasure driving, cruised about in cars in search of "pick ups" of the opposite sex. Petty thievery increased, as did runaways. During the first year of the war, there was a 20 percent jump in the number of children who appeared in court. In 1943 some civic-minded people formed the Council on Youth to address these problems. Through their efforts the schools began summer camp programs and provided evening dances. At Eastlake, where one half the total population consisted of small children, a nursery school was a godsend to working mothers.[18] But, curiously, the war left the city with a more heightened juvenile crime problem than had the Great Depression.

On a warm evening in August 1945, a crowd estimated at 50,000 gathered in Rodney Square to celebrate V-J Day. Their smiles and cheers reflected not only the intense relief of knowing family members overseas would soon come home, but also the anticipation of a better tomorrow in a prosperous, consumer-oriented economy. At Du Pont, for example, the average hourly wage had risen 42 percent since the war began, yet wartime restrictions and rationing had given workers few opportunities to spend their increased earnings. One of the most serious national shortages was in housing, since little had been built in the past 15 years. The second most common pent-up demand was for automobiles, which, like houses, had not been produced during the war.

The postwar period produced the greatest transformation in American history in the relationship between cities and their suburbs. Prior to 1945 suburbs had been subordinate to the cities that had made them possible. Cities provided more than jobs; they were the primary source of entertainment, shopping, education, and health care for their suburbanites as well as for their own residents. With the dramatic expansion of suburbanization after the war, suburbs ceased to be mere satellite bedroom communities and became instead competitors with the cities that spawned them in all of these functions. The key ingredient in this enormous shift was the almost universal ownership of automobiles, which made suburbanization not only possible but necessary, because the suburbs were designed with the automobile in mind whereas the cities had been built in and for an age of mass transit.

Widespread use of automobiles pulled people, activities, and wealth out of cities and then encouraged the recreation of cities in the image of the new suburban design. The older and more compactly built a city was, the more difficult the readjustment was likely to be. The context in which these changes took place and their effects are well illustrated in the case of Wilmington and its surrounding suburban developments.

Government regulations concerning suburban development were extremely loose in New Castle County, because until the 1940s nearly all the unincorporated parts of the county had been agricultural land. Housing contractors were restrained only by the prohibitions of the marketplace— would it sell? The government agency that was most concerned about the shortcomings of uninhibited development was the State Highway Department. In his 1941 annual report, the chief engineer called attention to the problems that burgeoning suburban communities posed for his department and for government generally. "It will come as a surprise to many people that there are communities in Delaware with a population nearly as large as the city of Dover having no local community government," he wrote, and cautioned, "that such a condition does not encourage or assist in an orderly and progressive development nor does it promote community pride and spirit." The suburban movement was in part motivated "by a desire to escape taxation" that caused an inequity for taxpayers in incorporated towns while it left suburbanites with inadequate services and unexpected problems. He blamed the trouble in part on silver-tongued real-estate developers who assured buyers that the Highway Department would take care of everything. "Moving to the country in spring or summer the suburbanite is frequently shocked on the approach of winter to realize that there are no sidewalks by which his children can reach the neighboring school, that the streets are muddy, rough and unlighted, and that no storm water drainage is provided, while other subdivisions may divert additional water to these streets or dam back the water [thus] flooding cellars or roadways."[19]

To deal with these difficulties, the Highway Department adopted new regulations in 1942 that required subdivisions to meet its standards for streets, sidewalks, and storm sewers before the department would assume responsibility for maintaining their roads. In addition, the department supported a bill in the legislature, entitled The Suburban Road Act of 1945, that, in essence, provided a substitution for local government. The act stipulated that whenever 50 percent of the freeholders in a subdivision requested street improvements, the County Levy Court would issue bonds and collect the necessary taxes to pay the cost of the Highway Department's work. But even after the act was adopted complaints about poorly planned, unconnected, hastily built suburbs continued to crop up in the State Highway Department's annual reports.[20] In 1947 the chief engineer pointed out that if the street mileage of Wilmington's 175 suburbs were combined it would nearly equal that of the city of Wilmington. Yet, unlike Wilmington, the suburbs were randomly scattered and laid out to no common standard. For instance, developers, unrestrained by law codes, ordinances, or bureaucrats, were free to ignore drainage problems. To save money and sell as many lots as possible on the cheap farm lands they obtained, builders routinely filled in low spots and blocked natural drainage, practices that led to flooded cellars and overflowing septic tanks.

The Highway Department was caught in a bind, however, for much as the engineering staff might deplore "the hurriedly-constructed community which we see rise practically overnight,"[21] the department was being pushed into building new routes in support of suburbanization both by its own commissioners and by the engineers' desires to alleviate traffic congestion. The best example of the consequences of this dilemma was the Kirkwood Highway, which had been conceived in the 1930s, at the insistance of a highway commission member from Newark, to be a link between that town and Wilmington, 12 miles away. At that time Newark was a compact college and industrial community of 4,500 people, joined to Wilmington by a narrow, two-lane country road known as the Capitol Trail. The Trail entered Wilmington through Elsmere. The highway engineer planned to replace this old-fashioned rural road with a four-lane highway that would improve Elsmere's automobile access to Wilmington, and provide a modern, high-speed connection between Wilmington and Newark, one of the county's principal towns. When the Kirkwood Highway was finally completed some 20 years after its planning, the results were quite different. It became the magnet for an instant strip city of retail sprawl surrounded by equally planless residential sprawl.

The significance of suburbanization in the Wilmington area during the 1940s is revealed in two statistics. During that decade, while the city of Wilmington lost about 2 percent of its population, the Wilmington metropolitan region gained 21 percent. In the first five postwar years, approximately 8,500 houses were built in the region, fewer than 700 of them in the city.[22] In the immediate postwar years not only homes, but jobs were moving to Wilmington's suburbs. The guns had not yet stopped firing in the Pacific when General Motors announced plans to build an automobile assembly plant on a 125-acre tract on Boxwood Road adjacent to Elsmere, Newport, and Richardson Park. General Motors' president, Charles E. Wilson, said that the plant, designed to build Buicks, Oldsmobiles, and Pontiacs, would be GM's first postwar plant and was part of his company's effort to decentralize production.[23] When the first car came off the assembly line in April 1947, the plant was employing 1,067 hourly rate workers,

Edgemoor Terrace, under construction in 1940, linked to Wilmington by the Governor Printz Boulevard. *(Courtesy of the Eleutherian Mills Historical Library)*

of whom 70 percent were veterans.[24] Just three years later the Chrysler Corporation Parts Division opened a 16-acre storage center at Newark, Delaware, which was expected to employ 500 workers.[25] The Du Pont Company was also employing more people outside the city. In addition to its pigments plants at Newport and Edgemoor, Du Pont constructed a gigantic campus-style Experimental Station across the Brandywine from the company's earliest powder mills.

Between 1948 and 1960, the economic growth in the chemical and automobile industries produced the greatest building boom in the history of New Castle County. The boom was supported by other factors as well, including a residue of unsatisfied aspirations from the constructionless

Depression and war period, federal mortgage policies that favored new construction, the baby boom, and society's preference for new construction over old. This last factor was related to the rapid changes that were taking place in home utilities and technology, affecting especially kitchen and bathroom designs, heating units, and lighting. Older homes were not only less fashionable because they had high ceilings and dark narrow corridors; they were also more likely to have coalburning furnaces, exposed wiring, large awkward bathtubs set on porcelain lions' claws, and gas ranges that required a match to light. According to the values of young middle-income families ripe for suburbanization, such features were not quaint but obnoxious.

As the State Highway Department kept pointing out, most new houses were being built with only the meager planning provided by individual developers. The state legislature had created the Regional Planning Commission of New Castle County in 1931, but the commission had little power. New Castle County did not enact a building and plumbing code until 1949 and had no zoning ordinance until the 1950s.[26] In the absence of externally applied restraints, builders responded to the pressures of the marketplace. They built what would sell, where it would sell. The market supplied its own planning. The suburbs were in nearly every case extensions of the status and the ethnicity of the urban residential areas nearest to them. Builders needed no zoning ordinance to tell them that upper-middle-class families would not buy a house on the flats close by the Marine Terminal, or that automobile workers would be eager to use their V.A. benefits to buy inexpensive tract houses close to the GM plant. Topography and existing land use provided the "planning," which meant that the suburbs became an extension of the growth pattern of the city. The locations of the Du Pont Experimental Station and the GM plant fit perfectly into the existing pattern. The GM plant was located along the same railroad siding that had made Elsmere a working-class suburb a half century before. The trolley suburbs already built near there were themselves extensions of the working-class ethnic neighborhoods of southwest Wilmington. The opening of the Kirkwood Highway encouraged builders to extend working-class-style suburbs on the flat ground east of the highway still further from the city. When the Du Pont Company located a large technical facility on Chestnut Run west of Elsmere, builders responded with a flood of middle-income developments on the rolling land west of the Kirkwood Highway. Likewise, Du Pont's Experimental Station, which employed many middle- to upper-income scientists and technicians, was located on the border between Brandywine and Christina Hundred, close to both the elite Kennett Pike area and the rapidly growing Concord Pike suburbs, the latter a continuation of the city's bourgeois Baynard Boulevard section.

Ten years after the developers of Edgemoor Terrace had pioneered in suburban mass-construction, these same techniques were revived in the construction of Fairfax, a 700-unit development located in Brandywine Hundred. The builder kept his costs low by offering a minimum of variety in his two-story, six-room colonial houses, which he sold for $15,000 apiece with little or no down payment and an FHA-backed mortgage. In addition to houses, he built a half-mile-long colonial-style shopping center, complete with a cupola, fronting the Concord Pike. This included a supermarket and a variety of other stores catering to homeowners' needs. A group of low-rise apartment buildings, also in pseudocolonial style, separated the shopping center from the rest of the community. Thereafter, builders often used a strip of apartment buildings as buffers between their highway-oriented commercial developments and single-family houses. Renters, they found, were less fussy than buyers about accepting a site that overlooked a shopping center parking lot or the bleak view of rear service entrances to stores. At the beginning of the 1950s there was also a boom in garden-style apartments, usually located on existing bus lines just beyond the city limits. The ease with which these several thousand units were filled testified to the severity of the housing shortage and the public's preference for new construction.

Fairfax both started and epitomized the home-building trends that were to characterize the 1950s. Builders found farmers eager to sell as the suburbs encroached on them. It was difficult to justify continuing to farm when a builder was willing to buy the land for more than the farm could produce in a decade. The construction of suburban developments proceeded according to a pattern that, although unwritten, was as sternly felt as the old city gridiron. It flowed like lava from a volcano outward from the city limits, seeking out first the major arteries, then the secondary streets, and finally the back roads.[27] Styles changed from two-story colonials to split levels in the 1950s, but the process remained the same.

The development of suburban public school districts further strengthened the movement to the suburbs, reinforced the socioeconomic clustering within suburban areas, and reduced the social ties and sense of community between the city and its surroundings. Until the late 1940s, many suburban children attended elementary school in their own local districts, then transferred into Wilmington for high school. As they became more populous, however, the suburban districts built high schools of their own. Under Delaware law each school district had the choice of subsisting on state funds or becoming a "special" district, in which residents could bond themselves in order to supplement the state's school allowance. Districts thus could choose either to offer basic educational services or to provide enriched curricula at the expense of their own taxpayers. For example, the Mt. Pleasant Special School District, which included the eastern portions

An Edgemoor Terrace house of 1941. *(Courtesy of the Historical Society of Delaware)*

of Brandywine Hundred, epitomized the educational values of the middle class. Its district included many scientists, engineers, and white-collar management personnel. The school board there had no difficulty in convincing taxpayers to support extra bond issues in the name of quality education. The district's reputation for modern schools and good educational programs was in turn used by real-estate brokers and developers as a selling point to attract more educationally minded families to the area. The wealthy people along the Kennett Pike, by contrast, typically sent their children to private schools and understandably showed less interest in their public schools, while the moderate-income families who predominated south of Wilmington were content with schools built solely on the state's appropriation.

Next to the garage, family room, and backyard barbeque, the public school became the most familiar symbol of suburban life. The change from one- and two-room rural schoolhouses to large, bright, modern multi-use buildings was the educational manifestation of the shift from farmhouses to tract developments. Initially these new schools merely rivaled those in the city with regard to programs and teachers' benefits, but by the mid-1950s several of the suburban districts had developed, or were in the process of developing, school systems that surpassed that of the city, and the number of suburban children attending the city's kindergartens and high schools declined.

Suburban school construction thus began a shift in the city's school population that increased the percentage of working-class and poor children, a change that was greatly accelerated in 1954 by the Supreme Court decision in *Brown* v. *the Board of Education of Topeka, Kansas, et al.*, which ended racial segregation in public education. Although two of the cases examined by the court involved black students in northern Delaware—one an elementary student in rural Hockessin, the other a high-school student in the steel-mill town of Claymont—northern New Castle County outside the city of Wilmington was nearly all white and was becoming increasingly whiter as suburbs pushed out the vestiges of rural community life. In contrast to the county, Wilmington's school population in 1954 was 20 percent black. Between 1940 and 1950 the number of black residents in Wilmington increased by about 3,000, or 21 percent, while the number of whites had decreased by over 5,000. It was in the city, therefore, that the impact of the Brown case was most felt. Indeed, all aspects of the movement to abolish segregation had far more impact on Wilmington than on its suburbs.

Ever since Reconstruction in the 1870s, Wilmington had operated a segregated school system, but when the Supreme Court announced its decision in May of 1954 the city's school administrators worked rapidly to desegregate by the opening of school the following September. Desegregation was carefully planned. Most principals took no vacations that summer, for they were busy reassigning students and teachers and visiting homes to explain the reassignments and to dispel parental fears.[28] The administrators took care to assign high-quality black teachers to previously all-white schools. By these means they turned what might otherwise have been a wrenching community experience into a relatively painless one. This was a considerable achievement, especially in light of the fact that Ku Klux Klan activities in downstate Delaware at that time were capturing national headlines.

Although the desegregation of the Wilmington schools was a model of smooth acceptance, school administrators were aware that desegregation accelerated white flight to the suburbs. One administrator estimated that during the first five years following desegregation Wilmington lost 5,000 of its white inhabitants, mostly middle-income people who could afford to move to the suburbs.[29] By the end of the 1950s, the Wilmington public schools were more than 50 percent black, and the city schools faced a complex series of problems. Young white teachers were choosing well-paid positions in the new suburban districts rather than entering the city schools. Among the remaining white teachers, some retired, while others were ineffective in dealing with the growing numbers of black children. To maintain the system, Wilmington had to hire more black teachers—some excellent and well-trained; others, unfortunately, poorly trained graduates of small, segregated southern colleges. To deal with these problems, in 1959 the Wilmington public schools launched an extensive project designed to improve the ability of the schools to serve their expanding population of mostly poor black children. By then, only a few of the city's public schools had populations that were predominantly white or middle income. In those parts of the city that remained white, such as heavily Polish southwest Wilmington and the upper-income Highlands, many children attended either parochial school or private schools. Those portions of the city that had been Jewish or white Protestant and middle income, such as the 9th Ward, were, therefore, the most drastically affected by the racial change.

Retailers were also responding to the suburban pull. In the trolley-car age the optimum store location had been in the heart of center city, where trolley lines converged. In the automobile age, before the construction of limited-access interstate highways the best location was a large plot of open land along a major arterial highway, at the point where the city and suburbs joined. Sears, along with two of Philadelphia's largest department stores, John Wanamaker and Strawbridge and Clothier, built stores at various locations at the edge of Wilmington in the postwar period. Strawbridge's store was the focal point of the Merchandise Mart, Wilmington's first large shopping center, a collection of stores nine city blocks long facing a parking lot for 5,500 cars on the Governor Printz Boulevard, at the entrance to Edgemoor Terrace. Opened in October 1952 at a well-attended ceremony featuring the governor, plus movie and TV personalities, the Merchandise Mart was typical of the postwar retailing revolution. It was designed to attract and to accommodate automobiles, not only from a single city but from a wide potential market including northern Delaware, southeastern Pennsylvania, and eastern New Jersey.[30] The success of suburban shopping centers spelled trouble for the merchants on Market Street. But at first the problems of downtown appeared to be easily resolved by a parking lot or two and a bit of streamlining of traffic flows. In the same month that saw the opening of the Merchandise Mart, an article in the local press cautioned that Market Street might be in trouble but then optimistically noted that "once circulation is restored the patient will revive."[31]

The problems facing Wilmington's Market Street, like those of Market Streets and Main Streets all over America, were not to be so easily resolved, however. The automobile brought not only a revolution in transportation, but also a revolution in the use of space. Cities built to serve the needs of walkers and trolley riders could not readily adapt to the demands of the automobile. For one thing, the automobile and its sibling, the truck, replaced not only the intracity trolley systems, but the intercity railroad system as well. Thus, while some automobile drivers were going to the downtown area, others were simply going through it. Yet the highway system inherited from the past was like the spokes of a wheel, with the downtown areas as the hub. Therefore, it placed both to and through traffic on the same roads, a situation comparable to having the trains and trolleys share the same tracks. In addition, there was the awkward problem of parking. Whereas trolleys and trains continually circulated and never got off their tracks, cars were owned by thousands of individuals, each of whom wished to leave his car as close as possible to his destination, which in most cases was in center city.

There were two discernible stages in the adaptation of the city to the automobile. The first stage, roughly the decade from 1945 and 1955, was characterized by attention to the widening of existing highways, the creation of shopping centers at the points where major highways entered the city, and the concentration of downtown merchants on quick fix solutions to inner-city traffic snarls and parking problems. Wilmington, responding as many American cities did to the downtown crisis, created a parking authority that was empowered to bond the city for the purpose of constructing parking facilities. After a slow start, the authority broke ground for the city's first parking building designed to hold 500 cars on 2 January 1957.[32] Moving traffic through Wilmington's narrow downtown streets proved to be a more difficult problem, however. Downtown merchants agitated to get rid of the farmers and hucksters whose trucks partially blocked traffic flow on King Street. The merchants assumed that if King Street could be widened and made one way and Market Street the opposite way, traffic would move through the city expeditiously. A succession of mayors took up the cry of the merchants, but to no avail. The farmers, whose market days went back to the city's founding, could not be moved.[33]

By the mid-1950s, it was evident that efforts such as these were inadequate to the scope of the problem of traffic control in older cities like Wilmington. The success in making existing highways more useful to the automobile had served only to enlarge the number of cars beyond the capabilities of these very improvements to be effective. Recognition of this fact led to a new approach to traffic flow, the federally financed interstate system of limited access, high-speed highways. But before we turn our attention to the role of interstate highways in Wilmington's history, it is necessary to consider another federal program of the postwar years: slum clearance. In 1949 Congress adopted a housing bill sponsored by Senator Robert A. Taft of Ohio, a conservative Republican. Unlike the housing legislation of the 1930s, the 1949 act came at a time when the construction industry was going full tilt, especially in the suburbs. The purpose of the law was not, therefore, to revive a sagging industry, but rather to redirect residential construction toward upgrading decayed urban neighbor-hoods.[34] The law provided that the federal government would pay two-thirds of the cost of acquiring and razing buildings on large blocks of land in blighted areas. The cleared land could then be sold to private developers who would erect desirable modern houses in place of slums. The net effect would be to increase city tax revenues and provide better housing for city residents.

The 1949 housing act was pioneering legislation that proved to be an inadequate instrument to meet the complexities of city problems. Five years after it had been enacted, only 60 projects were under way in the entire country, none of which had gone beyond the land-acquisition stage.[35] The most obvious flaw in the law's provisions was the assumption that middle-income housing would sell in areas that had become blighted. Each city met this difficulty in a unique fashion. In Pittsburgh, for instance, slum clearance was incorporated into a much larger civic commitment to the complete revitalization of the city's urban core, a program that had the active support not only of the city officials, but of Pittsburgh's Mellon family and other prominent industrialists.[36] Meanwhile, in Newark, New Jersey, an aggressive housing authority director, determined to maximize his city's involvement in the program, ignored the city's hard-core slums and instead demolished less blighted areas in order to ensure that develop-ers would find the cleared land attractive as residential sites.[37]

In Wilmington slum clearance had a slow and painful history. Instead of giving fresh vigor to the city, the slum clearance program combined the contradictions of federal policy with the city's own problems to produce highly unsatisfactory results. The area that was the most obvious candidate for slum clearance in Wilmington was the east side. Already perceived as a blighted area by the Governor's Housing Commission of 1932, by the 1940s much of that section had become an overcrowded slum. Many of its small rowhouses were owned by white former residents who had moved on to better parts of town and rented to the blacks who remained. During World War II, landlords had a bonanza as black servicemen's families and war workers who moved to the city found that the housing available to black people was strictly limited to either the east side or to two housing authority projects in South Wilmington. Spurred by the resulting demand, with only the most modest outlays of money, landlords converted small single-family houses into multi-family apartments. A house valued at no more than $4,000 in 1940 might yield $225 a month in rent by the 1950s.[38] Houses that had been on the verge of decay quickly deteriorated with overuse, and an area that had always produced the most health problems in

A building at Eastlake, the Wilmington Housing Authority's World War II development in north Wilmington. *(Courtesy of the Historical Society of Delaware)*

the city became even more unhealthy. By 1945 the east side revealed sad signs of blight—broken windows, unhinged doorways, collapsing plaster ceilings, delapidated, overused wooden privies.

The first line of defense against these conditions was the city's Board of Health, which for several years struggled to enforce the health code and to condemn the worst buildings as unfit for human habitation. During one sweeping inspection in 1945 the board identified 600 houses for condemnation. But the board was understaffed and condemnation proceedings went more slowly than the decay. The city forced a few owners to sell their delapidated houses for back taxes, bought the properties at auction and demolished them, but this random process was very slow.[39] The board also compaigned to force owners to rehabilitate their properties, but again with only modest results. In 1951 the board reported that it had selected an area three blocks wide for intensive inspection and that within a short time 74 percent of the owners whose houses had been identified as substandard had made some repairs.[40] Another report showed that between 1943 and 1951 only 36 houses had been razed in Wilmington, but, on the positive side, 392 properties had been connected to the city sewers.[41]

This progress was much too slow according to seriously committed housing reformers, who often accused the city health commissioner of foot-dragging. The Reverend F. Raymond Baker, a white minister and officer of the Citizens Housing Association, used his pulpit at the 2nd Baptist Church to castigate his fellow Wilmingtonians for their apathetic disregard of slum conditions. [42] Put on the spot by this and other attacks, the health commissioner responded that he was loath to condemn a building until its residents could find alternative housing better than "hovels and shacks." [43] This was, unfortunately, not easy to do, since in the decade that followed the war virtually none of the new housing being built was available to blacks. The east side's slum problem was further complicated by the fact that interspersed among the poorly maintained rental properties were owner-occupied houses, proudly maintained by people who had struggled all their poorly paid lives to gain the security, satisfaction, and independence associated with home ownership.

There was no one right way to deal with the slum problem. Perhaps, given the time and strong government support, the health commission could have succeeded in its efforts to improve living conditions on the east side, razing hopelessly dilapidated structures and forcing landlords to supply at least a minimum standard of amenities for their poor tenants. Some wealthy person or group might have taken up the challenge by buying up blocks of cheap houses, improving them, and renting at a low profit margin. One organization, The Citizens Housing Corporation, founded in 1925 by a Quaker businessman and later subsumed under the Woodlawn Trustees, did undertake such a program on a modest scale. [44] In 1947 the Rev. Mr. Baker asked "a number of wealthy, public-spirited individuals" to take on a similar commitment to housing reform but to no avail. [45] Instead, the matter was decided by a series of federal housing laws that decreed that 22 blocks in the heart of the east side be demolished and replaced with middle-income residences.

Slum clearance and public housing went together. Federal housing officials recognized that there was no point in tearing down slums if their residents had no place to go that was any better. In Wilmington public housing was segregated and mostly white, and the board of the Wilmington Housing Authority long remained deeply split over the issue of maintaining segregation. Several factors were conspiring to undermine the position of the segregationists, however. By the early 1950s, segregation was under attack in the federal courts, and public housing was federally funded. Furthermore, in the growing national economy fewer white families could qualify for public housing or wanted to remain in it, whereas a great many blacks still had incomes well below its maximum levels and had far fewer housing options.

In 1951, while local reformers were directing the public's attention to the east side, the Wilmington Housing Authority was negotiating with the city and county and with the Federal Public Housing Authority for permission to construct its first postwar low-income projects. As in 1941, location was the first and most difficult problem. No one wanted to live near public housing. When the WHA requested authority to build outside the city, the mayor of Newark, whose town was burgeoning from annexations of its rapidly multiplying suburbs, proclaimed that if the county were to agree to such a plan he wanted a ten-mile circle drawn around his town to keep public housing far away.[46] Confronted by a wall of opposition, the housing authority took the path of least resistance and built its new units adjacent to their earlier projects, all-white Eastlake and all-black Southbridge.

In 1953 the WHA began a protracted debate on their segregation policy in reaction to pleas from the Citizens Housing Association and the Catholic Interracial Council. Municipal Court judge Thomas Herlihy, Jr., appeared to settle the matter in favor of integration in a decree announced in June 1953,[47] but it took several months and the appointment of a new board member by Governor Caleb Boggs before the Housing Authority voted three to two to desegregate Eastlake.[48] Although the way finally seemed clear for slum clearance to begin, it was to take more than another six years before the bulldozers were unleashed on the east side.

Postwar Wilmington produced no political leaders with the vision and capacity to make the most of the federal renewal laws. In 1951 the state legislature designated the Wilmington Housing Authority as the city's redevelopment agency. The director of the WHA, Dudley Finch, was an able and conscientious professional administrator, but he lacked the instinct toward political power necessary to successful navigation through the murky waters of slum clearance and redevelopment. Finch had come to the Wilmington Housing Authority in 1949 with more than 20 years experience in managing buildings from banks and apartments to housing for military personnel. His was a practical expertise, and he liked the Wilmington job because he wouldn't have to "bow down to the politicians."[49] Fearless, honest, and unprejudiced in his dealings with tenants, he was proud of the high quality of construction and maintenance at Eastlake and Southbridge. But because Finch did not like the give and take of politics, he was not well suited for the task of leading Wilmingtonians through the complex stages of urban renewal. Finch would have been an excellent second-in-command in an urban renewal leader, but he found himself in the role of leader.[50] In some cities, most notably New Haven, Connecticut, under Mayor Richard Allen, the mayor supplied leadership for redevelopment. But in Wilmington in the 1950s, the position of mayor was a part-time job with little authority and did not attract first-rank politicians. It was not until 1964 that the mayor was given control over the city departments. In the meantime, city council, with its disparate, parochial interests, remained the most powerful political institution in the city. The want of strong coordinated leadership in Wilmington led to mistakes that plagued renewal efforts.

The choices available to lower-middle and middle-income families during the first wave of post-war suburban housing are typified in these three photographs, each taken about 1950. *Above left:* Munroe Park Apartments just beyond the city line in Christiana Hundred on the Kennett Pike. *Below left:* Fairfax along Route 202, the Concord Pike, in Brandywine Hundred. *Above:* a new house on New Castle Avenue, south of Wilmington in New Castle Hundred. *(Courtesy of the Historical Society of Delaware)*

During 1953 the WHA selected a 22-block area on the east side centered on Poplar Street for Wilmington's first plunge into urban renewal. The area, designated "Poplar Street Project A," contained 638 structures, nearly all of them two- and three-story houses, with small shops at each street corner. Student researchers in 1954 counted 364 outdoor toilets there and found that 45 percent of the houses lacked hot water, while 70 percent had no central heating. Conversions from single-family homes to apartments had expanded the number of dwelling units to 970. Ninety-six percent of the residents were black, fewer than 200 houses were owner-occupied, and there were 88 businesses of various kinds.[51] The area seemed well suited for renewal. It was only a few short blocks from Market Street, and it contained a number of good-quality community service structures, including a brand-new elementary school, a well-built junior high school from the 1920s, four churches, and a settlement house. These buildings would be left standing when the houses, described by the WHA as 97 percent dilapidated, were torn down. In the spring of 1954, James W. Follin, director of slum clearance and redevelopment for the Federal Housing and Home Finance Agency, toured Project A and proclaimed himself to be very pleased with Wilmington's choice. The city was "on the ball," he said, and its projected clearance area had "marvelous and unusual opportunties for both rehabilitation and redevelopment." "Much of what I have seen in Wilmington has good structural foundation and need not be demolished," he told reporters.[52]

To assist its slum clearance effort the WHA hired Carolyn Weaver, a social worker, to become the redevelopment authority's liaison with residents and owners of east side properties and with interested civic groups. Through her efforts the League of Women Voters became active in support of urban renewal. Weaver proselytized for slum clearance, enthusiastically proclaiming that once the bad old housing was torn down its former residents would be moved back into good new housing. Not surprisingly, many people believed what they were told, but the facts were otherwise. While it was true that under the law former residents would have first option on the new housing, it was also true that no developer could make a profit by constructing new housing within this group's ability to pay. Furthermore, federal regulations precluded the construction of low-income public housing units on slum clearance land. As a practical matter, the slum dwellers were going to be ousted never to return.

The false promises made to east side residents haunted all later efforts at urban renewal in Wilmington, causing friction within its management and confusion and bitterness among its constituents. As late as May 1970, when the housing authority was seeking city council's permission to alter the renewal plan for the east side by replacing a proposed retail area with a high-rise apartment building, Dudley Finch engaged in the following exchange. A black councilman introduced a former east side resident, who recalled the unfulfilled promises of the past and wanted to know what the rents would be in the proposed apartment building.

FINCH: I know that was never really promised officially.
RESIDENT: This is what they told us because I was one of them.
FINCH: Yes, but I did not, did I?
RESIDENT: No, sir.
FINCH: No.
RESIDENT: But this is what was told us, to us, at the time. Now, what I'm saying now is . . . I work with these people every day, and they still have no place to go. They still live in run-down houses . . . can these people pay it because the ones they just built . . . are a hundred dollars . . . and a lot of people can't afford this, and this is not low income to me.
FINCH: I agree with you. A lot of people cannot afford the housing which is called Title 263 housing, which is the next step up over public housing, and actually we don't have any public housing in

the area for the lowest-income families. We are faced with various regulations under which we can build housing, public housing . . ."[53]

It was no doubt scenes like this one that Finch had in mind when, reflecting on the results of slum clearance, he later said, "Sometimes I'm almost ashamed that I got into it at all, because what did it do, really?"[54]

While Carolyn Weaver's wishful thinking was misleading east side tenants, the homeowners and small businessmen in the area were organizing the East Side Home Owners Association to prevent the wholesale demolition of their houses. The homeowners got little support from anybody. The News-Journal papers, which dominated Wilmington's press, attacked them as irresponsible and immature and accused them of "playing a pressure game to get a good deal more than their properties are worth."[55] Some city councilmen sympathized with the homeowners and resented council's impotence over shaping renewal plans.[56] But although city council could and did retard implementation of urban renewal, they were under heavy pressure not to discard completely a plan that promised to bring new construction and additional revenue to their city. Wilmington's slum clearance plan was also debated in the State House of Representatives in connection with authorization for city bonds necessary to finance the city's portion of the cost. East side homeowners tried in vain to get support from legislators, few of whom worried about the fairness of the proposed compensation. No one would take the complaints of the homeowners seriously. A Democratic representative from Wilmington attributed the opposition to "a few tin horn politicans who receive big rents from . . . houses with no baths or hot water," while a liberal Republican member from the 9th Ward claimed that urban renewal would curb disease, delinquency, and other social ills affecting his city.[57] Thus blocked in the legislative assembly, the owners next tried the courts.

Mary Randolph, like many women on the east side, was a domestic. Her house at 603 Spruce Street, just inside the southeast edge of the renewal area, was "a good, sound, sanitary, and modern building" that met every requirement of the city health code.[58] In May 1957 she filed a suit in Delaware's Court of Chancery alleging that the laws under which her property was about to be taken from her were unconstitutional. *Randolph v. Wilmington Housing Authority* was an important case, a last-ditch effort to prevent the total demolition of residential properties on the east side. Mrs. Randolph's case rested upon several points. Denying that the entire 22-block clearance area was a slum, her suit urged the state to use its police power to condemn dilapidated buildings rather than to destroy the good with the bad. Under the state's redevelopment law, her lawyer argued,

Housing of the late 1950s. *Top:* Middle-income oriented Graylyn Crest, the Wilmington-area's first split-level development, located in Brandywine Hundred. *Bottom:* Riverside, a low-income housing development created in 1959 by the Wilmington Housing Authority to absorb people displaced by slum clearance. *(Courtesy of the Historical Society of Delaware)*

private property was being taken not for a "public purpose" but for the ultimate benefit of private developers. In April 1958 the Delaware Supreme Court decided by a vote of two to one in favor of the Housing Authority. In the opinion of the majority "neither the exercise of the police power nor the operation of private enterprise has abolished the slum" and therefore the state had adopted a way to eliminate slums that combined its public power of eminent domain with private redevelopment. "It is said that the dispossession and relocation of the residents of the area will merely shift the slum to other parts of the city. This is pure speculation. . . . We must assume that the Authority will bend every effort to relocate them in a suitable manner, in suitable housing."[59]

The third justice, Daniel J. Wolcott, who himself lived in a very old house in the town of New Castle, remained unconvinced by the Housing Authority's assertions that foresaw only public benefit from the clearance program. Whereas the other justices had cavalierly dismissed the notion that the police power could be used to condemn and rehabilitate dilapidated buildings, implying that such a procedure had proved unworkable, Wolcott noted that there was no evidence that such a process had been given a fair trial. The urban renewal law, far from being primarily directed at clearing slums, as his colleagues claimed, was really concerned with redevelopment and was, therefore, a misuse of the state's powers of condemnation, since it would take one group's private property for the ultimate benefit of another—private developers. By agreeing to this slipshod use of eminent domain the court was undermining "the constitutionally guaranteed right to own property." "The act," Wolcott said, "is an instance of the modern trend to do everything by governmental authority and to force the public to comply with social planning."[60] But Wolcott's view was a minority one, and it was ignored both by the public and by decision makers. In truth urban renewal was an idea whose time had come. Its many advocates felt no need to have more facts to justify their assumptions. Enough studies had been done already; now was the time for action.

As soon as the court announced its opinion, Dudley Finch began the tedious process of appraising properties and finding new homes for the area's residents. Housing reformers were jubilant. The battle for urban renewal had been won. In three years, they predicted, the dismal east side would be transformed into a clean, healthy, modern residential environment. Wilmington would turn the corner from slow decay toward vibrant resuscitation. Everybody would be better off. The residents would have better houses, the city would get more tax revenue, the construction trades would be kept busy, and Wilmingtonians would no longer be embarrassed by a downtown slum. These benefits seemed even further assured by the Eisenhower administration's Housing Act of 1954, which was designed in part to help those displaced by urban renewal. The law called for the construction of more public housing and for the liberalization of FHA policies to permit government-backed mortgages for older houses as well as for new ones.

While the housing reformers had been fighting the battle for slum clearance on the east side, another battle was being waged over the fate of the city's west side. Again federal dollars were at stake and the future of the

Views of Wilmington's east side in the 1960s. *Above:* The buildings on 4th Street between Walnut and Poplar Streets were demolished as part of the Poplar A slum clearance project. *Right:* The buildings in these photographs still stand, on 9th Street and Spruce Street respectively, immediately adjacent to the demolition area. *(Courtesy of the Historical Society of Delaware)*

city seemed to be in the balance. At issue was Wilmington's participation in the interstate highway program.

The interstate highway system had its inception in 1944, when Congress approved legislation calling for the construction of 40,000 miles of interconnected highways. The law was a statement of intent rather than of immediate purpose, because the program was left unfunded. In the years immediately following the war, Delaware's neighboring states, New Jersey and Pennsylvania, built toll roads. The New Jersey Turnpike, a major conduit for traffic through the heavily traveled Northeast corridor, presupposed a new Delaware River bridge at its southwestern terminus on the shore of the Delaware, just below Wilmington. A colonial charter, subsequently upheld by the federal courts, gave Delaware sovereignty over the entire breadth of the river within a twelve-mile radius of New Castle. The contemplated bridge would therefore be almost entirely within Delaware's jurisdiction.

While New Jersey's highway authorities were planning that state's turnpike, Delaware's highway department worked with them in planning its largest undertaking since the days of the du Pont Highway, a major suspension bridge over the Delaware. The effect that the proposed bridge might have on traffic volume in the Wilmington area could only be guessed at, but it was certain to be substantial. When the Delaware Memorial Bridge was completed in 1951, Congress was still several years away from enacting interstate legislation. In the meantime, how was all the traffic generated by the bridge to be moved to and through Wilmington? The Church Street-Governor Printz solution of the 1930s would no longer suffice in 1950. Therefore, in 1948 the Highway Department, in concert with the U.S. Bureau of Public Roads and the City of Wilmington, undertook a traffic survey designed to produce a new "master plan of arterial streets and highways for the Wilmington metropolitan area." The study found that local and nonlocal traffic followed different paths. Route pattern studies and interviews with drivers showed that 23 percent of the vehicles passing through Wilmington's east side on Church Street had no local beginning or destination. This traffic was pursuing the linear route, U.S. 13, created during the 1930s. By contrast, traffic with a local origin and destination followed lines that radiated out from center city like spokes of a wheel, going especially toward the most developed suburban regions along the Philadelphia Pike or toward Elsmere and Newport.[61]

In 1952 the Highway Department published another study that was, in effect, their recommendation for new highway construction based on the survey of four years before. The engineers proposed two new routes, labeled A and B, to cope with the traffic problems of Wilmington. Route A was to carry both through and local traffic through west Wilmington. The route would go from the Du Pont Highway, south of the city, across an as yet unbuilt Christina River Bridge, along a new highway located between Adams and Jackson streets, nine blocks west of Market Street, and then across the Brandywine and north to Pennsylvania parallel to the B & O Railroad. Route B, an exclusively through-traffic route, would replace the Church Street route. Route B was to bypass the city to the east, crossing the marshland of Cherry Island to link the Du Pont Highway to the Governor Printz Boulevard. The department gave priority to Route A, because it would address the problems of both local and through traffic. They planned to build both routes in stages as funding permitted. Implementation of Route A would, the Highway Department argued, relieve urban congestion and "afford convenient and direct service to the fast growing suburbs north of Wilmington."[62] These conclusions seemed reasonable enough, but a glance at the destination map from the survey on which they were based showed that the northern suburbs were most densely strung out to the east between the Governor Printz Boulevard and the Philadelphia Pike—an area that could be more easily connected to Route B than to Route A. The department was giving priority to the route that would require considerable demolition and disruption in the residential neighborhoods of west Wilmington over the route that would by-pass the city to the east and connect with existing suburbs.

Following the completion of this report, the department hired the nationally known New York consulting firm of Parsons, Brinckerhoff, Hall and MacDonald to draw up plans for routes A and B. In December 1950 the Parsons firm published maps and drawings that showed a limited-access overhead freeway along the Adams-Jackson route cutting a swath across the city and Brandywine Park. Although the proposed route went through a largely residential area far from the city's east side industries, the consultants claimed that the implementation of their plans would keep business and manufacturing in Wilmington. They also predicted that Route A would enhance property values in its wake.[63]

The publication of the consultants' map in the local press brought down a storm of criticism from west side Wilmingtonians. Spokesmen for the State Highway Department took refuge in the argument that the report had come from disinterested outside consultants, obscuring the fact that they had preselected the route themselves. Opponents were accused of short-sighted selfishness in the face of expert opinion. But the opponents appeared to win the day. Residents of the west side, many of whom were politically well-organized first- and second-generation Polish and Italian Americans, joined with the largely Polish contingent of Maryland Avenue merchants to demand that city council kill Route A. Eight hundred people turned out to a public meeting at P.S. du Pont High School to protest the plan. City council voted unanimously in support of its own constituents against the State Highway Department and its hireling experts. Mayor James F. Hearn, attempting to conciliate both sides, called Route A "a dead duck" but conceded that a new Christina Bridge was necessary. Nobody talked about Route B.[64] One week after the mayor's transportation advisory committee voted in favor of the Christina Bridge compromise, the world's sixth largest suspension bridge, built at a cost of $44,000,000 was opened by the governors of Delaware and New Jersey at a ceremony a little more than two miles southeast of Wilmington.

Meanwhile in Washington highway-related interest groups and government agencies wrestled with basic issues of the funding and location of the proposed interstate highway system. Some highway experts envisioned the system as a giant rural route that would skirt cities and towns to maintain the greatest ease of travel at the lowest land-acquisition and construction costs. This policy, which had become a canon of good highway construction, had been used initially in the plotting of Delaware's Du Pont Highway before World War I. Other experts disagreed. Noting that the cities were the greatest generators and destinations of traffic, they insisted that as a matter of simple utility it was essential to bring the proposed superhighways as close to the centers of cities as possible.[65]

One of the major actors in the drama of bureaucratic infighting on highway issues was Frank du Pont, the Eisenhower administration's Commissioner of the Bureau of Public Roads, the agency charged with the implementation of highway plans. Du Pont, the son of the highway pioneer T. Coleman du Pont, was the moving force in the construction of the Delaware Memorial Bridge. In Washington he vigorously advocated policies that would ensure federal control over the funding and construction of the interstate system. He was also convinced that the new highways should go to the heart of urban areas, since this was where the traffic was and where bottlenecks were notoriously disruptive. The stretch of Route 13 through Wilmington on Church Street was doubtless in his mind as a horrible example of the miseries of forcing heavy through traffic to use narrow city streets. Ultimately, du Pont's point of view carried the day, for when the Congress adopted the Interstate and Defense Highway Act in 1956, it provided that the federal government would pay 90 percent and the states only 10 percent, and that the highways would be constructed both around and through the nation's cities.[66]

Although the 1956 Highway Act represented a series of compromises among various interest groups, one set of interests had not been included in the deliberations: that of the cities. Only two years after the federal government had reinvolved itself in urban renewal activities on a larger scale than ever before, through the Housing Act of 1954, Congress adopted this major new legislation, destined to become the largest public works project in human history. The Highway Act was bound to have a dramatic effect upon the reconstruction of urban places. Yet its creators gave little thought to the possible integration of urban renewal with interstate construction. Without guidance mandated by law, each city and state was free to interrelate its highways plans into larger urban renewal goals, or not, as its leaders saw fit. In New Haven, Connecticut, a city roughly the size of Wilmington, a strong mayor committed to urban renewal made the interstate highway a part of an overarching city redevelopment plan. The highway was deliberately located so as to separate the city's industrial waterfront from the renewal area in the downtown shopping and office district. Ramps from the interstate highway led directly to new parking buildings in a design that encouraged motorists to use the interstate to get to center city's stores and offices.[67] Most cities, however, were not so fortunate. Instead of being used in tandem with slum clearance to revive

Wilmington's west side in the 1950s. The houses with neatly kept gardens in the foreground located near Front and Jackson Streets were among those demolished to construct I-95. *(Courtesy of the Department of Transportation, State of Delaware)*

downtown areas, the interstates were just one more federal bulldozer tearing at the remaining fabric of sagging urban interiors.

Wilmington had no tradition either of strong mayors or of strong government initiative. But the city had a long tradition of private *noblesse oblige*, dating back to William P. Bancroft in the late nineteenth century and Pierre S. du Pont in the early twentieth. Du Pont, together with his relatives and associates, had been at the center of the city's response to the Great Depression. By the mid-1950s, however, Pierre du Pont was dead and his siblings and associates were aged and no longer willing or able to provide civic leadership. Frank du Pont, one of the most able and dynamic members of the family's younger generation, was widely respected in Delaware, but he was busy running the Bureau of Roads in Washington. Hugh Sharp, Jr., a nephew of Pierre S. du Pont, then a young man with little experience in either business or government, had replaced Frank du

Pont as the principal Republican member on the State Highway Commission. Sharp was not a highway engineer and was by no means capable of playing so dynamic a role in highway affairs as had T. Coleman and Frank du Pont. According to his own account, Sharp's lack of expertise made him a willing follower of the Highway Department engineers, while he focused his considerable influence on reducing the inefficiency inherent in the department's political patronage system.[68]

Of the 41,000 miles of highway proposed in the Interstate and Defense Highway Act of 1956, 40 were apportioned to Delaware. In making their plans for the allocation of these 40 miles, the state highway engineers maintained the strictest secrecy. They later claimed that this policy was necessary to prevent land speculation, but one might infer that the department also wished to eliminate public debate by presenting the public with a *fait accompli*. Everyone knew that the Delaware portion of the interstate system would connect to the Delaware Bridge, but little else of the department's plans were known until February 1957, when the News-Journal papers published a map showing that the proposed route of the interstate expressway would have two branches—one from the bridge westward to Maryland, the other northward through Wilmington along Union Street.[69] The accompanying article said that the engineers had considered several other possible routes but had concluded that this one was the least costly and least disruptive means of carrying traffic through the city. The article also announced that the State Highway Commission had already approved the route selection. The next step would be a meeting between Highway Department officials and the city's street and sewer department to work out details. After that the Highway Department was required by federal law to conduct a public hearing and to secure the approval of the city council before bids could be accepted and construction started.[70]

The suddenness of the announcement shocked area residents, who suddenly realized that a very important decision for the entire community's health had been made behind closed doors. A few days later, Richard Haber, the Highway Department's chief engineer, told an audience of concerned citizens in New Castle that there was no way that public opposition could change these plans, because the federal government would build the highway even if the state disapproved it.[71] Soon after, the News-Journal published an article under the headline "Delaware Becoming Traffic Pattern Hub," which began, "Whether Delaware likes it or not, it is rapidly becoming the hub of one of the busiest traffic patterns in the world."[72] The article went on to point out that the federal highway program was designed to cure urban traffic strangulation. While no attributions were included in the article, sophisticated readers might have assumed that Frank du Pont was the probable source of these assertions, since they reflected a broad view of Wilmington's part in a national system and since some members of the du Pont family owned the News-Journal papers through their holding company, Christiana Securities.

From that time on, events moved swiftly. Announcement was made that the required public hearing would take place at P. S. du Pont High School that spring. Alarmed homeowners along the proposed right of way, which included moderate to upper middle income residences, organized and hired Thomas Herlihy, Jr., formerly a Republican mayor of the city and currently a judge in its municipal court, to represent them. Herlihy's own house, in Wawaset, was little over three blocks west of the proposed route. In Herlihy the homeowners had as counsel one who was a knowledgeable and notable public figure.

The public hearing was part of the legal process necessary for the state to participate in the federal highway building program. A transcript of the hearing, or hearings, was to be sent to Washington as part of the information package on Delaware's expressways. Although the law required that the hearing take place, it did not require that the majority of those attending the hearing should agree on the course of the highway, or even agree that there should be a highway at all. In city after city, people who lived in the path of a turnpike project objected with all their vigor, but generally to no avail. Sometimes, as a result of citizen protests, the direction of a highway might be altered slightly to preserve some park or landmark originally slated for demolition, but no hearing could hope to have more effect than this. The law had given the initiative in assigning expressway locations to state highway departments, and in the absence of powerful opponents, such as a strong mayor or governor or opposition from big business, those alignments could not be challenged successfully. But when Wilmington's hearing took place on 10 April 1957, the 1,000 angry people who turned out with their hand-painted signs proclaiming "Dam the Ditch," "By-Pass—Don't Trespass," and "Home Values Down the Drain," did not realize that the question of whether an expressway would go through the west side of the city was already decided.

The expressway decision caused the biggest crisis in Wilmington's government in the twentieth century. Complicated and diverse issues emerged slowly, almost grudgingly, as events unfolded. It is difficult to say, nearly a quarter of a century later, who was right and who was wrong, but it is possible to identify the few people who influenced the outcome and what arguments most persuaded them.

In the weeks between the first announcement of the project and the public hearing, Chief Engineer Richard Haber and his lieutenant, William Miller, addressing various audiences, confused the issue by suggesting that

I-95 wends its way through Wilmington along the Adams-Jackson Street corridor in this photograph, taken in 1968. *(Courtesy of the Department of Transportation, State of Delaware)*

the Highway Department was considering alternative routes for the freeway. Miller announced that the ideal route would take the highway down Market Street, since the department's studies showed that 80 percent of the traffic entering the city was aiming for the downtown area.[73] Meanwhile his boss, Richard Haber, told reporters that the department was seriously considering at least three routes: Union Street, the Bancroft Parkway, and the old Route A along Adams-Jackson streets, the last of which he called "still the best route."[74] The Bancroft route, which lay only a few blocks west of Union Street, appeared to be the most probable, however, because its

I-95 passing through suburban Brandywine Hundred, north of Wilmington, near Claymont, in this photograph taken in 1968. *(Courtesy of the Department of Transportation, State of Delaware)*

right of way included a wide median strip, eliminating the need to destroy many homes. Efforts to deflect the department away from a west side alignment in favor of one running through the east side slum clearance area parallel to the Pennsylvania Railroad received short shrift, as Miller explained that an eastern route was also being planned, but only as a carrier for through traffic.[75]

The first local governmental body to get involved in the controversy was the state legislature. John E. Reilly, a Democratic state senator from

Wilmington, tried to rally support in the legislature to block the highway from going through the city. Although this maneuver failed, Reilly did persuade the Senate to hold a hearing on the subject on 18 March 1957. There, Chief Engineer Haber spoke. First telling the senators that the Wilmington City Council would have final authority over the decision, he then noted that outside consulting engineers had proposed several possible alignments through Wilmington and pointed out that the highway was being designed to serve the greatest possible number of people in Wilmington and its suburbs. A spokesman from the Bureau of Public Roads reminded the senators that freeways had raised property values in Los Angeles, Houston, and other cities. Finally, Thomas Herlihy, Jr., had his opportunity to question the chief engineer. Wasn't it true that in drawing its plans the State Highway Department had consulted neither the city nor county planners? Yes, it was, but Haber explained that the New Castle County Levy Court had no authority to interfere with highway plans. How about the costs of land acquisition? The chief admitted that his planners had no idea how many houses would be destroyed or what the effects of the noise and air pollution might be. Zeroing in for the kill, Herlihy asked, "What real evidence have you presented that this expressway will benefit the communities involved and will not be a blighting factor on the communities instead?" Exasperated at being put on the spot, Haber exclaimed, "Don't confuse me with facts—my mind is made up. There is nothing at all you can say—you can quote anything." Regaining his composure, the chief engineer said that the federal program offered "an opportunity to provide Delaware with the finest state highway in the United States," that it would aid suburban commuters, would provide a stimulus to downtown revitalization, and would be neither an "eyesore" nor a "blight."[76]

With the Highway Department presenting a moving target, opponents and proponents of the west side route braced themselves for their confrontation in the auditorium of P. S. du Pont High School. In spite of the department's suggestions that several routes were still under consideration, the public hearings in April considered only the Bancroft Parkway alignment. Three raucous, crowded meetings provided a poor forum for reasoned examination of the points at issue. Haber presented the department's position in what his opponents characterized as an "arrogant, high-handed, brazen, public-be-damned manner," while Herlihy was criticized by highway proponents for conducting a virtual cross-examination of the chief engineer.[77] All in all, there was much heat, but little light. The opponents could not match the Highway Department's technical data nor shake the department's insistence that the highway must go through the western portion of the city.

Probably the most effective speaker for the anti's was Maurice du Pont Lee, chairman of the City Park Commission. In defense of the Park Department's interests, Lee, a nephew of Alfred I. du Pont, had all the courtly manner and unshrinking determination conferred by a strong sense of *noblesse oblige*. The Board of Park Commissioners had for three-quarters of a century "been composed of outstanding civic-minded citizens who have voluntarily given of their time and . . . their substance, to create the park system."[78] And as chairman he was not about to yield one inch of the lands that his distinguished predecessors on the board had so wisely acquired. The Highway Department's map showed that the Bancroft Parkway route would cross two city parks, Canby Park at the southwest corner of the city and Brandywine Park. Lee urged the Highway Department to abandon the Bancroft alignment in favor of one that would run alongside the nearby B & O Railroad tracks and thus minimize the destruction of both parkland and residences. At one point in the hearing, the park commissioner argued that the parks were now more important than ever, because in case of atomic attack people would flee to them for refuge. Already, he said, his department had been quietly installing water fountains and restrooms against that doomsday eventuality. Survival might depend on maintaining every piece of urban parkland.[79]

Although the hearings did little to clarify the issues, they did publicize the controversy. Civic associations in Brandywine Hundred and in the city organized to fight the highway that had so suddenly risen up to menace the serenity of their communities. James Wilson, a Du Pont Company engineer who lived in a suburban community about one-half mile from the proposed alignment, served as engineering advisor for the anti's, while W. Garrett Burckel, leader of the civic association of a suburban community near to the highway route, aroused other Brandywine Hundred groups to the fight with his letters to the newspapers and speeches to community organizations. A former resident of Hartford, Connecticut, Burckel had seen that the real-estate improvements promised by proponents of new highways had not materialized there, and he was convinced that the same would be true in Wilmington. Brandywine Hundred opponents questioned the wisdom of locating the interstate highway in a densely population area instead of away from the built-up portions of city and suburbs either farther to the west through "chateau country" or east of the city through Cherry Island Marsh.[80]

Jim Wilson was not alone among Du Pont engineers in opposing the highway. Many of the big company's engineers lived in Brandywine Hundred and had little reason to welcome an alignment that appeared to be hastily conceived and that spared the well-to-do at the expense of the middle class. The general manager of the Du Pont Engineering Department heard so many complaints about the road that he called Wilson into his office and asked him about his involvement in the controversy, but did not try to pressure him into abandoning the cause.[81] Recognizing how obstreperous the Du Pont engineers might be, representatives from the State Highway Department asked if they might come to the Du Pont Building and present their case to senior members of the company's engineering staff. The general manager of engineering gathered his chief assistants about him to hear the presentation by William Miller, the Highway Department's deputy chief engineer. When Miller had finished, the manager pushed back his chair and said, "Well, boys, I think Miller and his group are on the right track."[82] The highway engineers knew that they had won a valuable convert.

The most active supporters of the interstate, aside from the Highway Department, were professional real-estate groups such as the Wilmington Real Estate Board and the Home Builders Association, both of which predicted that the highway would be a catalyst for an advance in real-estate prices and additional home building.[83] The Wilmington State Police and Wilmington's Board of Public Safety also spoke on behalf of more highways as a means to relieve traffic congestion. On 1 May 1957, an announcement appeared in the press of the creation of Delaware Citizens for Freeways, an organization composed primarily of real-estate men and builders, led by Leon Weiner, a developer, and Garrett Lyons, a Wilmington Democratic political boss. The most formidable proponents of the highway, however, were the writers and editors of the News-Journal papers. The newspapers' editorials consistently praised and justified the highway plans, and Bill Frank, the papers' most popular columnist, wrote highly favorable pieces on the plans in his column, "Frankly Speaking."[84] Amid a deluge of letters to the editor, editorials, columns, meetings, groups forming pro and con, events moved swiftly toward their culmination in the Wilmington City Council, the only agency of local government with the legal authority to reject or approve the highway.

The city council was, at the moment, on the verge of a major shift in its political composition. After years of Republican control, in 1951 the Democratic party had a strong resurgence in Delaware. Working from their traditional base of support among rural and city voters, the Democrats captured control of the state legislature and the governor's office. They then proceeded to rewrite laws to favor their party. One such law replaced district elections with at-large elections for the Wilmington City Council. The first city council elections under the new law took place in November 1956, and resulted in a Democratic sweep of all twelve council seats. Eugene Lammot was the first Democrat to be chosen as mayor since the deepest days of the Depression in 1933. The new mayor and council were not scheduled to take office, however, until eight months after the election, on the first of July 1957. In the meantime, the old council, which had a slight Republican majority, remained in power.

Council met weekly on Thursday nights. To pass, the highway ordinance required an affirmative vote in two successive meetings. In early June 1957, as the days of the old council waned, some Republican members announced their intention to postpone action on the controversial highway measure until the new Democratic council took office. Council members had not even received copies of the State Highway Department's report on its proposed routes until the afternoon of 13 June, only hours before the third from last meeting of the old council. That evening, in the presence of about 75 highway opponents, council declined to take action on the matter. The Highway Department report, which few councilmen may have even read at that time, proclaimed the Bancroft Parkway route to be the most desirable, but mentioned three possible alternatives also in west Wilmington, including a Union Street alignment and old Route A, the Adams-Jackson Street corridor route.[85]

The next council meeting, on 20 June, was the last chance for the old city council to take a first vote on the issue. One hundred twenty people packed the stately wood-carved council chambers to witness the scene. The nine Republican councilmen filed into the chamber from their weekly majority caucus meeting. A resolution was presented calling for the Bancroft Parkway route. It was unanimously rejected. Another resolution was presented—this one for the Adams-Jackson route, old Route A, in the heart of a densely populated white ethnic neighborhood. Sensing a clever trick, the audience became restive, and boos rang out as the deputy highway chief, William Miller, and Hugh Sharp, Jr., the Republican highway commissioner, presented arguments on behalf of the second resolution. Thomas Herlihy, Jr., rose and demanded more time to consider this route, since no hearings had been held on it. But the Republican councilmen knew that protest was in vain. Council president Frank J. Obara, a plumber who lived two blocks from Jackson Street, pleaded with his fellow Republicans to reject the second resolution. He praised the residents of the Adams-Jackson area for their strong sense of pride in their homes. "I could eat a meal off the floor in any one of those houses along that route," he said. According to the Highway Department, the Adams-Jackson alignment would require the destruction of 369 houses; the Bancroft route only 189. Adams-Jackson encompassed two Protestant churches and was adjacent to two Catholic churches, Sacred Heart and Saint Paul's, both of which had many parishioners living in the right of way. "May God have mercy on those who vote for this proposal," Obara prayed, but the council president knew the outcome already. The vote was seven to five in favor of the resolution, with two Republicans, including Obara, voting in the negative.[86]

Four days later Herlihy had his only opportunity to present the Delaware Expressways Committee's position before a meeting of the State Highway Commission. The meeting took place at a restaurant in Dover, where Herlihy was made to wait while the commissioners had their pre-luncheon cocktails. The attorney made his presentation to the tune of clanking dishes and scraping silverware as the commissioners ate their meal. The humiliation rankled.[87]

On 27 June 1957, 300 people jammed the council chambers for the last meeting of the old city council. Herlihy and Maurice du Pont Lee spoke against the route. Representatives of Polish-American societies denounced it, the pastor of Saint Paul's Roman Catholic Church argued against it, the Maryland Avenue Businessmen's Association protested, as did the Tax-payers' Protective Association, a neighborhood group. The vote was seven to six in favor of Adams-Jackson. No further legal obstacles stood between the State Highway Department and its favorite alignment.[88]

How had it happened? How had a council made up largely of white ethnic Roman Catholics voted to tear up a two-block-wide portion of the west side, which would oust many of their own people from their homes? Why did the Highway Department not put the expressway on the east side, where it could have been integrated into the urban renewal plans? After all, Robert Moses, the famed New York city planner whose testimony had helped convince Congress that the interstate highways should go through cities, had specifically tied the urban highway concept to slum clearance and renewal.[89]

Eleven months after the votes in council, Frank Obara, the retired council president, wrote a letter to Tom Herlihy, who was then preparing a civil case on behalf of clients who lived along the route of the proposed freeway. Obara recalled how council had been "whipped into line" to support a proposal that had come "as a complete surprise to the whole council," and said that he was willing to repeat his story in court, under oath. He charged that a job offer had been made to him on condition that he go along with the resolution, and that councilmen from the east side taunted him with the argument that "You didn't go along with us on the move to kill the Poplar Street Slum Program, and they are going to tear down the East Side; Why should we go along to save the West Side?" Although Obara held firm against these pressures, other councilmen who had gone on record against the freeway did not. One in particular had told him in genuine agony that he must vote against his conscience for the highway, because "a certain party [who] had done him a lot of favors" had

One of the Du Pont Company's post-war suburban complexes at Chestnut Run, southwest of the city. (*Courtesy of the Eleutherian Mills Historical Library*)

called in his chips. "I was dumbfounded to learn that anyone could get a man, who for weeks had stated his position on the freeway question, to vote against his own convictions," Obara wrote.

Stunned by the impending turn of events, Obara went to the City-County Building on the evening when he would preside for the next to the last time over city council. "I shall never forget the evening," he wrote. "A member of the State Highway Commission came to the office of the Clerk of Council about 7:30 P.M., just one-half hour before our regularly scheduled Council Meeting. . . . After Council had disposed of routine matters in [Republican] caucus, the resolution for the Adams-Jackson monstrosity was brought out of the Highway Commissioner's pocket and was read to the members of Council. I venture to say that two-thirds of those present had never seen or heard the contents of that resolution prior to that evening." With no questions asked, the Republican councilmen voted and it was instantly clear that the resolution would win. "The people in the audience didn't have a chance," Obara concluded.[90] Nor did the Democratic city council that met the following week and voted to rescind the agreement, for the courts later held that the votes of 20 and 27 June had constituted a valid contract on the part of the city.

The commissioner who had come to the caucus meeting with the Adams-Jackson resolution in his pocket was Hugh Rodney Sharp, Jr. Sharp had been powerfully impressed by the arguments of freeway advocates in general, and by those of the Delaware's highway engineers in particular.

He believed it to be Wilmington's best interest for the freeway to run west of center city but as close to downtown as possible. He was not concerned about the possible hardship to residents of the Adams-Jackson region. Those who lived in the immediate path of the highway would simply have to move. After all, as another commissioner put it, somebody had to be inconvenienced.[91] As for the area adjacent to the freeway, Sharp was certain that it would rise dramatically in value and attractiveness. The expressways that he had seen in California were flanked by grass, shrubs, and flowers and by big luxury apartments. Sure that the same things would happen in Wilmington, Sharp was fond of saying that if it had not been for the potential charge of conflict of interest, he would have bought up land alongside the urban freeway. Sharp remembers that when he went before the caucus he saw an opportunity to appeal to the lame-duck councilmen to put the petty politics of their short-sighted constituencies behind them in order to support a measure that was in the best interests of the entire city. In retrospect, he can't think of a better place for the interstate.[92]

Hugh Sharp carried great weight in Republican circles, and the councilmen doubtless believed that the commissioner was speaking for the whole Greenville aristocracy who were the angels of the local Republican party. But it was not Sharp who was making the behind-the-scenes deals that Obara mentioned. That task fell to politicians lower down the line who were close to the police, the real-estate developers, and construction men. These were the people who had the most to gain from the highway, and these were the interests who cashed in their chips to get the votes that swung Wilmington's biggest highway deal of the century.[93]

There were yet other aspects of this battle, however. Routing the highway east of center city instead of west would have spared a great deal of residential destruction, integrated the highway into the city's major urban renewal projects, and served the transportation needs of the city's industries. Furthermore, since either an east or west side route was going to run north-south, either could be made to serve the already heavily suburbanized Brandywine Hundred. The only as yet undeveloped part of the county likely to be affected by the interstate system was the region between the Maryland border and the proposed cloverleaf intersection just west of the Delaware Memorial Bridge—an area totally unaffected by the route choice through Wilmington. Opponents of the west side highway kept raising these points throughout their debate with the Highway Department. At a rally at Saint Paul's R. C. Church held the night before the final vote in city council, an Adams Street home owner asked Commissioner Hugh R. Sharp why the department did not build an east route. "That's a good point," the commissioner replied, "and I don't deny it's an extremely appealing argument. There's no real answer, except that FA1-2 [the designation given to the west side route] would take care of today's local and through traffic."[94]

One man who thought he knew the real answer to the question was Irving Warner, a descendant of one of Wilmington's most distinguished old mercantile families. Warner was 75 years old in 1957. As a young man, he had trained in engineering before entering his family's shipping business, which dealt largely in masons' and builders' supplies. The Warner Company stood to profit from highway construction. An enthusiastic and inveterate motorist, Warner's familiarity with many of the turnpikes and freeways that already existed in America gave him points of comparison for the State Highways Department's plans for Delaware. He did not like what he saw, and tried by every means at his disposal to thwart the highway builders. He wrote to Delaware's U.S. Congressman Harry G. Haskell, Jr., he wrote letters to the editor of the News-Journal papers, he wrote to Bertram Tallamy, Administrator of the interstate program in the Bureau of Public Roads. Always his message was the same: Wilmington was not large enough to require or to absorb two freeways. Unlike sprawling Los Angeles, Wilmington was small and compact. There should be one interstate through the city, and that on the east side of town where it would do most good and least harm. But his friends in Greenville did not want an east side highway. In Warner's opinion, it was they who were "using political force to foist on Wilmington the routing of FA1-2 through its heart."[95] These powerful men, he wrote, "dominate the political parties of Wilmington. City officials who desire future political preferment must do their bidding. . . . The domination extends to the Delaware State Highway Department. It dictates the editorial and news policies of our Wilmington papers."[96] These wealthy people feared that if a west side route were not built now, someday the federal government might require the construction of another west side interstate—this one through Chateau country itself. As he told Congressman Haskell, himself one of the elite, "all my life I have seen the residents of the County dominate city affairs, always to the detriment of the city."[97] The Adams-Jackson route was only the most disastrous instance of that interference, in Warner's view.

The highway engineers and federal administrators had different explanations for FA1-2. A route through the city would be useful for mass evacuations in case of nuclear attack, they said, although the absurdity of this notion was perhaps so evident that they did not bring it up often. The News-Journal editors enthusiastically prophesied that the highway would eliminate commuter traffic jams. "You'll be home sooner and a great deal happier! Imagine what it's like to arrive at work whistling after a quick top-of-the-morning ride."[98] But an independent traffic survey in 1959 showed that even in rush hours it took no more than ten minutes to go from center city to any point at the city's edge, hardly a big-city-style traffic problem.[99] Another argument used by proponents was that the west side highway was absolutely necessary to save the downtown. Benjamin F. Shaw II, a highway commissioner, expressed this view in its most pristine overstated form at the dedication ceremony for the Walnut Street Bridge, where he warned that "unless we can get something built in downtown Wilmington, we will become a ghost town, strangled with waves of traffic."[100] In his enthusiasm, he had perhaps forgotten that traffic is the least of a ghost town's problems.

Of the five decades that now separate us from the Great Depression, no decade has proved more crucial for America's cities than the 1950s. Those ten years produced massive relocation of people; whites from cities and towns to suburbs and blacks from rural South to northern cities. Compared to the make-work programs of the New Deal or the war on poverty during the 1960s, federal programs of the Eisenhower years, especially slum clearance and highway construction, had far more significant long-range effects on the internal fabric of our cities. Sponsors of slum-clearance and interstate highway legislation intended these programs to benefit cities; the one to encourage private redevelopment of underutilized, blighted urban land, the other to make cities accessible to the new interstate highway system. Yet these programs have been strongly criticized by students of city life, because they tore down more than they built up, left slum dwellers with poorer housing than before, destroyed old neighborhoods, and further encouraged the multiplication at the urban heart of the cities' worst enemy, the automobile.[101] In short, critics claim that the 1950s policy-makers attempted several types of major surgery on cities without first undertaking a comprehensive analysis of the diseases from which their patients were suffering.

The effect of this legislation need not have been so destructive, however. Both the slum-clearance and highway laws gave considerable latitude to local leaders in deciding how these federally financed programs could be harnessed to serve an existing comprehensive community momentum toward redevelopment. Some cities were better able to incorporate federal programs into their plans than others, usually because they had some positive combination of entrepreneurial vision, powerful politicians who saw their own best advantage in a healthy city, planners sensitive to the idiosyncrasies of the community, and an absence of interest groups so powerful as to shape plans to fit their needs alone.[102]

It was Wilmington's misfortune to have nearly all the elements leading to helplessness before the power of these federal programs. As throughout the nation, for Wilmington the 1950s were a crucial decade; a decade in which the city's population fell by nearly 14,000 while that of its metropolitan district increased by nearly 100,000. Wilmington's inability to bend federally funded slum-clearance and highway construction programs to serve the needs of the city as a whole, or even to coordinate them to decrease their destructive impact has proved to be costly. The problem was that in the 1950s, when these basic redevelopment decisions were made, Wilmington did not have a strong government with planning capabilities, and neither its private sector nor the elite philanthropists of the past rushed in to fill the gap. Whether one thinks that the construction of the interstate along the Adams-Jackson alignment was in the city's best interests or not, it is clear that the means by which the decision was reached were hardly democratic or carefully planned from the total context of the community's best interest. Yet at no time did any of the public decision makers, the state legislature, or the city council attempt to relate the highway plans to other developments in the city, such as urban renewal, nor did they seriously study alternative routes. Instead, they simply took the advice of the highway engineers, who neither by training nor experience could be relied upon to examine the problem in a broad context. It is ironic that the Philadelphia Regional Plan of the 1920s had been comprehensively conceived, even though little of it was realized, while the far more important interstate highway system of the 1950s received no such coordinated study.

Why was this so? Some of the blame can be fixed upon federal policies that did not encourage a coordination of slum-clearance and highway policies, but the law did give considerable latitude to local governments. In that context two reasons for Wilmington's failure to plan appear preeminent: the weakness of Wilmington's city government, and the virtual abdication of responsibility by the city's elite. These two phenomena resulted in uncoordinated, lethargic implementation of the Eisenhower Administration's major programs in urban renewal and highway construction in Wilmington. Unfortunately, major and irreversible decisions had to be made during this decade of local drift. The professional people involved in these decisions were usually competent. Dudley Finch was an efficient, incorruptible public servant as head of the Wilmington Housing Authority, and the engineers working for the State Highway Department were also able men. The problem was at the top, at the level of political control.

There were many reasons why Wilmington should have had a weak government. The city was perhaps too small to tempt the most able, ambitious politicians to run its affairs. But it was the chief city of the state, and a person who made an outstanding record as mayor might aspire to the governorship or the U.S. Senate. More important than the city's size were the internal weaknesses in Wilmington's charter. Ever since the failure of reformers to secure a new charter in 1921, Wilmington had limped along with a charter that kept the city in near-bondage to the state legislature and made the office of mayor close to powerless. Any change in the city charter required a two-thirds vote of the legislature, a body dominated by rural interests.

During the 1950s, against a background of growing power in the Democratic party throughout the state, Wilmington's politicians took cautious steps to strengthen city government. In 1953 the legislature raised the mayoral term from two to four years and for the first time gave the mayor power to hire and fire city department heads, subject to veto by a two-thirds majority of city council. But mayors continued to govern the city on a part-time basis. On 1 July 1953, Republican August F. Walz took the oath of office as Wilmington's first four-year mayor, but later resigned the post to become the city postmaster. His successor, Democrat Eugene Lammot, ran a private insurance business and was a member of the state senate while serving as mayor. Walz appointed the city's first planning commission in December 1953, but only after getting approval from the state legislature. The five commissioners—a real-estate broker, the chief engineer of the Delaware Coach Company, a druggist, a retired State Highway Department engineer, and the business agent for the carpenters' union—were authorized to develop a "comprehensive development plan" for the city but had no power of implementation. Not until 1962 did the city hire its first professional planner.[103]

Prior to World War II, Wilmingtonians had less cause to complain about their government, because tasks that in most cities fell under the aegis of city government—developing the city square, rebuilding the school system, organizing relief in the Depression—were being performed by the du Ponts. By 1950, however, Pierre du Pont was eighty years old, and his brothers Irénée and Lammot, who had succeeded him as president of the Du Pont Company, were seventy-four and seventy, respectively. Alfred I. and T. Coleman du Pont were long since dead, and family paternalism had largely died with their generation. Young du Ponts were inclined to concentrate on mastering the ever more complicated nature of the chemical industry or to give their attention to such fields as horse rearing, flower growing, antique collecting, and real-estate development. During the 1950s there was no one in the du Pont family who filled Pierre du Pont's shoes as a public benefactor. More significantly, no one individual or group in the city combined the power, imagination, and interest in Wilmington that were needed during the crucial decade of federal intervention to make the best use of federal programs for the city's development.[104]

One can observe the portents of the passing of the generation of paternalists in two pieces of correspondence addressed to Pierre's younger brother, Irénée du Pont. The first is an undated letter from a group of homeowners who lived along the route of the interstate highway and who still clung to the old paternalistic relationship with the rich. "We . . . turn to you because of the countless times you have demonstrated a deep interest in your neighbors," they say, and go on to note that the old people in the neighborhood are very distressed. Already a house of prostitution has moved into their area—a sign of the ruin to come. "Rightly, or wrongly, the Du Pont Company is being generally blamed . . . because a certain gentleman [who] is a director of the Du Pont Company and also a commissioner of the State Highway Department . . . is the person who allegedly stampeded the 'lame duck' City council in its waning hours." They concluded with a reaffirmation of the capitalistic system, imploring his help against the "vultures who seek to fatten themselves upon our pain."[105] Like the working-class residents of Adams and Jackson streets, Maurice du Pont Lee also urged Irénée du Pont to intervene in saving the city from the highway. Irénée replied to Lee in April 1957 that he had not heard about the highway plans until his recent return to Wilmington from his home in Cuba. "I think that such a cavern would be useless, wasteful as well as unsightly," the most respected living du Pont replied. "I hope pressure can be brought to bear not to overdo high speed roads."[106] Later, however, Irénée underwent a change of heart, or at least concluded that he no longer had the capacity for civic involvements, for in response to a later appeal from cousin Maurice related to the same issue he wrote, "I would like to help out in your problem of protecting the park lands around Wilmington, but I have very definitely concluded that at my age and difficulty of both hearing and seeing I cannot make the effort . . ."[107]

On 7 January 1959, one week after a chancery court decision against the west side homeowners, the wreckers began dismantling houses in the Adams-Jackson corridor. Within a year the bulldozers were at work along the east side's Poplar Street as well. The arguments were over; the time of salvage was gone; the era of rebuilding was yet to come.

CHAPTER 4

When We Needed Unity
the Most: 1960–1968

When I look back to the '60s my mind tends to merge everything into WYEAC—it became all-consuming. There was more going on, but frankly, it's hard to remember.

Richard Pryor, Director, Catholic
Social Services, 11 June 1980

It should not be surprising that the leadership of our community elected to invest money and energy in this social experiment. Wilmington has benefited historically from extensive research experiments. When one considers what was required to develop a manmade fabric and synthetic leather, the investment to find a solution to complex human problems is quite understandable.

Edward J. Goett, President, Atlas Chemical Industries, testimony, U.S. Senate Permanent Subcommittee on Investigations of the Committee on Government Operations, October 1968

The rapid expansion of suburbia and the controversial decisions on urban renewal and highway construction that characterized the 1950s were but a prelude to the 1960s, the most disruptive and disheartening, yet, ironically, the most hopeful decade in Wilmington's long history. To use a cliche not wholly inappropriate in a state that touts the blue hen as its symbol, this was the decade when "the chickens came home to roost." It began with bulldozers and ended with National Guard jeep patrols. In between, the city was convulsed by riots and torn by discord; but it was also heartened by the efforts of an able, hard-working mayor and a coalition of major business-men to rebuild the downtown and resuscitate the community's confidence in its future. These tempestuous experiences were hardly unique to Wil-mington; indeed, they formed the common experience of nearly all Amer-ican cities in the decade of the Great Society, Black Power, and the war in Vietnam.

The first step toward solving a problem is the recognition that a problem exists. In Wilmington's case the conviction that postwar prosper-ity had been but a mixed blessing grew very slowly during the 1950s. At first glance the downtown seemed to be thriving. The several new bank buildings and other large office structures all built or projected within a block of 9th and Market streets during the 1950s obscured the decay that was eroding the residential and retail neighborhood adjacent to the new highrises. It was indicative of the optimistic spirit of the times that in the mid-1950s intelligent, well-meaning, and well-informed people assumed that if only the worst 22 blocks of old rowhouses on the east side were plowed under and replaced, the entire downtown area would be rejuve-nated. At the time it also seemed reasonable to assume that the construc-tion of an interstate highway through the near west side would raise property values, stimulate new urban construction, and revitalize down-town shopping. Even the monumental historical problem of race seemed to yield to quick solution when the Wilmington public schools integrated without incident in the fall of 1954.

But these seeming triumphs of prosperity, common sense, and good will were already looking a bit frayed by the late 1950s, and by 1960, in spite of the city's shiny new buildings, integrated schools, urban renewal, and highway plans, Wilmington had unmistakably entered a spiral of decline. Recognition of this fact came slowly. City school administrators were aware that an increasing percentage of the city's children were poor, black, and often from broken homes. In 1959 the public schools acknowl-edged these problems when they inaugurated a major three-year project to retrain their teaching staff to deal more effectively with disadvantaged children. Meanwhile, in another realm, Richard Sanger, a writer for the News-Journal papers, exasperated that his series of columns exploring the possibility of bringing a downtown mall to Wilmington raised little enthu-siasm, tried to wake up the city to its peril. "Let's face it," he wrote, "the city is decaying."[1] He found the evidence all about him. Market Street merchants were demanding a reduction in their property taxes because their sales were down. Blight was spreading "like dry rot" from the east side to the west side faster than the urban renewal bulldozers; yet he claimed, the city's efforts to deal with these problems were "chaotic."

There were even reports, Sanger warned, that an unnamed national magazine had selected "Wilmington as a horrible example of what happens when there's no coordination in municipal planning." Another telling sign of Wilmington's slide was the federal census bureau report showing that the city's population had dropped by 13 percent between 1950 and 1962, dipping below 100,000 for the first time since 1910. Meanwhile, the population of New Castle County as a whole had reached 307,446, a gain of 40 percent, while the increase in some suburban areas was more spectacular yet—142 percent in Brandywine Hundred and 125 percent in Pencader Hundred, adjacent to the town of Newark. The populations of just two suburban hundreds, Brandywine and Christina, added up to 105,373, nearly 10,000 more than the 95,827 who inhabited the city.[2] Wilmington was in danger of becoming the hole in the county doughnut. One did not have to be inside the school system or familiar with census data, or even sensitive to the shabby look of Market Street to be aware of the city's plight. The sight of 22 acres of vacant, rubble-strewn land surrounding Poplar Street just two blocks from the downtown retail section and the rat-infested swathe of boarded-up, abandoned houses awaiting destruction along the Adams-Jackson corridor made the point more convincingly than any statistics.

The block upon block of empty lots on the east side, looking like Berlin at the end of World War II, represented more than an embarrassing eyesore. The Poplar Street area, which has yet to be completely "renewed" 20 years after its demolition, had been the most concentrated black neighborhood in the city. Even as it was in the process of being destroyed, the city was receiving sizable numbers of new black families, mostly from the farms and villages of downstate Delaware and Maryland's eastern shore. This migration was related to the greater use of seasonal migrant workers and to the mechanization of agriculture on the Delmarva Peninsula as in other parts of the South. In the case of Delaware and Maryland, the introduction of large-scale poultry production, a form of agriculture that requires relatively few workers, was especially significant. During the 1950s while Wilmington's white population loss was over 22,000 the city gained nearly 8,000 blacks, more than half from migration rather than natural increase.[3] Continued migration, coupled with the displacement of about 800 households from the urban renewal area created a tide of black residential movement into other parts of the city.

The projectors of urban renewal had assumed that the displaced families would be relocated in one of two places, either of which would give the former slum dwellers better housing without disturbing the existing pattern of segregated housing. Those who had owned their own homes or could afford to buy were expected to select new houses among those to be

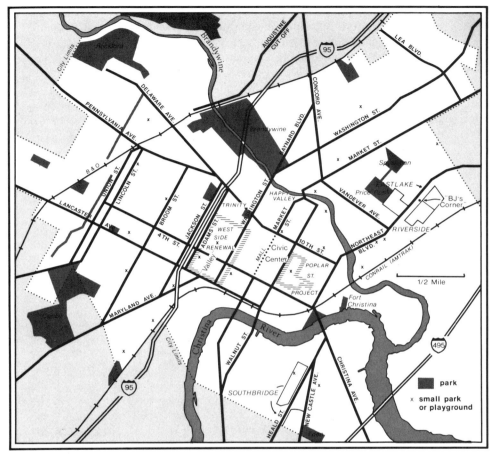

Wilmington during the 1960s, including public housing projects, urban renewal areas, the Civic Center, and areas of regentrification. *(Map by Marley Amstutz, Cartographer)*

constructed in the urban renewal area. Those who had been renters and had no means to buy would be rehoused in a newly constructed 400-unit low-income housing project called Riverside, located in northeast Wilmington near the Eastlake project. Riverside was not so well situated as Eastlake, however, for it was located between the Governor Printz Boulevard, a heavy truck route, and the Pennsylvania Railroad tracks, adjacent to very rundown workers' housing from the late nineteenth century. The assumptions about the relocation of the east side's displaced residents proved incorrect, for they failed to take into account several factors about the relocation of the Poplar area's population, including the continuing migration of new black family units to the city. It was also assumed, falsely as it turned out, that blacks would choose new low-income project housing over the older housing available to them through the private market, and, most fallacious of all, it was assumed that new construction in the urban renewal areas would be promptly erected and would be priced within the means of the former home owners from the area. Events proved otherwise.

Those involved in the renewal project recall that roughly one-third of those moved from Poplar A did go into the Riverside project, another third moved into privately owned rental housing, mostly on the city's near west side between Market Street and the Adams-Jackson freeway, and one-third simply disappeared.[4] West center city, an area ignored by those who planned both the urban renewal project and I-95, became the chief victim of both. With astonishing rapidity this moderate-income white ethnic enclave of largely owner-occupied houses was transformed into a neighborhood of poor black renters. The houses in west center city were, on the whole, larger, newer, and more architecturally varied than those on the east side; most of them were very neatly kept and many maintained rose gardens in their small backyards, but the process of conversion into apartments rapidly increased the density of population and reduced the neighborhood's economic and social stability. The west side's numerous white churches, Protestant and Catholic, and small corner grocery stores and taprooms, many owned by and patronized by Poles or Italians, were also victims of the rapid change.

By 1960 the near west side had a stricken look. Homeowners along the Adams-Jackson route were then in the process of selling their houses to the State Highway Department, but the department had no funds to tear them down immediately. Thus, a two-block swathe running the whole course of the west side was instantly transformed from well-kept homes into rows of decaying, boarded up houses, prey to rats, vandals, and arsonists. Walking home from work one evening in 1960, newspaper columnist Richard Sanger, who as a child had lived in a gracious turn-of-the-century Queen Anne style house on Adams Street, was shocked to see "symptoms of blight and decay" that "reach their most blatant severity in the area within and immediately along the Adams-Jackson Freeway route." From the hill on 6th Street he "marveled at how quickly these conditions can fester."⁵ Rats the size of alley cats moved into the abandoned buildings and roamed the area, frightening the remaining inhabitants.⁶ The decay extended much beyond the two blocks of Adams and Jackson streets. Two churches were in the direct path of the freeway: Zion Lutheran, which was burned out by arsonists before it could be demolished, and Saint Paul's Methodist. Neither had put up a struggle against the highway plans, because their congregations were no longer rooted in the neighborhood. The two Catholic churches located just outside the freeway route, Sacred Heart and Saint Paul's, had many parishioners still in the area, however. Another casualty of the freeway was a Polish club near 2nd and Adams streets that claimed 300 members.⁷ An 83-year-old barber who had come to Wilmington from Poland in 1902 remarked, regarding his eviction, "this freeway is worse than the Russians," and a 99-year-old woman forced to leave her once-proud Delaware Avenue home told a reporter, "they are mutilating Delaware."⁸

Falling sales on Market Street and falling houses on Adams Street represented a tragedy to some, an opportunity to others. Slum landlords took the money they were paid for their east side properties and reinvested in the city's most depressed housing market—the near west side. They converted single-family houses into small apartments and rented them to their old tenants or to recent migrants unfamiliar with city life. It did not take long for the remaining homeowners to sell their houses at cut-rate prices to escape. The entire process, which seemed to happen overnight, was tragic for everyone except the landlords. The largely black, universally poor newcomers had no institutions, no traditions in this environment that could assist in their adjustment and give them a sense of community. In this regard their situation was very different from that of blacks on the east side, where there were black churches, lodge halls, settlement houses, clubs, and other organizations formed by black Wilmingtonians in the course of more than two centuries in the city. The sections of the east side surrounding the Poplar Street Project remained the home of most of Wilmington's black middle class, people who were proud of their neighborhood and of their homes and were the leaders in their churches, lodges, schools, and in politics. The result was that whereas the east side maintained its composure even in the wake of Project A, the west side fell prey to intraracial gang warfare and interethnic conflict.

Other parts of the city were not immune from these changes. The eastern portion of the 9th ward, in the area close to Eastlake, Riverside, and Price's Run Park, was another region ripe for an abrupt shift in the racial make-up of its residential neighborhoods. This was the area adjacent to Vandever Avenue that had had its beginnings with the construction of the Pennsylvania Railroad shops during the first decade of the twentieth century. It was here for the first time in Wilmington that one encountered the charge of "blockbusting," the practice of real-estate men hastening whites into panic selling at cheap prices to middlemen who resold to blacks at far higher prices. Blockbusting was, by all accounts, relatively uncommon in Wilmington, and the chief factor responsible for the opening of the Price's Run section to black house-buyers was the integration of the Eastlake public housing project and of the Wilmington public schools nearly simultaneously in 1954. These decisions ensured that the neighborhood's hitherto all-white George Gray Elementary School would quickly absorb a large number of black children from "the Project." In the wake of these changes, those among the predominantly working-class white families who inhabited the area and could afford to move away did so. By 1963, 300 black families reportedly lived in the Price's Run area, including the highest proportion of middle-income black homeowners in the city—a fact that suggests where the black homeowners from the east side renewal had relocated.[9]

The movement of black families into the old white working-class neighborhood of the 9th ward east of Market Street had a further ripple effect on residential patterns in the traditionally more middle-class neighborhood west of Market Street in the vicinity of P. S. du Pont High School. The families who had moved into new houses in that area during the 1930s and 1940s had been drawn there in part by the area's excellent public schools. In the postwar era, young middle-income families were attracted instead to seek homes in Brandywine Hundred, which featured more modern house styles and schools that rivaled any in the city. Given the dynamics of the postwar housing market and suburban school building programs, even the most favored middle-class urban neighborhood could merely hold its older residents but could not attract similar newcomers. In the 1950s blue-collar white families moved into the area, but by the 1960s moderate-income blacks were moving in as well. The population shift changed peoples' perceptions of the public school population and curriculum. As each year P. S. du Pont High School received more students, both white and black, who were not academically motivated, the educationally oriented families remaining in the district became more eager to move to the suburbs. They were escaping not so much from blacks as from what they regarded as deteriorating school environments. By this process a large residential area of relatively new medium-sized duplex houses was demoted a few notches on the socioeconomic scale. But unlike west center city, this area remained largely one of owner-occupied single-family resi-

Henry Belin du Pont, the leader who inspired the Greater Wilmington Development Council's efforts at civic revitalization during the 1960s, shown at the controls of his airplane in 1957. *(Photograph by Cornell Capa, for* Life Magazine. *Courtesy of Cornell Capa, and Mrs. Henry Belin du Pont)*

dences, a factor that has maintained its stability as an integrated neighborhood.

The same process of change might have affected the southwestern and far western residential sections of the city, but, surprisingly, it did not. In the far west, the Highlands region near Rockford Park retained its well-to-do character, in part because many of its residents sent their children to private schools, partly because the area was more physically cut off from less affluent neighborhoods, and because many houses in the Highlands were large and ill-adapted to lower-income housing. In the southwest, by contrast, the houses were in many cases smaller and older than those in the 9th ward, but their predominantly Polish and Italian residents were strongly rooted in their churches, parochial schools, and other local ethnic institutions. Many younger Polish and Italian families did move to suburbs, but enough remained to maintain the character of their neighborhoods. These people valued community as much as the original 9th ward residents valued educational achievement. Therefore, their community retained a stability that the other did not.

Suburbanites were generally impervious to the changes that were taking place in city residential neighborhoods. Since the state of Delaware had no open housing law, the bankers, real-estate brokers, and neighborhood civic associations could easily prevent the sale of suburban houses to blacks in the name of maintaining property values. Black penetrations into the suburbs were rare. Generally speaking, in Wilmington, as in other American cities, prejudice and poverty kept blacks in the "inner city," living in the oldest, most cramped, least modernized houses.

In the summer of 1957, a realtor already known for his role in the integration or "blockbusting" of the formerly all-white Price's Run area near Eastlake assisted a black family to move into Collins Park, a suburb along New Castle Avenue that the realtor described as "not a preferred area."[10] When teenagers stoned the house and shot the owner in the leg, the blacks moved out. Two years later another black family, the Rayfields, moved to Collins Park. George Rayfield, a former resident of the east side, worked for the Du Pont Company's plant at Carney's Point, New Jersey and ran a small garbage collection service on the side. He was the father of two daughters; the elder had already left home to teach school in Baltimore, the younger still lived at home with her parents.[11] The Rayfields, who bought their house for $13,500, moved in during February 1959. They awoke the next morning to find a crowd of about 300 people, some carrying fire bombs, gathered in their front yard. Callers began phoning the Rayfields with one short, angry message, "Get out." Understandably afraid, the Rayfields called the state police, who brought four trained dogs to help protect the house.[12] In the fracas that followed the arrival of the police, seven people were arrested and two slightly hurt. The police erected a barricade some distance from the house. A rumor swept the community that the presence of blacks would lower property values by $2,000. Headlines concerning the incident appeared in the local newspapers. But after a few days it seemed that the people of Collins Park were reluctantly accepting their new neighbors. Leaders of the United Automobile Workers Union called for "fair play" toward the Rayfields, the crowds dwindled and the opponents of integration turned to the law in hopes of forcing the black family to move out.[13] Then, on the night of April 7 an explosion shook the Rayfield house, wrecking the kitchen and rendering the house uninhabitable. Early police reports suggested that the stove had accidentally exploded and that no foul play was involved.[14] But when another explosion destroyed what was left of the house a few months later, it was no longer possible to regard the incident as accidental, and police hastily arrested seven area residents on charges of burglary and conspiracy in connection with the case.[15]

The razing of the Rayfield's house in Collins Park was a brutal signal to blacks to stay out of established white suburban developments. Those black families who had the money for a down payment on a suburban house remained trapped in whatever undesirable city housing that whites had deigned to permit them. Only one Wilmington real-estate developer, Philadelphia-born Leon Weiner, seized the opportunity to make a profit by building suburban housing for blacks. In a business that generally produces cautious imitators of the proven, Weiner, the innovator, was a maverick. Weiner combined a social conscience and a willingness to experiment with new building ideas with a good nose for profit-making ventures. In 1959 he demonstrated these traits when he announced his intention to construct Oakmont, an open occupancy community of 261 homes to be located on 20 acres along New Castle Avenue just south of the city line. The development, of small sixteen-foot front houses, priced at $11,500, was clustered in rows. Oakmont was the first construction aimed at black buyers in the Wilmington suburbs, and the area's first development in what is now called the "townhouse" row style.[16] Because it was located close to the South-bridge Housing Project, Oakmont posed little threat to established white suburbs, but it did signal the movement of blacks into the New Castle Avenue corridor. In Wilmington's segregated real-estate market, "open occupancy" meant all-black.

The attempt to integrate Collins Park, midway between Wilmington and New Castle, had failed. But this area of moderate-priced houses close to the Marine Terminal, factories, and expressway interchanges was nonetheless ripe for integration, because it was one of the first suburban areas that contained housing that many black families could afford. Attempts at integration in the middle section of New Castle Avenue had produced violence, but attempts at the city's edge proved noncontroversial. Because of their rarity, Oakmont and similar break-throughs in the suburban racial pattern brought little residential integration. Most blacks who could afford to buy a house purchased in the city. Whether they bought on the east side, the northeast, or the southern suburbs, they brought with them neither blight nor lower housing values. Meanwhile the many blacks who lived a marginal existence on welfare or pick-up jobs remained in the inner city, where they presented an irresistible temptation to slum landlords, whose acquisition of whole neighborhoods could and did bring blight with astonishing rapidity.

The facts were that very few black families in Wilmington could afford the cost of a new house and that Oakmont had absorbed what little market they offered. Knowledge of these facts was hardly likely to hasten the much-hoped-for redevelopment of the 22 rubble-strewn slum clearance blocks on the east side. In 1959, just prior to the demolition, the principal of the area's new Drew Elementary School described his school's community thus; "The economic level of this community is low, with income mainly derived from the Department of Public Welfare, domestic work for women, and longshoring for men. Frequently, men hanging out on the corners or outside confectionary stores are paid 'lookouts' or 'runners' for numbers banks . . . There has been an increase in the number of fatherless homes and of juvenile pregnancies."[17] The destruction of east side housing did nothing in itself to improve the neighborhood adjacent to it, according to another school administrator who surveyed the area two years later. Walking cautiously along broken sidewalks, she found that the houses surrounding Project A were in grave need of paint and repairs. The most commonly found stores were taverns and liquor stores. Groceries displayed the "number" of the day prominently.[18] The area still had many positive features—strong churches and some well-kept houses—but in the real-estate environment of the early 1960s, the redevelopment area could not attract people whose incomes gave them choice in housing. No matter how close Poplar Street might be to downtown employment, no one would choose to live surrounded by a slum. Throughout the United States, this same problem frustrated urban renewal policy. The law assumed that once residential slum land had been cleared, its proximity to major downtown businesses, banks, stores, cultural activities, and entertainment would make it attractive to private developers. This assumption failed to account for two factors: the overwhelming popularity of the suburbs, which had already begun to replicate commercial, retail, and entertainment functions traditionally found only in the downtown, and the hostility of white people toward living near to or among blacks.

Project A posed an awkward series of problems for city officials. The Wilmington Housing Authority had hoped that its Philadelphia-based consultants, Jackson-Cross Real Estate and Jack M. Kendree Planners, could propose the best path for redevelopment. Enthusiastic reports by these nationally respected experts would attract the capital necessary to get redevelopment going. Outside experts generally provide positive reinforcement for large-scale redevelopment plans, but Project A daunted even the most optimistic planner. The muddled analysis submitted by Jackson-Cross illustrates that firm's efforts to balance real-estate realities with their desire to discover redeeming features on Wilmington's east side. The report began with the warning that although "capitalizing on this opportunity will not be easy," failure to revitalize such a large area so close to the city's core would "almost irrevocably commit the central city area to secondary status for many years to come." Following the lead of Jack Kendree's planning study, which had urged that redevelopment be res-

idential in character, Jackson-Cross declared that, assuming that everything possible was done to package the property in its best light, the 22
blocks' "highest and best use" would be for housing. They acknowledged,
however, that serious obstacles might compromise this optimum plan. One
such obstacle was Wilmington's poor urban renewal structure. The Wilmington Housing Authority, the city's redevelopment agency, had no
power to coordinate the activities of other city departments and agencies.
Furthermore, Wilmington's economy and real-estate market were already
in a mild downward trend. The Du Pont Company had cut back its labor
force in 1956 as part of a "profit improvement" campaign, and this in turn
had slowed down the rapid growth that the Wilmington area had experienced in the decade following World War II. Furthermore, there was a
strong trend in the private residential real-estate market toward Pennsylvania Avenue and Delaware Avenue on the west side, where several
high-rise luxury apartment buildings were either just completed or under
way. These projects more than satisfied the current demand for new
downtown apartments in the middle-income range. [19]

The most serious obstacle to successfully attaining Project A's "highest
and best use," however, according to the Jackson-Cross study, was Wilmington's unbending pattern of racial segregation. The few blacks who
could meet the minimum annual income of $5,000 required by the FHA to
be cleared for a home mortgage were already finding houses to buy either
in other parts of the city or in open occupancy Oakmont. The imperma-
nency of many of the jobs available to blacks had given the group as a whole
a rocky record of defaults on mortgages. In addition, the real-estate industry was wedded to the so-called "law of conformity," which held that
similar structures, functions, and races must be grouped together. It
seemed, therefore, that blacks could not afford the proposed "best use"
middle-income housing, and whites did not need it or want it. While
Jackson-Cross tried to sound optimistic, they could not escape this
dilemma.

The real-estate consultants' solution was to tie the renewal of Project A
to a much more extensive and costly renewal of the entire center city. The
report claimed that "it is possible for middle and upper income groups to
be attracted to this site if certain major and heroic steps are taken in the
central business area. Without these steps, it is our opinion that the only
proven demand will be in the lower income groups," which, translated into
racial terms, meant that without a gigantic turn for the better in the
downtown retailing district, there was no way that the Housing Authority
could woo whites into Project A and fulfill its potential "highest and best
use." Such a heroic effort would, according to the Jackson-Cross writers,
depend upon the city's ability to marshal all its resources. "If a strong

The Honorable John E. Babiarz, Mayor of Wilmington, 1961–1969. *(Photograph by Willard Stewart, Inc. Courtesy of the Honorable John E. Babiarz)*

renewal plan is backed by a strong citizen group, if certain leading institutions and industries commit [themselves] to an expansion of the Central Business District with additional civic, office, and possibly some retail facilities . . . then the highest and best use . . . might be within reach."[20]

Why should the city labor to achieve "the highest and best use" of these 22 brick-strewn blocks? Presumably to do so meant the most expensive conceivable development, which was not necessarily either the most needed or the best suited. Jackson-Cross did not use the term "heroic" lightly. In their opinion not only the existing project area but the 15 blocks from 4th to 9th street that separated Project A from Market Street would have to be rebuilt in a fashion that middle-income whites would find alluring. This undertaking was going to be especially difficult since the trend of new construction was along Delaware Avenue, towards the higher-income west side neighborhoods. But Wilmington appeared to have a terminal disease, and the doctors had just advised that only another major operation could rescue the patient from an impending death that was partly the result of his first operation. No one was in a mood to question the diagnosis. The gross cost of preparing the Project A redevelopment site had been over three million dollars, of which the city's investment of one-third was largely "in kind," in the form of improvements to the streets and underground utilities. City officials were understandably eager to translate this effort and expense into tax-paying property.

There was a brief flurry of controversy over the report, led by a few inner-city councilmen and the League of Women Voters. Leaders of the league felt betrayed, because they had been enticed into doing battle on behalf of Project A with the understanding that the land would be redeveloped as low-income housing for its former residents. A spokesman for the league announced that her organization approved, in principle, the construction of middle-income housing in the city, but not in the location already promised to others. A city councilman made the same point more succinctly when he said "The colored people need places to live worse than anybody else."[21] The News-Journal papers, however, took the view that the best interests of the city lay in pursuing the highest and best value formula of middle-class housing, lest "slum conditions" return.

It was at this portentous moment that Francis X. (Pat) Splane, Mayor Eugene Lammot's assistant, organized a group composed of a few key middle-level-managers from the Du Pont Company and the Wilmington Trust Company plus News-Journal columnist Richard Sanger to work with the mayor's office on urban redevelopment.[22] The group organized a sober presentation for the city's major executives that was held in September 1960 in the Gold Ballroom of the Hotel du Pont. Business and community leaders watched a slide show entitled "Which Way Wilmington?" and listened to an authority on urban development from M.I.T., who told them that only a Herculean effort could bring Wilmington back from its "long, cold slide into mediocrity."[23] Following the meeting, 174 people signed application cards for membership in a new organization to be called the Greater Wilmington Development Council. The News-Journal papers gave the event major publicity and the new organization appeared to have the support of the most important men in Wilmington's largest banks and corporations; but as Sanger noted on the editorial page of the *Journal-*

Every Evening, "The thought that haunts those of use who feel Wilmington has already dallied too long with its urban problems is that somehow the spark won't catch."[24]

The Greater Wilmington Development Council (GWDC) seemed like the U.S. Cavalry, arriving just in the nick of time. Leading executives demonstrated their support by accepting major posts in the GWDC. Edwin P. Neilan, President of the Bank of Delaware, was the first president, and nine other high-level businessmen served on the executive committee of its board of directors. Although his role in the formation of GWDC was often obscured by his reticence, H. B. du Pont, a nephew of Pierre, was really the pivotal figure in the early history of the GWDC.

H. B. (called Hank by his friends) had followed the family tradition in taking his undergraduate work at M.I.T. Following college he spent a few years designing engines at General Motors before joining the Du Pont Company in 1928 as assistant treasurer. By 1940 he was a vice president, and a member of both the board of directors and the executive committee. The fact that he was never chosen to head the company may be attributed to his intense shyness and discomfort in public situations. He did, however, become the president of Christiana Securities Company, the du Pont family holding company, after the death of his uncle Lammot du Pont in 1952. This position gave him power over the News-Journal papers, which were a Christiana subsidiary. An enthusiastic sportsman, du Pont devoted a great deal of his energies to his twin hobbies of sailing and flying. In the 1920s he had built Wilmington's first airport for his own private use. Whereas both Walter Carpenter and Crawford Greenwalt, the presidents of Du Pont during the war and postwar years, focused their attention on business matters to the exclusion of most civic affairs, H. B. was very much aware of the city's plight as he sadly watched Wilmington's decline from his 9th floor office window. Because he spent a good deal of time sailing at his summer home in Connecticut, du Pont was familiar with the efforts being made to revitalize the coastal cities of that state. He had seen how Mayor Richard Lee's dynamic policies had galvanized business and political power to achieve great new things in New Haven, and he had seen downtown malls in Bridgeport and elsewhere.

At the first hint of a business-government alliance in Wilmington, H. B. du Pont was pushing his relatives and the Du Pont Company to become involved from behind the scenes. His enthusiasm won over skeptical business acquaintances and relatives, including his cousin Irénée, Jr., who, in common with other Du Pont executives, was reluctant to involve the company in civic enterprises. Irénée, Jr., believed that business corporations should restrict their public role to that of supplier of goods, services, and jobs. Irénée, Sr., had taught his son that it was perfectly proper for an individual to give his money or talent toward the nonprofit but worthy causes of his choice. If his charitable efforts proved ill-founded the only harm done was to his own pocketbook and possibly his reputation. But when a large corporation abandoned the natural constraints of the marketplace to play Lady Bountiful the result might be disastrous for all concerned. The magnitude of the intrusion could make a well-intentioned but unwise gift backfire resoundingly on recipient and giver alike.[25] Since the 1920s the relationship between the Du Pont Company and Delaware has been one of delicate balance, where, as one study put it, "the elephant takes care not to dance among the chickens." To prevent bad publicity, the big company stayed out of local affairs in its small state.[26]

In twentieth-century Wilmington the Du Pont Company was the proverbial big fish in the small pond. Du Pont executives had always liked it that way. Wilmington was a comfortable town with plenty of rolling open land to the north and west for the good life, small enough to get in and out of easily. The elite all knew one another. Their children attended the same schools. They met at the same fine clubs. Overtures were not made to attract other big companies to the area. In 1959, for example, when the Army Corps of Engineers were considering the development of a new ship channel along the Delaware River, which might in turn invite new industry to New Castle County, the News-Journal papers published the following cautionary editorial comment. "Industry is vital. But it is not the plants but the office headquarters of heavy industry which have contributed most to the payrolls and economy of this community." The editors feared that "the character" of northern Delaware "as a good place to live as well as work" might be jeopardized by further industrialization.[27] GWDC reflected the concerns and style of this upper-management leadership. Although its founders encouraged broad-based membership, decision-making power resided in the nine-man executive committee, representative of the city's most powerful business leaders. In keeping with the interests and outlook of this group, the organization's basic thrust was toward the reconstruction of the central business district.

When GWDC came into being, Wilmington had just elected a new mayor, John E. Babiarz, the son of Polish immigrants who had grown to manhood on Wilmington's east side. A modest, pleasant man whose eyes twinkled when he smiled, Babiarz had a knack for making friends. On his return from active service after World War II, Babiarz joined his father-in-law's bedding company and became active in the VFW and the Democratic party. He was one of the party's "Young Turks" responsible for putting city elections on the November ballot, the key move that switched Wilmington from the Republican to the Democratic column, because it greatly increased the voter turn-out.[28]

Although Babiarz proved to be a good coalition builder and quickly consolidated his control over the badly fragmented city Democratic party, nothing in his background indicated that he had the ability to manage a city in crisis. Babiarz was no Richard Lee; he lacked the drive and the charisma of the nationally publicized New Haven mayor. But in Babiarz Wilmington had found a mayor willing to devote all his time, his political power, and his considerable intelligence to meeting the greatest series of challenges ever to confront anyone in his office. Behind the facade of his administration, a boyhood friend of the mayor from the Polish neighborhood, Leo Marshall, and Frank Biondi, a young attorney, were creating a Democratic machine that could be relied upon to deliver votes, reward its friends, and punish its enemies. In addition to this power base, the affable mayor also got on well with the businessmen who ran GWDC, particularly H. B. du Pont. The new mayor lost no time in confronting the city's major political problem, its outdated city charter. In his inaugural address, Babiarz called for a new charter that would free Wilmington from interference from Dover and provide strong executive leadership. He appointed a charter commission, chaired by Frank Biondi, that proposed that Wilmington adopt a modified form of Philadelphia's strong mayoral charter. The charter received the support of both parties and was accepted by the electorate in 1964.[29] It had taken a crisis to do it, but half a century after reformers had first pointed to the ineffectuality of its government, Wilmington finally had an adequate organic law. For the first time in its history, Wilmington had a powerful mayor.

The moment had also come when the politicians and businessmen of GWDC agreed that Wilmington should have a full-time professional city planner. In the past city planning had seemed to be a luxury, but new federal regulations controlling eligibility for urban renewal funds made planning imperative. The mayor and the business leaders chose Peter A. Larson, then 37, the director of planning in nearby Delaware County, Pennsylvania. The choice could hardly have been a better one to ensure cooperation between the city administration and GWDC. Larson inspired confidence. He was handsome, articulate, politically astute, and well-trained. A graduate of Dartmouth College, where he majored in pre-architecture and art, he also had a advanced degree from the University of North Carolina in regional planning.[30] Whereas Larson had been hamstrung in Delaware County by political bosses who made their decisions behind the scene, he was impressed with the commitment of Wilmington's business and political leaders to accomplish fundamental planning goals. While he was under consideration for the planning post, Larson was invited to dinner to meet the city councilmen. His dinner partner was Frank Biondi, whom he knew to be the intellectual power within the

A conceptual drawing showing redevelopment plans for Wilmington's east side from a brochure produced by the successful bidder, Wilmington Renewal Associates, in 1961. *(Courtesy of the Greater Wilmington Development Council, Inc.)*

mayor's inner circle. Larson was impressed with Biondi's fresh incisive mind. He especially liked the young attorney's candor in telling him which of the councilmen seated around the table were crooks.[31]

Like GWDC, Larson saw revitalization of the central business district as the overarching goal for his office, and like the Jackson-Cross Company he saw the reconstruction of the King-French streets section adjacent to the Poplar Street urban renewal area as the key to that revitalization. In this regard Larson was following the classic planning technique of balancing the natural trend for development to go westward with a countertrend eastward.

The new planner had hardly arrived when he was faced with his first major test. On 4 July 1960, the General Service Administration had announced the federal government's intention to construct a 12-story federal office and courthouse behind the old federal building on 13th Street between Market and King streets. It was rumored that the judges had selected the plot on account of its proximity to the Wilmington Club where they ate lunch. Everyone else was thoroughly dissatisfied with the location. Babiarz's predecessor, Mayor Lammot, who had been trying to pump life into the streetside Farmers Market, suggested an alternative spot at 7th and French streets; but a representative from the U.S. Government General Services Department told a meeting of local business and political leaders that the mayor's suggested site was "crummy." The federal government, he announced, was not duty-bound to cure blight and would refuse to invest seven or eight million dollars in a run-down area.[32] Stung by the rebuke, Mayor Babiarz pushed a measure through council that declared the blocks east of Market Street from 4th to 9th and King to Walnut streets an urban renewal area and appointed an architect, W. Ellis Preston, who drew up a broad plan for east side development. This was precisely the policy advocated by the Jackson-Cross study to tie Project A to the central business district. At an October 1961 press conference, the mayor presented the architect's plan to create a new city civic center on the scale of Rodney Square. The plan included not only the federal office building, but new city-county and state buildings clustered together on a mall. He announced that General Services had reconsidered and would cooperate with the city's proposed Civic Center plan.[33] A few weeks later, GWDC published a similar, even more elaborate plan in the local press. The GWDC plan included a broad mall featuring a reflecting pool that formed the imposing approach to a four-story civic auditorium flanked by high-rise government buildings and mid-rise parking garages. The accompanying article reminded skeptical Wilmingtonians that "the level at which Wilmington sets its sights as it embarks on programs of rehabilitation and renewal can play an important part in the success or failure of these programs."[34] This was the program to which Peter Larson had now to turn his attention.

The troubles seemed endless. In the fall of 1961, the Wilmington Housing Authority offered Project A for development bids. The winning bid would be chosen on the basis of how closely it matched a set of preestablished criteria for practicality, attractiveness, proposed density of population, and conformity to federal regulations. Five companies submitted proposals, including two with local connections. Ernest DiSabatino and Sons, a long-established Wilmington firm, acting in collaboration with a New York-based funding agency proposed to construct a supermarket, a motel, and shops, all contained within a superblock that would include houses for sale and rent at three price levels. The City Redevelopment Corporation of Jenkintown, Pennsylvania, offered a plan that included housing for the elderly, a theater, and a swimming pool, and a Washington, D.C., builder proposed to build a 16-story office building. The winning bid was that of a local consortium called Wilmington Renewal Associates, led by Leon Weiner, the developer of Oakmont, the open-occupancy suburb. The consortium's architect, W. Ellis Preston, had only recently completed the plan for the Civic Center, and his firm announced that their proposal had been conceived in unity with the Civic Center and hinged upon the city's commitment to it.[35] The Preston plan was almost entirely residential in character. It consisted of 550 rental units, some to be contained in a large Y-shaped mid-rise building, the others in various garden apartment styles, together with 190 rowhouses, which were for sale, surrounding a public park. Among Weiner's other associates in Wilmington Renewal was Michael Poppiti, chairman of the city Democratic party. Although the DiSabatino group complained that their rivals had had an inside track on the bidding, Weiner got the contract.

By selecting the plan that depended most upon the Civic Center project, the Housing Authority was forcing the city to engage in a more extensive renewal program than had been originally contemplated. The Poplar Street-Civic Center plan was contingent on the cooperation of the Federal Housing Administration, the General Services Administration, the state general assembly, New Castle County, and the city government. Delays by any of these agencies and governmental bodies could—and did—hold up the project not merely for months, but for years. The old houses were torn down but nothing new was going up, because the developer was waiting for progress on the civic center. By 1963 the News-Journal papers, strong supporters of renewal, admitted in a headline that "Bitterness, Suspicion Fester Around Project A Wasteland." The small-scale retailers who had once operated in the area had given up on ever getting new customers, and long-time residents were selling their houses to slum lords to escape from the sight of rubble. A social worker at the Peoples Settlement in the renewal area told a reporter, "The people are bitter; they're hurt; they're disappointed. They think they've been let down. . . . The failure of the city to rebuild has deepened the bitterness. They say the city is trying to stall, to make the area into a big parking lot for suburbanites." Ezion Methodist Church, the oldest black congregation in the city, had to charter a bus to bring in its members, who had scattered all over the city when their houses were torn down. A black Episcopal priest blamed the despair on the fact that the major decisions were "being made in business offices outside the east side community."[36] The east siders were powerless to influence events. They were not represented in GWDC, and the Babiarz administration's control over city council reduced them to ineffectual sniping in City Hall. In the midst of these problems, city councilmen who appeared to be sympathetic to the plight of the neighborhood lost influence due to their own peccadillos. Two councilmen who had publicly criticized renewal plans were indicted for an attempted shakedown of Leon Weiner,[37] and William "Dutch" Burton, the councilman who represented the east side and the leader of the original homeowners' fight against Project A, was jailed for assault and battery on his girlfriend.[38]

Unlike Project A, where the argument could be made that most of the buildings that had been demolished were beyond repair, Project C, as the three-block-wide King Street to Walnut Street area was designated, contained a high percentage of structurally sound buildings.[39] The proposed Civic Center would displace, among others, King Street merchants who were paying over $90,000 a year in city property taxes. The area's long and colorful history was reflected in the variety of its buildings. Whereas the more prosperous merchants on Market Street had covered over the original 18th- and 19th-century facades of their stores with plastic tiles to keep them up-to-date, the stores on King and French streets had changed little from the turn of the century. Like their brethren on Market Street, King Street merchants were suffering from competition from the suburban shopping centers, but their businesses were in less direct competition with the suburban stores than were their neighbors' on the major shopping street. Auto suppliers, tailors, beauty parlors, furniture stores, and especially wholesale food dealers and meat markets still flourished in the vicinity of 4th and King streets. Their proximity to the city's farmers' market drew many shoppers to the area. After the demolition of Project A, the streets were less crowded, the shoppers fewer, and the area's down-at-heel look seemed more pronounced; but it was not a slum.

The area's 221 buildings had a great variety of uses. Some, such as the Adas Kodesch Synagogue and the German and Irish halls, had outlived their original functions, since the ethnic groups who built them had moved away from the neighborhood. But other buildings, like Ezion Methodist Church and the Mother Church of the African Union Methodists, were historic structures that were still very much a part of community life. Some buildings were architecturally significant, particularly the gracious old classical revival U.S. Customs House at 6th and King streets, which dated from 1841. Stores, churches, and social institutions, including the black-only Walnut Street YMCA and a day nursery sponsored by the Episcopal Church, intermingled with rowhouses that featured interesting Victorian decorative motifs.

In the early 1960s, no one had as yet demonstrated the possibilities inherent in the renewal of commercial buildings through rehabilitation, nor was the adaptive use of old structures the watch-word of city planning that it was to become during the 1970s. Boston's Quincy Market was still merely a collection of antiquated stone warehouses, as were many other old urban commercial neighborhoods that have subsequently been returned to vibrant life. The wisdom of the time was that mixed use was a bad thing, and the Project C area epitomized mixed use. Experience in the 1950s suggested that a neighborhood like this had nowhere to go but down. Middle-income whites would never be enticed into buying houses in Project A unless new buildings connected their enclave to Market Street, or so it was thought. Therefore, the old had to go to make way for the projected Civic Center. The prospect of a collection of government buildings on the site of the mixed-use neighborhood was viewed with great optimism by city leaders. When Mayor Babiarz appointed GWDC as the developer for the Civic Center, the *Evening Journal* prophesied that it "could be one of the most beautiful in the country."[40] Since H. B. du Pont was then president of both GWDC and Christiana Securities, owner of the News-Journal Company, this prognosis counted for something more than a mere pie in the sky prediction.

But while the mayor's office and GWDC were bending every effort to return prosperity to the east side, the city's economic base and social stability continued to erode. The 1960s were a confusing time for the urban poor throughout the United States. The hopes engendered by the civil rights movement and the promises of Lyndon Johnson's Great Society rhetoric clashed head on with the realities of poverty, joblessness, and the indifference or hostility of white America toward minorities, especially the hostility of those wearing police uniforms. In contrast to the immigrants who had found industrial jobs in nineteenth-century American cities, the migrants who now occupied their old neighborhoods looked out across closed factories, toward the big downtown office buildings that offered no places for them. The major welfare programs, old age assistance and aid to dependent children, were spending far more than ever before, yet these programs hardly touched the problem of black unemployment. No one even knew how many of Wilmington's poor were unemployed.

In 1964 the Community Services Council of Delaware, the planning arm of the YMCA, commissioned a demographic study of the state. The study showed that Wilmington faced very serious social problems. Although New Castle County as a whole was one of the richest per capita in the United States, Wilmington's residents did not share in that wealth. Young white families whose breadwinners had good educations and high-paying jobs had deserted the city for the suburbs, leaving behind the elderly and a rapidly growing population of poor, uneducated black families. By 1960 Wilmington's nonwhite birthrate was four times greater than its white birth rate, and illegitimate births were escalating.[41] Nearly one-quarter of the city's black families were headed by females, and about one-half of the employed black females worked in the lowest paying job in the economy, as domestic servants. In a country in which the annual mean buying power per family was nearly $10,000, that of urban blacks was less than $4,000.[42] Nearly 80 percent of the city's adult black population had not completed high school, and over 13 percent of the adult black males were unemployed.

These social conditions were closely related to poor housing and the declining economic base in the city; as a demographer put it, "The distribution of deteriorating and dilapidated housing generally tends to follow the

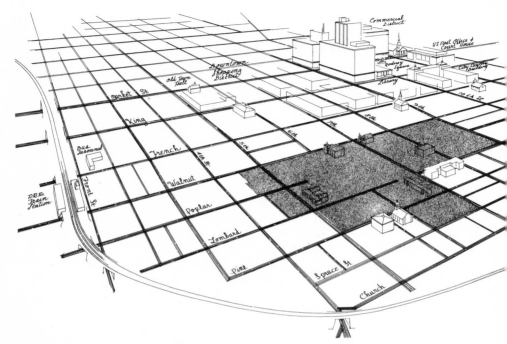

Drawing showing the location of the Project A redevelopment area relative to the Wilmington Central Business District from the brochure produced by the Wilmington Renewal Associates, 1961. *(Courtesy of the Greater Wilmington Development Council, Inc.)*

pattern of non-white residency."[43] This observation was particularly pertinent to the oldest residential areas, especially those adjacent to the Poplar Street slum clearance. The near west side, which the study called "Wilmington's major area of social transition,"[44] went from 88 percent white to 54 percent black in the eight years after 1960.[45] Another area of dramatic transition was the northeast surrounding Eastlake in the 9th Ward, which changed from 70 percent white to 85 percent black during those years. These "racial frontier" zones had few churches, voluntary organizations, or welfare agencies to assist their residents through this confused period. Yet, in spite of these handicaps, many of the black newcomers were struggling successfully to enter the middle-class mainstream of American life. In the northeast, for example, the shift from white to black had been accompanied by an increase in the percentage of owner-occupied homes from 63 percent to 75 percent, and even on the much-troubled west side, 55 percent of the black residents owned their own homes by 1968.[46]

A big question asked in American cities such as Wilmington during the 1960s was how to assist minority groups in their struggle with the problems of poverty. This issue was not merely one of altruism, because the social pathologies fostered by poverty and ignorance were threatening to destroy the city from within. In the case of Wilmington the problem was heightened, because the city lacked a strong core of black businessmen who might seize leadership and bridge the gap between what were called in the 1960s the white power structure and the black community. The only potentially effective organization committed to revitalizing the city was GWDC, but few among its leaders were willing to lend that organization's prestige and resources to direct confrontations with social problems. Most GWDC executives preferred to stick to planning and construction goals that could be measured on a balance sheet. A new building is a three-dimensional reality that cost a specific sum of money to build and will generate a specific income. But who knows when a residential neighborhood, a family, or an individual has been rehabilitated? One GWDC committeeman, Russell Peterson, a Ph.D. chemist and director of research at the Du Pont Company, disagreed with this philosophy. Peterson, who was to be elected governor of Delaware in 1968, was a native of Wisconsin, a state long identified with liberal causes. Peterson tried to sell his colleagues at GWDC on "people oriented" programs. Disagreement with Peterson's views among other Du Pont executives in GWDC evaporated when H. B. du Pont announced his support for the chemist's position. Peterson was placed in charge of GWDC's new Neighborhood and Housing Committee, which was assigned a GWDC staff person to initiate programs to help the poor.

In 1965 Peterson's committee committed GWDC to a three-year Neighborhood Improvement Program designed to improve inner-city housing and social conditions. Predicated on the notion that poor people would organize themselves to solve their own problems with a minimum of outside assistance, the Neighborhood Program was conceived as an experimental pilot effort necessary only to get the wheels turning, hence its brief duration. GWDC funded three store-front neighborhood centers, the West Side Conservation Association, the United Neighbors for Progress on the east side, and the Price's Run Service Center in the northeast. To secure neighborhood participation, each center created block clubs where residents were invited to meet to define and solve their common problems. The program also provided funds for housing rehabilitation. Aside from these common elements, each center was free to develop in its own separate way. Some directors devoted the bulk of their time to individual counselling, while others emphasized community organization.[47]

Unfortunately, after the three-year commitment there were no other groups or individuals except the federal government with the resources to continue the GWDC pilot projects on a scale grand enough to make much impact. Therefore, the project promised much more than it could deliver. In 1969 Harold Brown, a University of Delaware demographer, concluded in his evaluation that the Peterson group's efforts had brought only a modicum of help into the sea of troubles that afflicted the city's poor. Evaluators Brown and Robert A. Wilson noted that perhaps the most important result of the effort had been "the realization that complex social problems do not lend themselves to the assumed simple solutions on which the present program was predicated."[48] After an initial flurry of interest, attendance at meetings of the Block Clubs declined rapidly—partly, Brown believed, because "poor people tend not to be formal participators," but largely because their most serious problem, unemployment, could not be solved by a neighborhood club, however strong it might be. The Peterson committee found that each step it took sank it ever deeper into the complex problems of the poor. For example, when GWDC tried to respond to the need for employment with its Better Jobs Program, 900 people came to apply for work, but only about one-third of them had the stamina or skills to get jobs. Most of those who sought help from the GWDC-funded centers were referred to other health, social, and government organizations that had specific expertise to help with a particular problem.

Brief experience with these referrals revealed to Peterson's staff the lack of coordination among the multitude of public and private agencies with which the poor contended. Demonstrations of housing rehabilitation, another goal of the Neighborhood Program, had little impact among people who worried about where they would get their next meal. The most successful long-term result of the GWDC program's experience, according to Brown, was the creation of an Opportunities and Industrialization Center, jointly sponsored by local government and GWDC, which continued through the 1970s preparing people for the job market.

Brown and Wilson's most important criticism of the GWDC effort to assist the poor was their observation that the program had suffered because lines of authority and responsibility were left confused and undefined.[49] No one seemed to know who was empowered to make decisions: the GWDC executive board, the Neighborhood and Housing Committee, or the staff of advisory committees at the individual centers. Suspicious of the businessmen's motives, the professional social workers at the centers wanted to take GWDC's money without accepting their control. The GWDC people, however, expected to be kept informed and involved in policy decisions. These differing expectations left everyone's roles ill-defined. It is not surprising that an experimental program such as this produced administrative confusion; but considering that the people in charge were chief execu-

ing Street on Farmers' Market day, looking north from below 5th Street, in 1935, showing
me of the commercial area that was demolished by urban renewal during the 1960s. *(Courtesy
f the Eleutherian Mills Historical Library)*

tives of complex business bureaucracies, one must conclude that the
businessmen must have been very unsure of themselves in their role as
social reformers. One cannot help but compare the self-assured
businesslike way in which Pierre S. du Pont directed his charitable activities during the 1920s with the more tentative approach to social involvement among business leaders in the 1960s. In the case of Wilmington's
Neighborhood Project, the businessmen took on extremely complex problems without first doing the research necessary to establish realistic goals.
In the long run, the most effective of GWDC's social programs was the one
closest to the experience of businessmen, the Opportunities Industrialization Center, which trained hard-core unemployed people for industrial
jobs. By the end of 1968, the OIC had enrolled 352 students, 126 of whom
had found full-time employment.[50]

Violence was another broad social problem that eluded quick solution
either by GWDC or by the city authorities. As early as 1961, police noted
that the west side neighborhood known as the Valley, which ran north from

4th to 8th streets and between Washington Street and the I-95 site, had become the most dangerous and crime-ridden in the city. Drunkenness, petty gambling, and loitering were common. Gangs of youths often attacked police with bricks and bottles. The west side's people, young and old alike, feared to venture outside of their own neighborhood to see the rest of the city.

Gangs had long been a feature of Wilmington life. In the nineteenth century, youths from one part of the city courted attack if they crossed a bridge or street into a rival section of town. Ethnicity and socioeconomic differences had played a major role in gang warfare in those days. But the resurgence of gangs during the 1960s did not pit one ethnic group or social class against another. The new gangs, although highly territorial, were nearly always composed of young people who were both poor and black.

During the 1960s there were at least ten major gangs in Wilmington. The most important included the south side and west side gangs, the Jayhawkers of southwest Wilmington, the Mountain Dew Gang and Romans from the northeast public housing area, and the east side Stompers. The police tried with modest success to hold the gangs in check, but there were occasional street battles. Hostility between the west side and northeast gangs was particularly intense, and in April 1966 a west side youth shot and killed Beverly J. (B. J.) Keller, a popular member of the northeast's Mountain Dew Gang, near 16th Street Bridge in the northeast. Both the victim and his assailant were 18 years old.[51]

B. J.'s death drew public attention to the gang problem and gave direction to nascent efforts by the YMCA and Catholic Social Services to find positive outlets for gang members. Recognizing that the methods traditionally used by social workers were not reaching this group, the Y and CSS experimented with new approaches to "street" youth. In 1965, at the urging of Monsignor Thomas Reese, the director of CSS, the diocese of Wilmington authorized the creation of an Office for Inner City Development. The office was to be a rallying point for social outreach by both urban and suburban churches. Fr. Reese hired a young exseminarian named Edward J. (Ned) Butler to work for the Office for Inner City Development. Butler was to discover the office's potential for assisting the people living in northest Wilmington near the spot where B. J. Keller had met his death, where the diocese acquired some land that it planned to donate for community use.

In addition to his work for the diocese, Ned Bulter was studying for a graduate degree in sociology. He was much influenced by Saul Alinsky, the radical sociologist who taught the urban poor that they must organize themselves to demand social justice from governments, welfare agencies, and others who refused to treat them as anything except "cases" to be patronized. Butler saw himself as an agent for social change whose role was to foster the development of self-respect among the poor by assisting them in dealing with their problems. His involvement with the people of the northeast resulted in the creation of two advocacy groups, one for youths, the other for adults. The Concerned People of Riverside-Eastlake Extension, an association of mature female public-housing residents, succeeded in forcing the Housing Authority to relax some of its policies, most notably its prohibition against housing unwed mothers. Butler's other group, Concerned Youth of the Northeast, had a more controversial and well-publicized history. In a master's thesis based upon his experience in the northeast, Butler described his reactions to the young people of the community. He mentally divided them into two groups, the "classics" who were "school-oriented" and involved in musical or other organized activities, and the "trumpcats" or "street" youth who had dropped out of school, often had arrest records, and were involved in gang activity.[52] Butler chose to ignore the "classics," who already appeared to be set upon the straight and narrow road, to concentrate his organizing efforts upon the more volatile "trumpcats." While they were still shocked by the death of their friend B. J. Keller, this group became the nucleus for the Concerned Youth of the Northeast.

The YMCA, the Presbyterian synod, and the Council of Churches had embarked upon similar efforts to reach alienated youth in other parts of the city. Three inner-city Presbyterian churches established community service centers that promoted open-ended assistance of the kind proposed by Ned Butler. Following comparable methods, the YMCA hired a former "street" youth, Charles (Chezzie) Miller to work with the violence-prone young people on the west side, and the Council of Churches supported similar youth work in south Wilmington. The directors of these programs were eager to cooperate, for this was the period when the Christian religion was in the full flush of ecumenism. Added to the desire to build bridges between Protestant and Catholics were ties of personal friendship and shared ideals among the directors of these various programs. Richard Pryor, who headed the Catholic Office for Inner City Development, had been in graduate school with his counterpart in the YMCA, while Pryor's boss, Monsignor Reese, was friendly with the leaders from the Council of Churches.[53] These ties made possible the creation of a city-wide youth organization, called the Wilmington Youth Emergency Action Council (WYEAC), which had a program that was frankly experimental; its goals far-reaching yet vague. A writer in the Catholic diocesan newspaper, *Delmarva Dialog*, tried to sum up WYEAC's objectives with the statement that the program would "show a decrease in anti-social and lethargic activity and a corresponding increase in constructive and active involvement in the total community development."[54] To achieve such results with the city's "trumpcats," even under the most supportive conditions, was bound to be difficult, especially since honest men might disagree on what degree of improvement would justify the effort. The attempt to redirect gang life was destined to polarize the city's welfare community during a most critical period.

In 1964 Congress had adopted a comprehensive Economic Opportunity Act as the chief weapon of President Lyndon Johnson's much-publicized "War On Poverty." Title II of the act created Community Action Programs (CAP) to be funded by the Office of Economic Opportunity (OEO) in Washington. CAP proved to be the most controversial section of the Economic Opportunity Act nationwide, because the goals of the community programs were very loosely defined and because, unlike earlier government aid programs, which gave recipients no policy-making role, the CAPs were to be organized in such a way that the hitherto powerless poor would participate in determining their own fate.[55] In 1965 Mayor Babiarz created an organization called Community Action of Greater Wilmington (CAGW) to be Wilmington's CAP agency empowered to deploy OEO money.

In compliance with the spirit of the Economic Opportunity Act, Community Action of Greater Wilmington was an umbrella agency representing a variety of social organizations together with members elected from target city neighborhoods. The first president of CAGW was Mrs. Thomas Herlihy, wife of the municipal judge who had battled the State Highway Department over the location of I-95 in the late 1950s. Mrs. Herlihy was a liberal Republican with an outstanding record of public service, gained over many years. As a young matron she had entered the public arena as an officer of Wilmington's women's club and had gone on to lead the fight for juvenile courts in Delaware and to serve on the State Labor Commission. During the Eisenhower administration she was elected chairman of the National Committee for Children and Youth and was, in 1965, chosen National Church Woman of the year. These accomplishments and experiences had given Mrs. Herlihy the confidence necessary to lead such a large and disparate group as CAGW. A conscientious presiding officer, she was more concerned with keeping meetings orderly and following government procedures than with assuaging those who disagreed with these priorities. Nor would she permit potentially controversial matters to be evaded in public.[56]

By the spring of 1967, the religious agencies involved in youth outreach had convinced some members of the rival gangs in the northeast, the west side, and the south side to subsume their differences and join forces with the Wilmington Youth Emergency Action Council. Under the close direction of Ned Butler, WYEAC prepared a grant request for CAGW's consideration with the cumbersome title "An Experimental Project in Youth Self-Help Through Youth Determination with Adult Support." The group asked for $76,844, of which $66,739 was to be from OEO funds and the rest from other local agencies. Most of this large sum of money was to be used to pay the salaries of WYEAC's "youth organizers," ex-gang members who were to recruit street youth into WYEAC.

The relationship between WYEAC and CAGW was stormy from the beginning. Much to the audible consternation of the young blacks present at the CAGW meeting that took up the request, Mrs. Herlihy refused to take immediate action on it. Instead she sent the proposal to a subcommittee with instructions to reconcile the grant application's provisions with OEO guidelines. At a later meeting, CAGW voted to fund WYEAC in spite of Mrs. Herlihy's continued qualms about the use of federal poverty funds to pay salaries to those young men selected by WYEAC who already had jobs or who had serious arrest records. Her actions created an undertone of suspicion between her and the supporters and members of WYEAC that never disappeared. The WYEAC members, used to encountering red tape from welfare agencies and from the Wilmington Housing Authority, saw Mrs. Herlihy as just one more uncaring official to be defeated by whatever means was at hand. Ned Butler, their counsellor, deliberately fostered a combative verbal style in them as a means of building their self-respect. The result was that the WYEAC group came off looking to Mrs. Herlihy as if they were blackmailing the city and the CAGW into meeting their demands with crudely stated threats to violence. Mrs. Herlihy, on the other hand, must have appeared to those sympathetic to WYEAC as a sharp-tongued, rule-bound schoolmarm.

At that same time, in June 1967—a month marked by a series of racial disorders in cities throughout the United States—the U.S. Attorney for Wilmington concluded from interviews with neighborhood leaders that the city was ripe for unrest. He called the situation "shocking, frightening, and disheartening."[57] Nor was violence far away. One month later, after a week of serious rioting had devastated part of Detroit, Michigan, there were sporadic disorders in west Wilmington. In one incident blacks fired into a tavern in an Italian neighborhood west of I-95, but most of the "civil disorder," as Mayor Babiarz termed the shootings and explosions, took place along Jefferson, Madison, and Monroe streets in the heart of the near west side's Valley. A black social worker who was working with WYEAC on the west side saw kids looting a liquor store. When a police car arrived it was met by a well-organized barrage of bricks from a nearby roof; it "sounded like every window in the place was going to pieces."[58] The mayor took swift and decisive action to restore order. He instituted a curfew and

As a policeman stands guard, firemen fight blazes during the riot in Wilmington following the assassination of Dr. Martin Luther King, Jr., in April 1968. *(Courtesy of the News-Journal Papers)*

augmented the city police department with units from the state police, while 500 National Guardsmen were kept on alert at the New Castle County Airbase. Things quieted down quickly, however, and the guardsmen were sent home without having entered the city.[59]

In the aftermath of these brief disorders, Governor Charles L. Terry, a former state judge from Kent County, appointed a special committee to investigate the cause of civil unrest. After informal talks with residents of Wilmington's black neighborhoods, the committee members reported that conditions in the city's poor neighborhoods were atrocious and in need of immediate remedy. They found that the residents, having already endured successive false promises for a better tomorrow, had become either apathetic or impatient. The committee members were shocked at the outrageously high rents being charged for accommodations that amounted to "nothing but a hovel." Dependent mothers who got only $170 a month in welfare payments had to pay $100 of that money just for housing and utilities. Housing codes were not being enforced, while slum landlords flourished. Unions and employers conspired to keep blacks from getting jobs, the schools were poor, and there were inadequate services for work-

A common sight in Wilmington from April 1968 until January 1969, a National Guardsman standing guard with fixed bayonet in an inner-city neighborhood. *(Courtesy of the News-Journal Papers)*

ing mothers. The committee discovered that age played a major role in the suggestions they received for reform; in fact, age divided the black community. The older residents saw religion and existing social institutions as the keys to improvement. They wanted to increase evangelism and police patrols, to close down prostitution, and to keep young people in school longer. The youth, by contrast, found the police callous, were suspicious of white paternalism, and were angry because of their limited employment opportunities. But young and old agreed that the "white power structure" was directly responsible for the injustices suffered by blacks. In 1967 there was a Black Power conference in Newark, New Jersey. Its message reflected the belief among young blacks at the time that whites held all the cards and could end discrimination if they wanted to, while the only weapon available to blacks was to resort to violence.[60] This was the national mood among minority youth when WYEAC began its short, painful life in Wilmington.

WYEAC was the embodiment of Ned Butler's concept of self-help among the poor as applied to the most alienated, least responsible, least educated, least experienced, and therefore most easily radicalized group within the black community. It was a difficult target group with which to prove a sociological theory. Initially funded for ten weeks, WYEAC hired a staff of about 50 people, mostly members of gangs who had police records. George N. Brown, an ex-laundry driver in his late twenties who was a hero among Butler's northeast "trumpcats," was paid nearly $10,000 as Project Director. In his master's thesis, Butler attributed Brown's popularity among the younger "trumpcats" and his qualifications for leadership to such qualities as his "flashy, fast style of life, engaging personality," success with women, and ability as an excellent dancer. Butler described Brown as "a leader who had proven his capacity to give and take punishment by establishing what in local circles passed for a 'respectable' police record and a street fighting reputation."[61] Others with similar qualifications were appointed to posts with titles like Program Planner, Youth Organizer, Economic Developer, Legal Aid Specialist—all of which paid in excess of $6,000 at a time when beginning salaries for police, firemen, and school-teachers were around $5,000. WYEAC spurned office space in existing social agencies and set up its own headquarters in four city neighborhoods so that its operations could be completely independent. Its quickly trained youth workers were soon out on the streets engaging in what WYEAC called "soapboxing" with other alienated youth. Chezzie Miller, the YMCA's west side youth worker who became a youth organizer at $7,748 a year under WYEAC, explained to a reporter, "I attend meetings, cruise around, talk to the guys to try to find out what's playing today. My job is not to tell the guys what to do, but to try to stimulate their ideas and help them to make their own decisions."[62]

WYEAC epitomized the confusion of social policy, the sense of guilt, the desire for quick results, the optimism tinged with fear that characterized the response of white liberals to urban blacks in the 1960s. Its tactics could only be successful in the long run, and Wilmington did not have the luxury of time. Nonetheless, the program had supporters in powerful places. A *Morning News* article concerning the youth group's goals provoked Vice President Hubert Humphrey to write to the paper's president that it was "one of the most moving" stories he had read in some time. "It is so important that Wilmington youth are being given a chance to express themselves through positive outlets," the vice president said.[63] Some Wilmingtonians shared this view. Members of the Friends Meeting at 4th and West Street enthusiastically joined WYEAC members in converting an old building in their neighborhood into a club house. The Quakers, who mostly lived far from their old downtown meeting, were grateful for the opportunity to do something positive to help the young people who lived in the area where they worshipped. Within the business community, the most influential advocate of WYEAC and similar approaches to the poor was Edward J. Goett, President of Atlas Chemical Industries and an active Catholic layman. A major figure in the Greater Wilmington Development Council, Goett urged that GWDC support the experimental organization. Goett chaired a GWDC committee that investigated WYEAC and credited the youth organization with reaching more than a thousand young people, providing them not only with wholesome athletic and social activities, but also with training in managing their own affairs.[64] GWDC subsequently provided some funding for WYEAC, especially after CAGW cut down the amount of its support.

WYEAC's record was not so convincing to others, however. Following the 1967 summer disturbances, two black state legislators from Wilmington complained to leaders of CAGW that public funds were "going into the hands of persons contributing to racial unrest,"[65] a statement whose truth or falsehood depended upon one's perceptions. The Goett committee, and other friends of WYEAC, recognized that they were trying to enroll the most disruptive youths in the organization and argued that WYEAC members had to circulate around the west side attempting to quiet the rioters. No doubt some had done so, but there was overwhelming evidence that merely putting on a WYEAC jacket did not make a gang fighter into an instant pacifist; WYEAC members continued to appear on police blotters with embarrassing regularity. Even more distressing, WYEAC, instead of reducing the gangs, seemed merely to shift their focus. Gang rivalry persisted even within the umbrella organization and led on one occasion to a group of WYEAC members firing on a parked van that belonged to other WYEAC members. In addition, the organization spawned new gangs led by people who either rejected WYEAC for its ties to "the white power structure" or, alternatively, hoped to get in on the big salaries. One such organization, led by Leonard Flowers, a young black electrician with a long record of arrests, formed a militant gang called the Blackie Blacks, which achieved considerable power on the west side in early 1968. Flowers, like Miller and Brown, was a real "trumpcat" leader and hero. He had a long and serious police record, but he had once escaped a prison sentence because a judge was impressed by his bravery in saving six children from a burning building. He was a friendly, expansive person who frequently lent money from his numbers racket earnings to distressed westsiders with little concern for repayment.[66] The success of his new gang called into question the assertions of WYEAC spokesmen that theirs was the only organization representing black youth in the city.

The controversy over WYEAC paralleled and intensified a larger controversy over whether Wilmington as a whole was beginning a comeback or falling further into decline. Many signs pointed to the latter conclusion. The city was experiencing a serious breakdown in law and order. In 1967 robberies were up, Market Street was looking more haggard with every passing day, and the state legislature refused to pass an open-housing bill. Yet in spite of all the turmoil and bad news, there were signs that GWDC was making progress in its campaign to revive the city. Ralph Moyed, a writer for the *Evening Journal*, captured the confused, intense spirit of the times when he called 1967 "the Year of the City," a year marked by crisis but also by the hope engendered by increased cooperation among the city government, the business community, social agencies, and the federal bureaucracy in addressing Wilmington's problems.[67] 1968 continued—indeed, it magnified—the contradictory emotions of fear and hope that had characterized 1967. During these two years, Wilmingtonians believed that a great crisis threatened their city; and various groups strove to harness the momentum of change to fit their particular visions of the future.

Meanwhile GWDC concentrated its planning efforts on the civic center and the revival of downtown shopping. With the support of Mayor Babiarz, the businessmen's organization hired a consulting firm that issued a highly encouraging report proclaiming that if the city moved boldly it could attract a large retail mall to the King Street urban renewal site, adjacent to the Civic Center. The mall would be privately developed to serve an interstate region that would include one million people by 1980. Heartened by the report, the *Evening Journal* predicted that downtown could once more become "a vital urban core, a growing source of liveliness and livelihood."[68] Sounding the same note, Paul A. Wilhelm, the executive director of GWDC, told the Harvard Club of Delaware that "an exciting downtown is not just a planner's wild fantasy," but a necessity, since America could no longer support its ever-expanding suburbs. Wilmington, Wilhelm said, must quickly seize the opportunity to create the proposed enclosed mall that could make the city a shopping mecca for a million people in four states.[69] More immediately, there was good news for the downtown as several local enterprises embarked on major construction projects in the business district. In June 1968, while the Bank of Delaware was already constructing a new building on Delaware Avenue, the Du Pont Company announced its intention to build a $20 million, 19-story office building just west of its earlier Du Pont and Nemours Buildings.[70] The decision, said Du Pont President Charles McCoy, "demonstrates our confidence in center city."[71]

Meanwhile urban renewal was continuing in Wilmington's residential areas, although Project A was still far from redeveloped. The *News-Journal* accused the Housing Authority of a "time gap" on the east side similar to LBJ's "credibility gap" in Vietnam.[72] And, indeed, most of the project did look like a battlefield, but officials had labeled it "a learning experience" and were going ahead with several other, smaller, low- to moderate-income projects.

The problems encountered in Project A did call for a reassessment of urban renewal policies. In the 1950s urban renewal planning had combined massive destruction of old downtown residential areas with the construction of equally massive public housing projects intended to absorb displaced slum tenants. Those responsible for this policy had assumed that private developers would eagerly buy up the cleared land for any one of several higher and better uses than the existing slum housing. In many cities, however, including Wilmington, the cleared land did not prove to be as attractive to developers as had been expected, nor did slum residents choose to live in public housing if they could afford to rent even substandard living space within the private market. The lesson from this experience was that if center city housing was only attractive to the poor anyway, and if the poor preferred private market housing over public projects, then rehabilitation rather than slum clearance should be the key to residential redevelopment. Such a policy would eliminate the syndrome associated with Project A, where the expulsion of the old residents merely radiated the slum into other parts of the city.

Wilmington's city planner, Peter Larson, created his plan for west center city in light of these lessons. There, in contrast to the policies pursued so disappointingly on the east side a decade before, the plan was to improve the housing without removing the tenants. A survey showed that even by the city's stringent standards of age and deterioration, only 681 of the 1,586 structures on the near west side were substandard. Consequently, as Larson told residents of the area in December 1967, the city's renewal plan for the area called for the razing of only those few houses that were uneconomical to repair. Furthermore, the necessary renovations would proceed on a small scale so as to minimize the inconvenience to tenants. The Wilmington Housing Authority planned to rent some apartments and houses scattered throughout the area to its low-income tenants rather than continue to concentrate them in projects such as Eastlake and Southbridge.

The city's new plan would not only operate gently to improve specific housing units, but it would also make the whole west side area more attractive, convenient, and habitable for its residents. In place of the existing heavily traveled short blocks, the near west side was to be broken up into much larger, quieter, less congested superblocks filled with trees and places to play or stroll. In addition, Larson announced the city's intention to bring recreational facilities to this densely populated neighborhood. A new community park, complete with swimming pool and gymnasium, was to be built adjacent to the local elementary school, and a new community center was to be located at 5th and Madison streets, in the heart of west center city.[73]

Just as implementation of these plans for west center city was about to begin, a breakthrough occurred for the long-stalled east side renewal area. On 5 April 1968, the News-Journal reported that city council and GWDC had just created a joint public-private corporation called Downtown Wilmington, Incorporated, for the purpose of developing the regional shopping mall south of the projected Civic Center. Peter Larson and H. B. du Pont hailed the announcement as "the most important step toward revitalization of Wilmington in many years," calling it "the key to the full revitalization of the entire city." "Those of us who have been close to the planning of this project," H. B. du Pont told reporters, "are confident that it is feasible, and we are determined to implement it promptly and aggressively."[74] It was characteristic of the rapid swings between pessimism and optimism of the 1960s that on the same day the newspaper carried this hopeful story it also announced the sensational news that Dr. Martin Luther King, Jr., the most respected and beloved black leader of his time, had been shot to death by a sniper in Memphis, Tennessee.

The shock of Dr. King's death came at a particularly volatile time in Wilmington, for in spite of the recent spate of plans to improve the city, many of Wilmington's blacks remained convinced that "the system" was determined to keep them locked in perpetual poverty and isolation. These suspicions were particularly strong among westsiders, many of whom had fled the east side to escape an earlier urban renewal project. But beyond the west side there were other, more general, problems associated with housing. For at least three years, tension had been building over the issue of open housing. A few civic and religious groups, notably some Roman Catholic, Episcopal, and Presbyterian clergy, publicly deplored the concentration of blacks in the city and sought to end ghettoization. In March 1964 the reformers appeared to have won a significant victory when the Home Builders Association of Delaware announced its support for open housing. The victory was short lived, however, because the Wilmington Board of Realtors refused to bind its members to the agreement. Recalling the Collins Park incident of a few years before, the realtors were determined to act in unison on this sensitive issue, which required that their board move at the pace of its most hesitant members. Some realtors still demanded the right to refuse to sell a house to blacks even if the owner requested it, if, in the realtor's opinion, black occupancy might lead to a disturbance.[75] In 1965, in response to continuing pressure from liberals, the realty board issued a twelve-point open-housing policy under which realtors were committed to list any house as being under open occupancy if their client wished them to do so. Realtors reserved the right, however, to warn owners of the possible consequences.[76]

A few months later, the State Human Relations Council supported a bill in the Delaware legislature that would have made it illegal for an owner to refuse to sell his house to someone on the grounds of race. The realtors opposed the bill because owners would lose their freedom to sell to whomever they chose. The issue was further complicated when the only black senator, Herman Holloway, Sr., introduced a rival fair-housing bill, while the realtors backed yet a third. Equivocal editorials in the Wilmington press did little to reduce the confusion, and the legislature let the matter die.[77] Late in 1965 the legislature met again to vote on a compromise fair-housing bill that had the support of the socially conservative governor, Charles L. Terry, but even this watered-down version failed to get a majority.[78]

The next big push for open housing took place in the spring of 1967. By then both political parties had proclaimed their support for the principle of open housing, and Governor Terry had said that he would sign any bill that passed. This time the legislators were embroiled in a controversy over whether to include a "Mrs. Murphy clause," a provision to exclude small owner-occupied rental units from the law. When the bill lost by one vote, nine major employers, including Du Pont, Atlas, and Hercules, intervened and told the governor that although they would not endorse any specific plan, "the best interests of the state" demanded rapid positive action. Once more a bill was brought to the floor and passed the House of Representatives only to fail in the Senate, while Senator Holloway watched with tears freely flowing down his face.[79] In late 1967 the State Human Relations Council released a study that showed that during the three years of voluntary open listing, 50 percent of home sellers in the city, but fewer than 10 percent in the suburbs, had chosen it.[80] The issue seemed dead for 1967 until the NAACP revived it once more, in December, when it staged a march on Market Street to protest the action of a realtor who had taken a black couple's down payment on a suburban house and then sold it to whites.[81] Yet another demonstration, by two hundred people, failed to persuade Governor Terry to call the legislature into special session to act on the housing issue. By the beginning of 1968, blacks had endured a series of frustrating confrontations with the state government over open housing, each one more emotionally charged than the last.

Yet the same legislators who had refused for three years to give black Delawareans the right to buy a house of their choice had responded swiftly to Governor Terry's request for new laws to strengthen the government's hand in dealing with disorders following the brief disturbances in June 1967.[82] Armed with his new powers, Governor Terry maintained a tight curfew in Wilmington for one month after the disorders had ended, and when he finally lifted the state of emergency he took the opportunity to attack a newly formed middle-class black organization that he quite falsely accused of wanting violence.[83] Soon after, Terry told a conference of Southern governors that his tough approach to rioters had been effective. He proudly described how he had sent in the state police and called up the National Guard against the wishes of Wilmington's mayor: "we sent in the state police and they [the rioters] left the streets."[84] In a rare show of unanimity, both the Wilmington police and the city's black leaders took offense at Terry's remarks. The governor further exacerbated the tense situation at a press conference, where he explained that the city police had come through well but that adding the state police "served an important psychological role in preventing violence." He went on to warn that serenity was not at hand. "On the contrary, the evidence that reached me from many reliable sources, which I cannot disclose here, indicates that there are forces at work to keep alive the spirit of dissention and lawlessness . . . and to perpetrate worse mischief if the opportunity presents itself."[85]

Tempers were getting shorter all round. Just before Christmas 1967, Roy Wagstaff, president of the Wilmington branch of the NAACP, once more called on the legislature to adopt open housing. In a tone that the governor could only regard as threatening, Wagstaff said "unless the legislators face up to the need for open housing in Delaware, we probably are going to have a real hot summer in 1968" and advised that a housing law, while not a panacea, would "help in lessening the possibility of unrest among people who are literally trapped in their present housing."[86]

The spring of 1968 brought yet another ominous confrontation between black Delawareans and their state government. When the legislature threatened to cut welfare payments, a group of Wilmington's poor came to Dover, where they were met by a phalanx of state policemen on the steps of Legislative Hall, while a hundred national guardsmen were kept at the ready. Interpretations of the event served to increase hostility. Black leaders said that the protest had been an orderly effort to deal "with the power structure in Delaware in an atmosphere of equality and respect," while the governor told a Masonic luncheon group in Wilmington that the demonstrators "have had a taste of the state police" and hoped that "they never have to have a taste of the state police and the National Guard at the same time."[87]

Only a few days later, riots broke out in many American cities in the wake of Martin Luther King's assassination, and President Johnson hurriedly signed a national open-housing law. King's assassination provoked the most intense and bitter series of racial disturbances that the United States had yet witnessed in the 1960s. Sporadic violence began in some cities on the night of Thursday 4 April, the day of the civil rights leader's death. On Friday and Saturday, the rioting spread to include more than 40 cities. The most shocking and well publicized disorder occurred in Washington, D.C., where roving bands of black youths burned and looted, destroying many whole blocks of stores before they were brought under control by more than nine thousand regular army and National Guard troops on Sunday. But just as order was being restored in the nation's capital, an equally serious riot broke out in nearby Baltimore, Maryland, where six died and over thirty-two hundred were arrested during several days of sniping, burning, and looting. By 10 April, the last day of serious disorders in Baltimore, racial violence had been experienced in 110 American cities.[88]

When news of the King assassination first reached Wilmington, the city remained quiet in spite of local tensions over housing and welfare. Students broke a few windows in the cafeteria of Wilmington High School, but school administrators quickly calmed the situation by encouraging the city's high school students to plan a joint memorial assembly in Rodney Square. The next day students marched solemnly from their schools to the mass assembly, where 1,500 people paid tribute to Dr. King and heard a black representative call on his fellow legislators to "come forward and show their good will" on the housing issue. With students intermingled throughout the crowd, there was no opportunity to reunite them in groups to return to their respective schools, and a few who wandered downtown threw bottles and rocks at store windows.[89]

On Tuesday 9 April, the day of Martin Luther King's funeral in Atlanta, Wilmington schools and state offices were closed. That morning minor disturbances occurred along Jefferson Street in the west side's Valley. In an effort to keep the peace, Mayor Babiarz attended an emergency meeting at CAGW headquarters, where he promised young blacks to commit his office to the goals of more jobs, the enforcement of the housing code, cleaner streets, improved welfare payments, and a better-disciplined police force. Calling the Valley incidents "much less" than those of the previous summer, he declared a curfew but refused the assistance of state police and national guardsmen.[90] But the mayor's promises, delivered in a moment of crisis, crashed against the tide of rebellion. By the afternoon of 9 April, thirty fires had set old abandoned buildings ablaze in the west side, mostly in neighborhoods where the Housing Authority's promises of scattered site low-income housing were as yet unfulfilled. In one two-block area of Madison Street alone, 21 buildings were destroyed. Dense black smoke rose over the Valley, two police cars were fire-bombed, more than 40 people were injured, and 154 were arrested before state and city police, assisted by the National Guard, cordoned off a 20-block area. Viewing the scene, a young black clergyman shuddered at the horror of seeing his city in flames and at the weird gaiety that possessed the people watching the walls of gutted houses cave in.[91] Meanwhile, only a few blocks away, frightened commuters caused massive traffic jams as they scurried to escape back to their peaceful suburban neighborhoods.[92]

By comparison to the riots in Baltimore, Detroit, Washington, and Newark, New Jersey, the Wilmington riot was a small, short-lived affair that did relatively little damage. But in the consciousness of the community, both black and white, it loomed large. It loomed largest of all in the mind of Governor Charles L. Terry, who, when asked by the mayor for 1,000 guardsmen to secure the riot-torn area, had instead mobilized the entire state guard, 2,800 strong, and sent them to Wilmington.[93] The massive infusion of guardsmen quickly quieted the west side. By 10 April the rioting was over and Mayor Babiarz relaxed the curfew. Within four days of the trouble, workers were already cleaning up the damage and guardsmen were spending their time keeping out curiosity seekers. City officials later reported that the disorders had cost $162,835 in property damages and destroyed 20 abandoned buildings.[94] Those 20 buildings cast a long shadow.

For the remainder of 1968, Wilmingtonians lived in the shadow not so much of what had occurred but rather of what might have occurred or

The People's Pulse

Peoples Settlement Association & United Neighbors For Progress Publication
WILMINGTON · DELAWARE

OCTOBER   1968

THE ONLY CITY IN THE (FREE?) WORLD THAT HAS BECOME A POLICE STATE

WILMINGTON, DEL. - USA

READ OPERATION FREE STREETS

The People's Pulse, a publication of the Peoples Settlement Association on Wilmington's east side and United Neighbors for Progress, headlined their opposition to the occupation of Wilmington by the Delaware National Guard in this October 1968 issue. The photograph was taken on the street of a Wilmington Housing Authority project.

might as yet occur. Although both the mayor and governor were Democrats, similarities in their response to the problems of Wilmington stopped there. For Babiarz the riot emergency was over, the troops could go home, the curfews end. He demonstrated the direction of his concern by becoming the first mayor in the United States to join the march of poor people to Washington, D.C., called by Dr. King's successor, the Rev. Ralph Abernathy. Governor Terry, however, took an entirely different view. With informants in Wilmington warning him that more violence could erupt at any time, he insisted upon keeping the National Guard on patrol. Each night troops in battle gear drove their jeeps up and down the streets. By the end of May, Wilmington was the only city in the United States in which the guard was still on patrol. Most black people strongly resented the patrols, although some older blacks and many urban whites were grateful for the extra precautions against a possible recurrence of rioting.

The guard patrols coincided with a period of increased violence among young blacks. Early one morning in May, Leonard Flowers, the leader of the west side's Blackie Blacks, was murdered in front of the club's headquarters at the corner of 8th and Jefferson streets.[95] The shock of Flowers's death was keenly felt in the community, for he had been a modern-day Robin Hood, and like his medieval counterpart he had often been an outlaw. At the time of his death, he was awaiting trial for assault on a policeman during the April riot. Flowers had committed a lengthy list of offenses, including rape and burglary, but according to friends he had largely given up these practices and made the money that he so freely gave away in the numbers racket. While National Guard jeeps and police patrol wagons continually drove by, 400 young black people paid tribute to their hero and friend at a memorial service conducted in a vacant lot a block from the scene of the shooting. One youthful speaker summed up the main theme of the day when he told the crowd, "We gotta get ourselves together. We've been praying and marching, but we gotta get together to reach our goals."[96]

Many believed, however, that, far from getting itself together, the black youth movement was descending into chaos. True, some young blacks continued to demonstrate faith in peaceful efforts toward self-improvement. In one well-publicized case, a group of black girls calling themselves the "Blackettes" opened a coffeehouse in a Jefferson Street property loaned by the area's biggest slum lord.[97] But many other young blacks turned to antisocial acts to express their frustrations and racial militancy. The city fire inspector reported 99 vacant-building fires in Wilmington, mostly on the west side, between 1 August 1967 and 31, August 1968,[98] and police records showed that while the frequency of burglaries remained stable, robberies, including muggings, increased from 27 in August 1963 to 87 in August 1968.[99] More ominous still were the escalating incidents of gang-type violence, some involving members of WYEAC. Eleven paid WYEAC workers had been arrested during the disorders that followed Dr. King's death. Gangs continued to fight it out on the streets, with bloody results. The police uncovered arms caches, one at B.J.'s Corner in the northeast, others in WYEAC vans, and in June police charged a WYEAC employee with assault with intent to commit murder after he had suddenly appeared and fired his carbine into an occupied police patrol van.

This train of events involving WYEAC members climaxed in the "Cherry Island incident" of 31 August 1968, when police happened upon a group of six heavily armed black youths on Cherry Island. Wearing bandoliers and sporting black berets, the group were engaged in target practice in the marshland east of the city along the Delaware River. Three wore badges that read "I have already been drafted into the Liberation Army," and four of the six were paid workers in WYEAC. They had driven out to the marsh in a WYEAC van. As a police official later put it, "The manner in which these men were attired and their actions preceding their arrests seemed highly suspicious of having even greater implications."[100] The police later searched the homes of the six men, where they discovered rifles and more than 3,000 rounds of ammunition. It did not take a wild imagination to conclude that these discoveries were only the tip of the iceberg, especially in light of a police announcement to the effect that the city had become "an armed camp."[101]

The Cherry Island incident was one more confirmation that Wilmington was no safe place to be, and it tipped the wavering scales of public support against WYEAC. Calling for a "serious review" of the youth organization, Mayor Babiarz expressed his disappointment that this "good concept" had been corrupted by "an evil influence," and, reversing his earlier stand, he asked the governor to keep the guard in the city.[102] Thus vindicated, Terry replied that his sources had been warning him about the Liberation Army for some time and promised that he would not let the people of Wilmington down by removing the guardsmen.[103] In the wake of the Cherry Island incident, Delaware's senators and congressmen asked Senator John L. McClellan's subcommittee of the Senate Committee on Government Operations to investigate WYEAC. McClellan was at that very moment hearing testimony about Chicago's Blackstone Rangers, the only other OEO-funded enterprise in the country comparable to WYEAC.

The Senate hearing began 8 October 1968 and lasted for three days. Testimony revealed that the federal government had spent $164,930 and GWDC, the largest local contributor, $105,000 to support WYEAC. Among the witnesses, who included professional investigators and police, the most interesting were Mrs. Herlihy and Edward Goett. In restrained tones Mrs. Herlihy explained that she had resigned her position in Wilmington's Community Service Council rather than be a party to supporting WYEAC, an organization that she believed merely perpetuated and subsidized gangs. In her view the responsibility for creating and sustaining WYEAC lay with well-meaning but ill-informed whites who failed to recognize that the organization, by ignoring law-abiding young blacks, was proclaiming the most criminally inclined to be the "leaders" of black youth. "To have WYEAC considered as an example for black youth or as providing leadership for them is to consign black youth to the continued tyranny of the gang," she said.[104] She especially questioned the OEO and GWDC's policies of lavish funding for WYEAC at a time when Wilmington's job training center was starving for money, and she noted the hypocrisy of GWDC's support for this questionable program when its member businesses would not give jobs to the likes of WYEAC workers.[105]

Edward J. Goett, president of Atlas, represented GWDC at the hearings. As a big businessman, Goett was not accustomed to being on the defensive before anybody, and certainly not before the senatorial subcommittee, and his resentment showed through continuously as he sought to justify the business community's involvement in the WYEAC experiment. Speaking with Rodney M. Layton, a leading Wilmington attorney, at his side, Goett compared GWDC's investment in WYEAC to the chemical industry's investment in research and explained that an ad hoc subcommittee that he had chaired had determined that WYEAC was providing genuine services to youth with picnics, sports leagues, and similar activities. Forcefully denying the claim the GWDC had funded WYEAC "for the purpose of buying peace in the city," he declared that "this subcommittee could not possibly believe that a few gangs in the ghetto could intimidate an organization of the stature of the Greater Wilmington Development Council."[106] Responding to Mrs. Herlihy's criticism that GWDC had funded WYEAC in lieu of its member companies hiring ghetto youths, Goett later wrote to Senator McClellan that his own firm, Atlas Chemical, had employed 16 hard-core unemployed in the past year and a half as part of a joint GWDC-YMCA Better Jobs Program that had found paid work for a total of 292 people.[107]

Goett's testimony to the contrary, the record indicates that WYEAC had indulged in intimidation in its dealings with GWDC. In July 1967, during the disturbance of that summer, WYEAC had demanded a meeting with the mayor and the president of GWDC, James Grady of the Du Pont Company. The meeting was called so hastily that Grady had to leave a cocktail party to attend. Once there, he pledged $15,000 to buy vans for WYEAC. Later he explained his independent action to the GWDC executive committee, saying that "the atmosphere in the room was rather tense and I could sense being pressured into support of the program . . . I really did not think much of the quality of the program as it was explained but decided it was better not to question it," since he feared "serious adverse reaction" if he had requested time to seek the executive committee's approval.[108] At least some black leaders were also uncomfortable with the dynamics of the WYEAC-GWDC relationship, because black youth were gaining direct access to and becoming dependent upon the patronage of the "big guys" at 10th and Market streets. It was a topsy-turvy world when middle-class, well-educated blacks were shunned by the elite while street toughs were welcomed into their offices. Instead of engendering self-help among its members, WYEAC's relationship with GWDC induced an attitude typically Wilmingtonian that these "big guys" would take care of things.

Although GWDC's leaders stoutly defended their investment in WYEAC, signs of growing militancy among Wilmington's young blacks, culminating in the Cherry Island incident, triggered the businessmen's retreat from involvement in the organization. The Wilmington business elite's flirtation with black youth was, to use its own favorite analogy, an experiment that failed. Irénée du Pont, Jr., was willing to post bail for WYEAC workers and to entertain them in his office just so many times. More to the point, Ned Butler's philosophy that poor blacks must make a radical break from control by the "white power structure" was utterly at odds with the short-lived alliance between WYEAC and GWDC. Neither group could remain ignorant of their fundamental incompatibility, and both had reason to feel betrayed. Beyond the brave words of justification before the senators, GWDC quickly backtracked from its involvement with the youth program, while militant paramilitary groups that shunned all involvement with whites, such as the Liberation Army and Black Panthers, snatched the allegiance of many young blacks away from WYEAC.

The fallout for the city was severe, especially on the near west side. In the wake of the April riot, which had destroyed the west side's precarious business base of old-style corner stores, negative attitudes toward the Valley subtly altered official thinking about its future. Visionary grand designs were discarded. With some of the buildings that had been slated for rehabilitation destroyed, the Wilmington Housing Authority scaled down its mix of rehabilitation in favor of destruction, and the lower west side recapitulated the experiences of the east side. The superblock was reduced to a pale imitation of the original concept. A few streets were cut off to traffic, but there was little new landscape design to energize the area. In the Quaker Hill area near 4th and West streets, fine old houses were torn down for no other reason than that no one could envision their utility in a slum.

The most visible and oppressive sign of Wilmington's troubles remained, however, the nightly National Guard patrols. In December 1968 the *New Yorker* published an article in its well-known tongue-in-cheek style, describing the deadening effect of the nightly patrols in Wilmington. As he made the rounds with the bored guardsmen, the author, Calvin Trillin, noted: "As you ride through, it doesn't seem like they [black residents] have a feeling of resentment, it's more like pure hate." The patrols had polarized the community. A group of secretaries circulated a petition in support of the guard, while another group, called the White Coalition for Justice Without Repression, and a black-led group called Operation Free Streets, circulated counter petitions. A WYEAC worker asked Trillin a telling question: "How long would a white community allow a black army to patrol their streets?"[109] Leftists throughout the nation, linking their hatred for both capitalism and racism, concluded that big business, the military-industrial complex, as represented by the Du Pont Company, was responsible for this act of oppression. A New York group called People Against Racism staged a guerrilla theater performance in front of the Empire State Building to dramatize their conviction that Wilmington was "The Nation's First (Police) State."[110] In reality it was not the Du Pont Company that was maintaining the guard in Wilmington, but a Southern-style governor who had convinced himself that the chief city of his state had become a dangerous place and that his unprecedented enforcement of the law would pay off in votes come November. The political and social sensibilities of the Du Pont Company were in fact represented in the gubernatorial candidacy of Russell Peterson, the former Du Pont chemist with the liberal Midwest Republican background who had been GWDC's first activist on behalf of the urban poor. Peterson and the company he had formerly served viewed the military occupation as embarrassing and counterproductive. The Republican candidate for mayor, former Delaware congressman Harry G. Haskell, Jr., an independently wealthy son and nephew of important Du Pont executives from the days of Pierre S. du Pont, also opposed the guard patrols. Both candidates attracted strong support from Wilmington's blacks. Both ran far more costly, sophisticated, Madison Avenue-style campaigns than those to which Delawareans were accustomed. Leftist opponents of alleged Du Pont power would have found, contrary to their assumptions, that Wilmington's elite were solidly behind the liberals, Peterson and Haskell, rather than the conservative Terry.

The events of 1968 also shattered the coalition that since 1961 had tied together a Democratic mayor, whose power base was in the city's white ethnic community, and GWDC, the organ of the city's corporate and banking elite. The coalition had worked rather well, but it faltered in the end because of an obstinate governor and because the businessmen believed that Mayor Babiarz was too slow, too partisan, too unimaginative, and were convinced that one of their own could do better. The election results represented a more modern and liberal reversion to the days before the 1960s when the du Ponts and their friends had kept the Republican party in power with the votes of poor blacks.

On election day, to no one's surprise, both Peterson and Haskell won resounding victories, and on a cold rainy day in January 1969, Governor Russell Peterson did what his predecessor had pledged never to do, and sent the guardsmen home. The siege of Wilmington had ended, but the effects would not die so quickly. Archie Lewis, a black resident of the Valley, said it best. "When we needed unity the most, the sight of the guards drove a wedge that divided blacks and whites. They bred hate and mistrust that will take years to overcome."[111]

CHAPTER 5

Community in Conflict:

1969–1980

*By [a] variety of federal, state, and local conduct . . .
governmental authorities have elected to place their
power, property and prestige behind white exodus from
Wilmington and the widespread housing discrimination
patterns in New Castle County.*
        Evans v. Buchanan, 393 F. Suppl. 428 (1975)
        p. 438, opinion of judges John J. Gibbons
        and Caleb Wright

The riots of April 1968 marked the nadir of Wilmington's postwar decline.
For many months, even years, afterward the fear of further disorders,
augmented by news stories about frequent muggings, and the sight of
groups of black youths on Market Street, discouraged whites from coming
downtown except to go to and from work. The continued presence of
national guardsmen patroling the streets kept anxieties high and postponed
efforts to resolve the crisis. Urban real-estate values plummeted, while
downtown merchants had much more to worry them than their concerns of
a decade before about traffic congestion and the lack of parking. In the
decade that followed the riot, the city slowly regained some degree of
equilibrium, but the costs of Wilmington's precipitous decline have been
high and its reconstruction has been uneven. Improvements have been
limited primarily to additions to the city's healthiest sectors—its core
corporate, banking, and government center, and those scattered residential neighborhoods that have profited from the white middle-class back to
the city movement. Twelve years after the riot, the city's poor and its
center city merchants had yet to see much change in their situations. With

slower population growth and the loss of economic initiative—conditions that presently characterize not only New Castle County but the entire Northeastern United States—Wilmington has entered a period of relative stability that is likely to last for some time.

A city and its suburbs are complementary but often competitive parts of the same whole. Since 1968, when Wilmington reached bottom in its relationship with Greater Wilmington, the city has recovered some lost ground. In part this improvement stems from federal policy that has funneled money into urban redevelopment; partly it is due to the maturation of suburbia that has brought about more critical public appraisal of suburban living. This reappraisal has in turn precipitated the back to the city movement. Real-estate brokers who had once steered the chemical companies' transferees and other middle- to upper-middle-income home buyers away from the city were doing so no longer by 1980, and, with city living once again respectable, urban property values rose faster than those of the suburbs.[1] Other factors have been equally important: in 1978 court-ordered busing combined Wilmington's school population with that of northern New Castle County, scrambling formerly race- and class-segregated school districts. In addition, since 1969 the state legislature has permitted Wilmington to impose a wage tax on its nonresident workers, and the income from the tax has made city property taxes more competitive with those in the county. These and other factors have redirected the city-county relationship from one in which the city had lost its power to attract toward one in which city and county are on a more equal footing.

The most important public issues in Greater Wilmington during the 1970s, interdistrict busing, metropolitan government, and the future location of the area's major hospital, have all pitted the interests of the city against those of county residents. In 1978 a long-feared court-ordered busing plan destroyed the old county and city school districts in favor of one metropolitan district. The terms of the federal court's desegregation plan became the most hotly debated and deeply resented public issue throughout the Wilmington area. Only slightly less contentious was a decade-old plan to relocate the Wilmington Medical Center's major facility outside the city.

The major issues that influenced Wilmington during the 1970s all had their beginnings in the restless, liberalizing years immediately before. Among the plethora of reform causes of the 1960s the least controversial major steps taken by government in Wilmington's orbit were the reform of the city charter and the reorganization of New Castle County's government. The structure of county government in Delaware went back to colonial times, when the main county functions had been providing courts of law, maintaining roadways and giving alms to the poor. The small

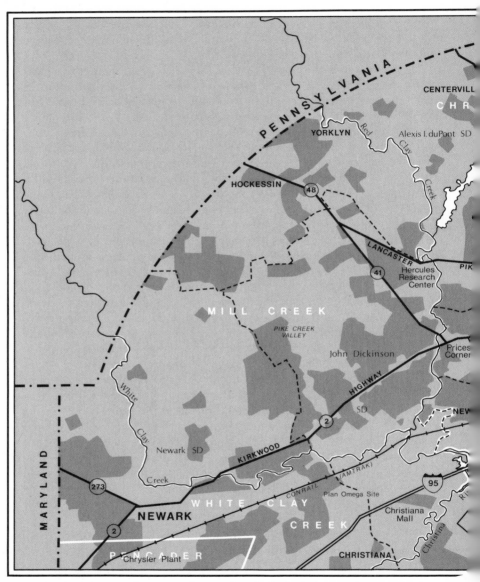

Northern New Castle County in the 1970s, showing hundreds, highways, and pre-1978 school districts. (*Map by Marley Amstutz, Cartographer*)

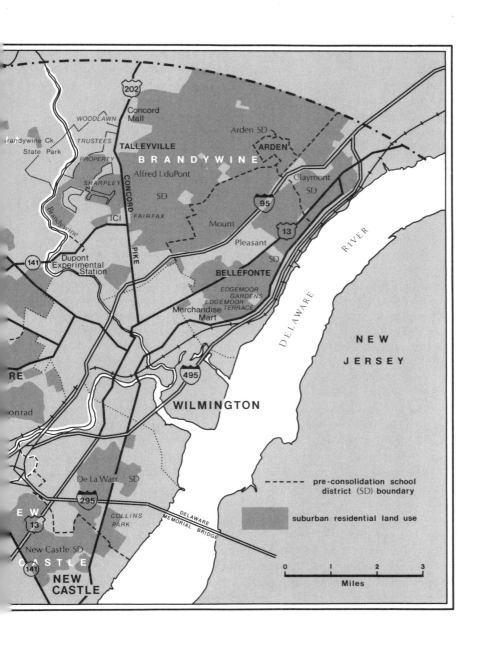

WOODLAWN

Brandywine Ck
State Park

TRUSTEES
PROPERTY

202

Concord
Mall

Arden SD

TALLEYVILLE

ARDEN

B R A N D Y W I N E

SHARPLEY

Alfred I. duPont

Claymont

SD

SD

95

ICI

FAIRFAX

Mount

13

Brandywine

141

Dupont
Experimental
Station

Pleasant

SD

BELLEFONTE

R I V E R

EDGEMOOR
GARDENS
EDGEMOOR
TERRACE

Merchandise
Mart

D E L A W A R E

N E W

J E R S E Y

495

WILMINGTON

RE

onrad

De La Warr SD

295

DELAWARE
MEMORIAL BRIDGE

E W

13

COLLINS
PARK

New Castle SD

C A S T L E

141

NEW
CASTLE

- - - - - -   pre-consolidation school
            district (SD) boundary

            suburban residential land use

0   1   2   3

Miles

elected body charged with raising the tax levies for these services and administering them was called the Levy Court. The Levy Court combined legislative and executive functions, but for all its power it proved to be an unresponsive and inadequate instrument for the governance of a heavily populated county facing the problems of supplying modern services. Several factors retarded the reform of New Castle County's government during the postwar years. Decades of Republican one-party control made innovation difficult, since entrenched politicians are notoriously hostile to the unknown consequences of change in the form of government. In addition, the willingness of state and city government to assume essential tasks that the county did not provide obscured the basic inadequacies of the Levy Court system. As we have seen, from the days of its streetcar suburbs Wilmington's municipal departments had supplied the city's most populous nearby suburbs with water and sewer service. Likewise, in the 1930s and early 1940s, the State Highway Department took control over roads formerly maintained by the county and accepted responsibility for roadways in the suburban developments. Fire protection was provided by well-equipped, state-subsidized volunteer companies. In addition, private companies supplied water to areas beyond the city water system, and suburbanites looked to housing developers to provide them with sidewalks, street lights, playgrounds, swimming pools, and similar amenities that would have been the responsibility of government within an urban setting.

The fact that builders offered such services only in their more expensive developments, rather than as a matter of right for all, did not seem to bother many suburbanites. People who moved to the suburbs did so at least in part to escape what they perceived to be the over-governed, over-taxed city. Aside from utilities such as roadways, water, and sewers, the major governmental service that suburbanites most demanded was a good school system, and Delaware's heavily state-subsidized local school districts supplied this need without the involvement of county government.

Yet, in spite of these considerations, weak county government was costly. Its limitations and impotence were most apparent in the areas of comprehensive planning, recreation, and police. Without planning, the generous use of land that characterized suburban development degenerated into sprawl that left pockets of wasted land, made for inefficiencies in the delivery of services and in transportation, failed to provide important services, and sometimes put incompatible land uses adjacent to one another. Without provision for parkland, people from the suburbs traveled to the city to walk through woods or across large unrestricted plots of grass at Brandywine, Rockford, and Canby Parks. The more people moved to the suburbs the more apparent these deficiencies became. The growing population in the suburbs, beyond the legal jurisdiction of the city police, also invited more crime, particularly burglaries. Fairness dictated that the people who lived in rural areas or in municipalities that maintained their own police forces should not be made to pay for a state police force enlarged to meet the needs of the unincorporated suburbs. Police, parks, and planning—the major areas left undeveloped by the Levy Court and unsupplied by either state or city—had become serious problems for the suburbs by the early 1960s.

Planning was not unknown in New Castle County, but it was nearly powerless. As early as 1931, when suburbanization was but a gleam in contractors' eyes, the state legislature had created a regional planning commission made up of ex-officio state, city, and county professionals as well as some citizen representatives. The commissioners were charged with creating a master plan for the future development of the unincorporated portions of New Castle County. They, in turn, hired a firm that made the county's first land-use map. In 1933, after studying the map, the commissioners issued their initial policy statement, in which they urged the Levy Court to discourage small, scattered plot development, since "the owner loses the very essentials for which he built in the open." Instead they sought to encourage developers to group houses together, making their blocks long and shallow with few intersecting streets.[2] But these were mere observations, without force of law, for the commission had no legal authority to enforce its will on the Levy Court or anyone else. During World War II, the state legislature empowered the commission to refuse developers the right to erect two or more houses without securing the commissioners' approval after a public hearing. But whereas cities such as Wilmington had from their earliest settlement laid out streets ahead of construction, the county's planning commissioners were not empowered to create their own plotting system but could only make suggestions on design and insist upon a few common-sense rules. The commissioners could prevent a developer from putting up a subdivision on marshy land, for instance, or from building deadend roadways with no room to turn around, but they could not control design.

In 1944 the commission published a rule book that included an ideal plot of an imaginary subdivision. The development was ideally located along the shore of a lake fed by a stream that intersected the community. The streets of the development followed a grid pattern and emptied onto two modern highways, one a four-lane parkway.[3] Excusing the fact that few areas could hope to replicate these ideal topographical features, still it is worth noting that virtually no development created after 1944 conformed to such general features of this plan as the interior street organization and the proposed relationship of suburbs to major highways. The image of suburban life created by planners of the 1920s and 1930s had idealized the notion of houses placed in parklike settings served by well-designed, tree-shaded parkways, but this image bore little relation to the large, close-packed tract subdivisions and highway strip commercial development that characterized suburbanization after World War II.

The county planning commission had been established during a period of relatively slow suburban development directed mainly toward upper-middle-class residential construction. Because it was given only negative controls, it proved powerless to prevent sprawl, flooded basements, erosion, and incompatible contiguous land uses. By the late 1940s, suburban residents were already complaining of irrational hodgepodge development.[4] Yet the state legislature refused to pass a zoning bill for New Castle County until 1941 and did not empower the New Castle County Levy Court to purchase and maintain parkland until 1953. During the 1940s and 1950s, zoning and planning remained separate, uncoordinated functions. Moreover, the work of the county planning commission was not integrated into that of related agencies such as the State Highway Department. In fact, no government agencies at any level were required to make their plans conform to the county commissioners' planning map or to clear their plans with the county planners.[5] By 1960 there were already sizable concentrations of new housing, especially in Brandywine Hundred, in the Price's Corner area, and in the area between Wilmington and New Castle. Developers were entreated to provide adequate playground space but were under no obligation to do so. Unplanned, unharmonious, traffic-stalling commercial development blighted and choked major arteries. The middle- and lower-middle-income areas were most affected and most powerless. Pleading against the erection of yet another commercial structure along the Kirkwood Highway between Wilmington and Newark, a suburban housewife told the County Zoning Commission in 1963 that developers were "pushing us from our homes. We came out here to get peace and quiet," she pleaded, "and now we have this jungle of horns, lights, and noise."[6] Her plight was far from unique.

The role of the county within the total framework of Delaware government was most ambiguous in the 1940s and 1950s. In a state in which county identification was very strong, the counties had progressively lost power to the state. Welfare, highways, and schools, the big areas of county control in the nineteenth century, were all under state control by the mid-1930s. Unlike a city government, the Levy Court had no charter and therefore was open to direct legislative manipulation. Its ill-defined functions were a catch-all of those duties left undone by the state and chartered municipalities. Designed to superintend a region of farms, dirt roads, and one-room schools, the Levy Court was hopelessly underpowered to cope with suburbanization. Furthermore, it was administered in a fiercely partisan manner in which each of the 750 to 800 county jobs were delegated on the basis of political patronage.

It was the political spoils system that finally doomed the Levy Court. For the many years that the GOP had controlled the state, city, and county, the force of competitive partisanship was absent from governmental affairs. But the postwar resurgence of the Democratic party brought changes. Wilmington's new city charter was one such change, county reorganization was another. In 1963 Democrats in the state legislature introduced a "ripper" bill designed to pad the Levy Court with members of their party. The more statesmanlike Democratic governor, Elbert Carvel, vetoed the bill and seized the opportunity to appoint a bipartisan committee charged to propose far deeper changes in New Castle government.[7] Composed of experienced public leaders, including H. B. du Pont, the committee was dubbed a "blue ribbon" body by the local press.[8] The creation of the committee coincided with a series of unusually awkward scenes in county government that gave an added impetus to the committee's work. In February 1963, when the Levy Court announced plans to double the size of its 22-man police force, even the Republican-controlled News-Journal papers protested that the existing force was already too mired in politics to be effective. Later that year the Levy Court was again embarrassed over its sudden firing of the county planner, a precipitous act that was followed by a series of petty charges and counter-charges that drew further unflattering attention to the county's unprofessional patronage system.[9]

The governor's committee approached their task with bipartisan support and a strong commitment to improve county government. Discarding the conservative option of merely fine-tuning the present system and the radical plan then popular among the county's Republican Greenville elite to subsume Wilmington and the other corporate municipalities into a single county-wide metropolitan government, the committee chose the middle ground of restructuring county government without discarding existing city and town charters. The committee heard testimony from various groups and hired a task force from the University of Delaware's Division of Urban Affairs to undertake background studies and to make recommendations. A consensus rapidly emerged among the committee members, and most of their decisions were unanimous. All agreed that the Levy Court must go, to be replaced by a system that clearly separated executive from legislative powers. They also assigned a high priority to replacing the spoils system with a merit system and creating professionally staffed departments to represent each major county function: finance,

The Honorable Harry Haskell, Mayor of Wilmington, 1969–1973. *(Photograph by Willard Stewart, Inc. Courtesy of William P. Frank)*

planning, safety, parks and recreation, and public works. Having agreed on the basic form of the new government, the committee encountered its only real difficulties in determining the political structure of the new system. After much negotiation they agreed that the county executive should be elected directly by county residents and accepted a plan for seven councilmanic districts that mediated between the ideal of the one man, one vote concept and the necessity of carving out districts that were unlikely to provide consistent majorities on council for either political party.[10]

Due to a legal technicality, Governor Carvel was unable to present the new plan to the legislature in 1964, and it was not until 1965 that the legislature adopted the measure, and it was 1966 before elections for the new government could be held. The Democrats had swept the state in 1964, electing Charles Terry governor and reelecting Babiarz as mayor of Wilmington, but 1966 proved to be a Republican year in New Castle County. The voters elected a Republican Du Pont Company lawyer, William J. Conner, as the first county executive and C. Douglass Buck, a grandson of T. Coleman du Pont, as president of a county council that consisted of six Republicans and one Democrat.[11]

On 3 January 1967, the Levy Court met for the last time, to see Bill Conner take the oath of office as the county's first executive in the lobby of the City-County Building on King Street. Among the spectators was the new executive's wife, Louise, a member of the state legislature since 1964. The Conners had come to Delaware from their native Minnesota in 1947, when Bill joined the Du Pont Company's legal department. At the University of Minnesota, the Conners had imbibed a doctrine of public service that underlay their later careers in local politics. Like their friend, fellow Midwesterner Russell Peterson, they became active in Republican party politics in their adopted state and identified with the party's liberal wing. Their political base was in the heavily Republican Brandywine Hundred, home of many middle-level corporation employees.[12]

The Democrats could take the credit for instigating charter reform in Wilmington, and reform and government reorganization in New Castle County, but it fell to Republican administrators to implement both changes. The Republicans' success in the off-year election of 1966 proved to be a portent of the nationwide GOP triumphs in 1968 that brought Richard Nixon to the White House and elected Russell Peterson governor of Delaware and Harry Haskell mayor of Wilmington. From 1969 through 1971, Republicans controlled the major state, county, and city offices, and local government enjoyed a brief season of cooperation that provided a good foundation for a new city-county relationship. During his two terms, John Babiarz had dramatically increased the visibility and importance of the office of mayor of Wilmington. But it was Haskell who first made full use of the powers granted to that office by the new charter. Under Babiarz the newly created position of administrative assistant to the mayor was underutilized, and patronage considerations continued to outweigh those of efficient administration. Consequently, the city's Democratic party became a well-organized machine, under the leadership of the mayor's boyhood friend Leo Marshall, and the Greater Wilmington Development Council took the initiative in planning the city's revitalization. During the Babiarz years, H. B. du Pont's activist leadership inspired GWDC and gave the organization clout with City Hall, while GWDC's bright young professional staff outshone their City Hall counterparts.

In the Haskell administration, all of this changed. Haskell and Babiarz represented two very different aspects of Wilmington society. Babiarz, a man of modest means and the son of Polish immigrants, was a politician with only local connections and local ambitions. Haskell, by contrast, the descendant of high-ranking Du Pont Company executives, was a former congressman, a major benefactor of the Republican party, friend to numerous national Republican leaders, and a man who yearned to be a U.S. Senator. A former aide has described him as a "big picture person" who, having run for mayor out of party duty, had surprised even himself by getting elected, and subsequently threw himself wholeheartedly into the task of saving the city.[13] To do this he brought to bear the most sophisticated executive structure that Wilmington government had ever experienced, coupled with the same blend of public relations and liberal idealism that marked the mayoralty of his friend John V. Lindsey in New York City. Like Lindsey, Haskell overcame the political limitations associated with a patrician background with studied grace. He was highly visible in the black community, where he appeared, coat slung over his shoulder, as a friendly sympathetic figure.

Haskell brought a new level of dynamism and competence to city government. This he accomplished in part by coopting staff people from GWDC. With the death of H. B. du Pont in 1970, GWDC lost a prestigious and concerned leader who had shepherded the disparate business community into civic action. Simultaneously, the new mayor was developing a strong professional staff to run the city. Several of his key staff members came from GWDC. Allen Rusten, a journalist who headed GWDC's public relations, became Haskell's administrative aide, and Patricia Schramm, who had resigned her job as GWDC research aide to complete a Ph.D. at Bryn Mawr, became Haskell's social planner.

When the new mayor was sworn in, the city faced serious and immediate problems. The months of National Guard patrols had devastated morale in the police department. Haskell moved quickly to bring new leadership to the department that dramatically improved the professionalism of the force and restored its effectiveness. The Haskell team could do little to improve other needed city services, however, unless the city first expanded its revenue base. The property tax was traditionally Wilmington's main source of income. Since the city was losing businesses and residents, while the number of religious, health, and charity-related tax-free properties in the city was growing, the revenue from property taxes was declining. Raising the tax rate was bound to be counterproductive since it would only drive still more businesses and householders into the suburbs.

The University of Delaware's Division of Urban Affairs convinced the mayor that the best way out of this dilemma was for Wilmington to emulate Philadelphia's recent imposition of a wage tax on suburbanites who worked in the city. The rationale behind the wage tax was that those suburban residents who used the city's streets, police protection, and other amenities should help pay for them. In most circumstances, however, it would have been impossible to convince a majority of the Delaware state legislature to vote for such a tax. But Harry Haskell managed to do the impossible. Because Haskell had provided financial support to Republican candidates for state offices for many years, numerous legislators from suburban districts owed him favors, and so the impossible was accomplished, and Wilmington got its wage tax in 1969.[14]

Both county and city now had professional bureaucratic structures capable of generating accurate, detailed information on the cost and effectiveness of their various parts. The most obvious conclusion from these comparisons was that even with the wage tax the city could no longer support some of its former activities. As recently in the past as the 1950s, the city had been the rich uncle that provided numerous services to its politically underorganized, sparsely populated suburbs. Suburbanites used the city's parks, its public schools, its library, its water. By the late 1960s, the city was a poor old uncle, while the county was booming. This reversal of roles had gone unnoticed and unchecked so long as the county was governed by the Levy Court, but with the advent of a more capable county structure it made sense for county government to absorb a greater share of the financial and administrative burden of local government.

As mentioned earlier, Greenville Republicans, including the business and editorial leadership of the News-Journal papers and Mayor Haskell himself, would have preferred to see metropolitanization of government throughout the entire county as the least costly, most fair, and most efficient alternative. The News-Journal ran a series of articles on the benefits that metro government had brought to other cities, highlighting especially Nashville, Tennessee, and the new Unigov merger of Indianapolis, Indiana.[15] For a time the journalists' publicity campaign against overlapping government appeared to generate some enthusiasm among politicians in both city and county, but the racial disorders of the late 1960s left city and suburban residents with too much mutual suspicion for complete consolidation. The two jurisdictions did, however, negotiate a series of piecemeal mergers. In December 1969 the city and county agreed to combine the maintenance departments of their shared public building, together with disposal of solid wastes, data processing, and property assessment functions.

Two months later a team of business administration specialists re-

cruited from local industry issued a report sponsored by the Delaware
Government Research Foundation, Inc., a du Pont family financed organization, that praised the cost-saving consolidations that had been
achieved.[16] The News-Journal papers interpreted this expert report as
justification for more mergers, but in fact the pendulum was beginning to
swing the other way.[17] As spring approached, the Democrat-controlled city
council balked at the complete merger of the city's park system with that of
the county, and William J. (Woody) McClafferty, Jr., the curmudgeonly
Democrat president of city council, who frequently sparred with the
mayor, was quoted as saying, "I think we'd be better off on our own."
Shortly thereafter, the county council, too, dropped the idea, charging that
McClafferty had created a bad atmosphere.[18]

Actually, the Democrats were not the only ones to resist consolidation. At the height of the merger movement, County Executive Conner
had also publicly opposed total consolidation in favor of merger on a
service-by-service basis. The newspapers might find New Castle County
wastefully overgoverned, but Conner expressed a sentiment widely felt
among suburban residents. With racial tensions still running high, the idea
of political consolidation was unpopular in the suburbs, while the city's
minority groups, believing that they were finally getting some power over
civic affairs, were opposed also. Most people of both parties believed that
overlapping services could be merged and waste eliminated without in-
terfering with the basic structure of either municipal or county government. The frustrated editorial writers at the News-Journal compared this
hesitation over centralization to "the dilemma of the donkey who starved to
death between two bales of hay because he couldn't decide which one to
eat."[19] In a review of 1970 written in January 1971, newsmen admitted that
the merger idea, "a hot item in early 1970—is colder than a week-old
fish."[20]

The merger effort had achieved some of the benefits of consolidation
while preserving the existing layers of government. The county's Department of Parks and Recreation took over responsibility for the city's major
parks, and the county agreed to replace the city's traditional subsidy to the
Wilmington Institute Free Library. In the area of public works, county and
city engineers virtually consolidated their water, sewage, and landfill
operations with a cost-sharing plan whereby both city and suburbs continued to make full use of the city's sewage treatment plant and landfill, but
at less cost to city residents. While the county was thus beginning to
shoulder some traditional urban responsibilities, the state helped the
county by completely absorbing the cost of welfare and the cost of maintaining the county court house—both county functions from colonial days.

To the citizen at large, the two most noticeable results of county reorganization were the reinvigoration of the county police force and the creation of the Department of Planning. From the poorly trained cadre of 20 policemen that Conner's administration inherited, the county government had created a professional force of 75 officers and cadets by 1970.[21] After a few years of sometimes acrimonious debates over territorial rights with the state and city police, the brown-uniformed county policemen became the acknowledged maintainers of law and order along the hundreds of miles of narrow winding suburban streets. Similarly, the reorganization of county government brought to an end the relatively powerless planning and zoning commissions in favor of a consolidated Department of Planning. The new department moved quickly to establish good public relations by publishing a series of attractive, colorfully illustrated, loose-leaf booklets that outlined the department's proposals on future development. Although much of the research for these booklets had been done under the old government, the publication symbolized the vigor of the new department.[22]

These planning documents presupposed the continuation of the rapid growth that had characterized New Castle County for the past 20 years and proclaimed the direction that the department proposed to take. This assessment drew its intellectual force not only from immediate past history but also from Jean Gottmann's provocative book *Megalopolis* (1961), which had described the Boston-Washington corridor as the most vigorous and important among several growing megacities in the United States. If Gottmann's predictions proved true, New Castle County could expect sustained growth as one of the best locations within that expanding conglomoration of industrial and technical economic growth that was expected to form the nucleus of the Northeastern economy of the future. Such expectations went hand in hand with an increased need for careful planning to maintain the proper balance and distance among industrial, residential, recreational, and other competing land uses. To meet this need, the Planning Department recommended that future population growth be focused within the corridor of as yet underutilized land between Route 40 and I-95 in the western end of the county south of Newark. Development would thus be channeled away from the piedmont "chateau country" region northwest of the city to an area just south of the already rapidly growing Wilmington to Newark corridor. In addition to following the existing path of development, the plan emphasized the untapped potential of I-95 as a magnet for housing and services.

Viewed from the perspective of only a little over a decade later, the planning assumptions of the late 1960s appear astonishingly inaccurate. No one anticipated the deceleration of population growth that was revealed by the 1970 and 1980 censuses or the fundamental population shift in the United States from the old industrial states of the Northeast and Midwest to the sunbelt states of the South and Southwest. Between 1960 and 1970, the city of Wilmington lost more than 16 percent of its population, the highest percentage drop in the city's history. Wilmington had contained more than 110,000 people in 1950; by 1970 its population was 80,000. Equally significant, New Castle County was no longer growing at the dramatic rate that had characterized the postwar years. According to the U.S. Census Bureau, the county's population increased only 3.4 percent during the 1960s.[23] This reduction in the rate of population growth increased suburbanites' ability to resist any efforts, whether by government or by private developers, to interfere with their residential environment. In practice this meant that the geographical and historical forces that had always been the controlling influences carving the suburbs into their various income areas continued to be the most significant factors in development. Suburban residents perceived efforts to impose planning concepts on the county as an undesirable infringement upon their rights. No matter what the stated objective of planning might be, the people of the suburbs equated such efforts with the idea of mixing various income groups together, which inevitably would be linked to racial integration. There were no more house bombings such as those in Collins Park in the 1950s, but resistance to residential integration in the late 1960s and early 1970s was no less effective.

By 1970 the older cities of America, such as Wilmington, Delaware, were in the midst of a housing crisis. The Wilmington Housing Authority, then more than thirty years old, owned, in addition to its "projects," numerous individual old houses throughout the city. Some of those it intended to raze, others, to rehabilitate. The concentration of bad housing close to center city made the urban housing problem obvious to anyone who ventured downtown. By contrast, the existence of a housing problem in the county went completely unnoticed. People's perceptions of the county excluded such a possibility, yet according to the report of a citizen housing committee chaired by Mrs. Richard J. Both, in 1971 New Castle faced "not simply a housing crisis, but a housing disaster."[24]

The Both committee report provided the first comprehensive study of housing in New Castle County ever undertaken. Mrs. Both personally was representative of the upper-income residents of Greenville, on the Kennett Pike. She had considerable social prestige as the wife of a high-ranking executive at the Hercules Corporation and as the daughter of a rector of Christ Episcopal Church, Greenville. In the wake of the racial disturbances in Wilmington, some members of Christ Church, including Mrs.

Both, had met to explore ways in which they might meet the needs of Wilmington's poor. After discussion with local officials, the group decided to concentrate its efforts in the neglected area of housing reform.[25] With members of other churches they formed the interdenominational Citizens Housing Alliance of Delaware, with the expectation that the alliance could be the catalyst for new solutions to the housing problem. Possible new departures included the encouragement of low-income housing in the county and the end of red-lining practices, whereby banks refused to grant mortgages in areas that they arbitrarily deemed undesirable. County council president C. Douglass Buck, also of Greenville, a supporter of the group's intentions, appointed Mrs. Both to chair an official county committee to study New Castle County's overall housing needs.

The results of the Both study, made public in 1971, were alarming. The committee discovered that although nearly 60 percent of Wilmington's suburban households received incomes of less than $10,000 a year, very little new housing was being constructed for this group. Furthermore, throughout the county there were pockets of dilapidated housing, the remains of presuburban rural communities and old trolley suburbs. These units were easy to overlook because they were scattered, not concentrated in one area like deteriorated urban housing. Noting the recent decline in housing starts in the county, the Both committee concluded that to meet the needs of its people, county government should request federal funds in order to construct public housing units for low-income residents. They proposed that a county housing authority be created to build the 1,500 units necessary to replace present unfit dwellings. In light of the success of a similar venture in Montgomery County, Maryland, they suggested that the public housing units be spread throughout the county, so that no one area would be stuck with the stigma of low-income housing.[26]

Almost concurrent with the Both report, the Nixon administration offered a recommendation designed to assist the faltering housing industry to find more cost-effective, less environmentally destructive ways of supplying houses for middle-income buyers. In August 1970, President Nixon sent Congress a message based on a study by the White House Council on Environmental Quality that predicted a national ecological disaster unless Americans found a better way to cope with suburban sprawl. The presidential report also deplored the tediousness of homogeneous, cookie-cutter-style, suburban developments. The council suggested that federal policy channel future construction into clusters or planned unit development centers (PUDs) that would cost less money to build and service yet provide more open space than did the traditional half-acre and quarter-acre suburban lot. At about the same time, federal housing officials announced that they would no longer permit city housing authorities to bunch low-income

Trenton Place, a street of late 19th century houses, became the core of "Trinity Vicinity," one of Wilmington's first areas of regentrification during the back to the city movement of the 1960s. *(Photograph by the author)*

housing units in certain areas of a city, a policy that had perpetuated and exacerbated ghetto conditions. Future federal housing grants were to be contingent upon a trade-off, requiring the scattering of low-income housing throughout a city and the region surrounding it.[27]

Although these federal policies were designed to deal with very different problems—a lagging home construction industry, expanding slums, and the overexpansion of public utilities—the typical suburban resident believed that they were all interrelated and all to be resisted. County residents had a history of protesting any new housing construction near their own homes that was either more dense or less costly than their own, regardless of whether good planning concepts were used or not. As the president of the Council of Civic Associations of Brandywine Hundred admitted in a talk to a civic group, the typical suburban resident had no interest in any goals that extended beyond "his picture window."[28] In 1962, for example, residents of Foulkwoods in Brandywine Hundred, who lived on 22,000-foot lots, opposed the proposal to construct a carefully planned superblock adjacent to their development, because each lot was to be only 10,000 square feet. The developer, the most experienced in the area, agreed to increase the lot size on the abutting properties. Residents ignored the proposed good planning concepts and looked only at lot size.[29] Similarly, in 1964 officials of the Alfred I. du Pont School District, representing that same area, appeared at a zoning hearing to protest plans to build apartment complexes in their district because of possible traffic congestion. Other opponents at the same hearing circulated leaflets with a funereal motif: an "In Memoriam" to "the anticipated peaceful passage of a way of life that drew thousands of families to this area of Brandywine Hundred and that was created by the investment of life savings, pride of property appearance and those hundreds of hours of hard but happy work."[30]

Suburban resistance to new planning impeded developers who wished to alter the homogeneous tract style. In 1963 Mill Creek Hundred, west of the Kirkwood Highway, was mostly farmland interspersed with a few scattered custom-built houses. In that year a group of four Wilmington-area builders purchased 1,000 acres in Pike Creek Valley, where they proposed to construct a gigantic new development using the cluster concept. The Pike Creek Valley development was planned to house 12,000 to 15,000 people and to include shopping facilities, schools, and a golf course. Like Columbia, Maryland, and Reston, Virginia, it was to consist of a series of clusters of houses and apartments designed to attract people from different age groups and economic levels.[31] The New Castle County zoning law was not designed for such a concept, however. Founded on the notion of lot size, the zoning requirements specified that all of Pike Creek Valley be zoned for dense habitation to accommodate clusters.

As the controversy deepened it took on the appearance of sparring among socioeconomic groups over questions of public policy, social privilege, and personal life style. The local press supported the developers' plans for Pike Creek Valley. An editorial writer for the *Journal-Every Evening* wrote that "minimum lot area zoning has produced development that is manifestly undesirable; it has encouraged the building of homogeneous communities, each home with its specified plot of ground (and no public open space thereby) and little variety among the houses." The editor noted that this type of zoning was wasteful of land, a resource that was "rapidly becoming scarce and expensive in these parts."[32] But the Polly Drummond Civic Association, near to the proposed development, announced its "vigorous opposition" to the high-density zoning request.[33] The civic association members liked their homogeneous neighborhoods zoned to keep out people less economically well-off than themselves. Middle-class suburbanites accused the well-to-do housing reformers, including the management of the News-Journal papers, of hypocrisy, because Greenville's elite were maintaining chateau country as a low-density area surreptitiously by preventing the construction of sewer lines that would have permitted more intense development. Eventually the builders and their opponents reach a compromise on Pike Creek Valley that permitted the construction of some apartments and townhouses and set some areas aside for traditional detached houses.[34] Interestingly, when the development began in the 1960s the detached houses predominated, but in the much tighter, more expensive building market of the 1970s, the builders switched exclusively to townhouses. By the late 1960s, construction was already moving away from free-standing homes, and the biggest construction boom in New Castle County during this time was in so-called "luxury" apartment complexes. These developments attracted people who did not want to devote most of their time and money to home and yard care. The new apartment styles featured wall-to-wall carpets, swimming pools, balconies, and similar accoutrements that appealed to young marrieds, the single "Mustang" set and older "empty-nester" couples.

Into this already suspicious suburban environment came Governor Russell Peterson's announcement in December 1969 that he had offered the federal government one hundred acres of state-owned land adjacent to the Ferris correctional institution, west of the city, for "Operation Breakthrough," an experimental housing project. There the federal Department of Housing and Urban Development proposed to construct clusters of multifamily townhouses using new, more efficient techniques and less costly materials. HUD had selected the Ferris site as one of only eight throughout the United States, and an enthusiastic Governor Peterson proudly touted Delaware's part in this demonstration of the "Nixon Administration's determination to end the severe housing shortage."[35] Although Operation Breakthrough was not designed to appeal to low-income families, local residents reacted as if the newcomers would be a scourge. The News-Journal, again sympathetic to experimental housing, published plans showing attractive, imaginatively designed modern townhouses, but federal housing projects had a negative, low-income image, and the local residents feared the type of people the development might attract.[36] Opponents brought suit against the state to prevent the governor from transferring the land in question to the federal government. Public meetings on Operation Breakthrough degenerated into confrontations between government officials and irate citizens. At one such meeting, a group calling themselves the Taxpayers' Revolt accused Governor Peterson, County Executive Conner and County Council President Buck of being on the take from HUD, to which Buck responded, "Which of you people out there are the revolting taxpayers?"[37] Buck was so annoyed by the negative attitudes expressed by these people that he threatened to introduce legislation in county council to block all new construction in the county until utility expansion could catch up. "If Greater Wilmington cannot develop and grow in an orderly manner it will continue to deteriorate from the inside out," Buck warned. Quoting from the Both committee report, he reminded critics of housing reform that "there are already 1,500 delapidated housing units and 5,000 substandard units in the county outside the city, so that the housing crisis has already leaped the city line."[38] But the suburbanites won their fight when HUD decided that if Delawareans did not want Breakthrough, the federal program could go elsewhere.

Similar opposition frustrated efforts to build low-income public housing in the county. Opponents postponed the creation of a county housing authority for over a year by blocking passage of a county building code, which was required for federally assisted financing. Once that hurdle was passed, the county administration hired Leon Weiner, who had a reputation as the most innovative, socially liberal developer in the region, to build the first projects. Weiner was to work with the county planner to locate sites and to construct low-income housing on the turnkey plan, whereby the private builder would turn over the finished buildings to the county government. Weiner identified three sites in various parts of the county, but in each case residents' objections killed his plans.[39] Dudley Finch, the director of the Wilmington Housing Authority and no stranger to scenes of acrimonious public debate, called one of the meetings with suburbanites the "most vicious" he had ever attended.[40] Only when Weiner had failed did officials create a county housing authority in 1972. The new authority aimed to construct hundreds of units, as outlined in the recommendations of the Both Report, and promised to spread the units throughout the county, including the high-income Greenville area.[41] But whenever specific sites were named, protesters came out of the woodwork in force. As Bill Conner characterized it, "time after time we put our toe in the water and the crab would grab it."[42]

The Wilmington area was only a microcosm of a national public policy problem. HUD secretary George Romney had tried to get away from his department's former policy of locating-low income housing in areas that were already overflowing with low-income people. The disastrous Pruitt-Igoe highrise in St. Louis, Missouri, where alienated ghetto residents had nearly destroyed the building from the inside had come to symbolize the futility of that approach. But HUD's efforts to change this policy met everywhere with the same type of opposition that characterized its reception in New Castle County. The issue of whether the federal government should insist on politically unpalatable scattered sites or allow the old policy to prevail was finally fought out within the Nixon cabinet between Secretary Romney and Attorney General John Mitchell. Not surprisingly, President Nixon sided with Mitchell. In June 1971 the president announced that "a municipality that does not want federally assisted housing should not have it imposed from Washington by bureaucratic fiat."[43] Federal policy would no longer attempt to integrate income level, the president said, although the government could continue to encourage racial integration within each income level. Because most minority people were poor, this policy meant that in practice there could be little integration.

Born in the midst of this policy, the New Castle County Housing Authority was destined for a short and unproductive life. The authority never built any public housing units, and in the mid-1970s its assets, mostly a few rental properties in communities just south of the city adjacent to low-income Southbridge, were absorbed into the county's Department of Community Development and Housing.

Local housing reformers turned to one other possible ally in their struggle to provide low-income people with good housing in the county: the Woodlawn Trustees, Inc. Woodlawn Trustees was the real-estate company that the Quaker philanthropist William Poole Bancroft, son of the founder of the Bancroft Mills, had created in 1901. Called the "Father of the Wilmington Park System," because his timely gift of parkland in the 1880s had begun the city's excellent system of parks, Bancroft expected his real-estate company to help realize his goal of providing the Wilmington area with parks to accompany its residential development. Although the Woodlawn Company's form was that of a profit-making organization and Bancroft did intend that it should make money, the purpose of this money-making was to permit the company to acquire additional parkland for Wilmington.[44] Early in its history, the company undertook two very different kinds of residential development. On its land abutting Rockford Park in the Highlands section of Wilmington, the company laid out generous lots, suitable for expensive houses to be sold at high prices. Meanwhile along

Union Street, in a vicinity toward which working-class housing was already moving, the company built nearly 400 row houses for rent to low-income working families. Some of the income from these operations went to a variety of local charities, including hospitals, homes for the aged, and the public library, but most of the income was used to purchase farm lands in the Brandywine Valley north of the city, between the Brandywine River and the Concord Pike.[45]

When Mr. Bancroft began buying land in Brandywine Hundred, he envisioned that the city would eventually expand to encompass his purchases. Most of the land he was buying would presumably become parkland; some portion of it might be used for residential purposes, as in his city real-estate operations. But at his death in 1928, Bancroft's real-estate purchases in Brandywine Hundred had not progressed to a point where his specific intentions were clear. Ten years before, the Woodlawn Company had been reorganized as Woodlawn Trustees, Inc., which made the company exempt from federal taxes and provided for continuity after its founder's death. In the years that followed, the trustees, including Bancroft's descendants and associates, not all necessarily Quakers, continued to buy land in Brandywine Hundred. During the Depression decade the trustees sold their first suburban lots for an upper-income development called Alapocas, adjacent to the new Friends School. In the 1950s, after the construction of Fairfax had opened the east side of the Concord Pike to intense development of middle-income houses, the trustees began to sell their lands on the west side of the pike. The land there is divided into two distinct topographical sections. A rocky wooded slope rises from the Brandywine River to a flat plain along which runs the Concord Pike. The trustees planned to maintain the slope as parkland and to sell residential lots on the plain. In the fashion of other suburban development companies, they partitioned their land into subdivisions, each with its own name and system of curvilinear roadways. Land along the west side of the Concord Pike had a natural setting capable of attracting more affluent buyers than those who settled in most other parts of Brandywine Hundred. In laying out the lots, therefore, the trustees followed the same pattern of appealing to upper-middle-income buyers that their company had pursued in its earlier development of the Rockford Park area and Alapocas.[46] None of the Woodlawn lands north of the city were developed as working-class housing.

In the 1960s social activist members of the Wilmington Friends Meeting drew public attention to the policies that Woodlawn Trustees were pursuing. Opponents noted that in his lifetime William Bancroft had devoted considerable attention to the construction of lower-income rental housing. They were disturbed that the trustees were running the company's affairs as a private business rather than as a philanthropic undertaking. In 1963 some members of the meeting questioned Woodlawn Trustees' tax-exempt status and criticized the trustees' policy of maintaining "insured compatibility" of income level and race within their developments. Again in 1965 Quakers picketed the offices of Woodlawn Trustees carrying signs denouncing the company as a "twentieth-century feudal lord,"[47] and in 1969 a band of Quakers held a religious vigil in front of the Alapocas home of Philip G. Rhoads, chairman of Woodlawn Trustees.[48]

Housing reformers found the trustees to be impervious to their complaints and suggestions. Bancroft's written and oral legacy was ambiguous, and the trustees chose to interpret their trust in a conservative fashion. They pointed to statements by William Bancroft to the effect that the trust was not intended to assist a variety of philanthropic aims but rather to achieve one principal goal, the preservation of woodland for public use along the Brandywine. They claimed, on the basis of their experience in real estate, that selling large, expensive lots would raise more money for additional land purchases than would the more intense division of the land for less costly housing. Nor did the trustees feel justified in experimenting with intermixing housing for different income levels, or different races. In this regard their policy was in accord with a survey in which residents of Sharpley, a Woodlawn development, had voted two to one against the statement: "I believe that any family of good character, able to buy a home in Sharpley, should be allowed to do so."[49]

In 1972 the Philadelphia Yearly Meeting attempted to adjudicate the dispute. A Quaker committee of inquiry found that the trustees had indeed put commercial values ahead of social ideals and recommended that Woodlawn Trustees build low-income housing on some of its remaining land in Brandywine Hundred. This the trustees refused to do. The following year Mrs. William Henry du Pont offered to buy a large old house on Woodlawn's Brandywine Hundred land to be a home for neglected children. Again the trustees refused, because, they said, such a use was incompatible with nearby upper-middle-class homes. Mrs. du Pont charged the trustees with racial discrimination and brought suit, but the trustees prevailed when she decided to abort her action and purchased land in Greenville instead.[50] Because Woodlawn Trustees, Inc., refused to bow to these pressures, another potential way to break the class- and race-segregated housing patterns of New Castle County was lost.

Even in the early 1970s, therefore, there was much reason to believe that the pattern would continue whereby Wilmington's population became progressively more poor and black while the suburbs remained white and affluent. Government had proven unequal to the task of countering this

Downtown Wilmington in the mid 1970s showing the reconstruction of the east side residential area in the foreground still separated from the Market Street area by a no-man's land of stripped landscape along Walnut Street, French Street, and King Street. (*Courtesy of the Historical Society of Delaware*)

trend, and to judge by the lengthy petulant opposition that had plagued proponents of fair housing legislation and the reluctance of most land developers and suburban residents to violate the doctrine of social compatibility, there was little reason to imagine that change might be on the horizon. Social compatibility, the euphemism for maintaining homogeneous ghettos based on race and income level, prevailed in the city as well as in the suburbs. The planning for Wilmington's Model Cities neighborhood in west center city, for example, was based on the assumption that the area would continue to be a low-income minority residential neighborhood far into the future. In fact, there were only a few areas in Wilmington, mostly in the Pennsylvania Avenue section, that did not appear to be becoming low-income minority neighborhoods. Surprisingly, however, other forces were already quietly at work to modify, if not reverse, this seemingly overpowering trend.

In the 1950s there was virtually no part of the city that seemed capable of holding its value as desirable residential real estate. Large, expensive houses of the past were torn down to make parking lots, or submitted to the luckier fate of being transformed into doctors' offices or apartments. Houses on Broom Street near Pennsylvania Avenue, an area that as recently as the 1920s had been among the most prestigious in the city, had become "white elephants," undesirable to those wealthy enough to purchase and maintain them. In center city there were abandoned houses of every size, including some formerly elegant mansions. Neither city government nor private sources could justify the cost of restoring this growing number of vacant buildings. The headline "Parking Lot to Replace Old Landmark" described a common occurrence.[51]

Then, in the mid-1960s, against all odds, a new, more optimistic attitude toward city living began to grow, at first slowly, then with increasing vigor, until by the 1970s one could truly speak of the back to the city movement as a potent force among the many dynamic influences that make up the real-estate market. It is impossible to single out any one cause as the most important in beginning or sustaining this trend. Nonetheless, in the 1960s and early 1970s, some prospective house-buyers caught on to the fact that urban houses were far cheaper than their equivalents in the suburbs, that many were often within walking distance to the major downtown office buildings, and that, having smaller yards than suburban houses, they required less effort to maintain. But all of these factors had been equally true in the 1940s and 1950s, when the suburban boom wreaked havoc with urban real-estate values. Nor was there a dramatic change in race relations during this interval. If anything, racial tensions and fears were more powerful in the late 1960s than earlier, and black penetration of formerly all-white neighborhoods was much greater. Some of the change resulted from disillusionment with suburban living or resulted from individual efforts to make a statement about human brotherhood during tense times, but the most significant new factors appear to have been the rising cost of suburban real estate and a growing aesthetic movement throughout the United States that favored architectural preservation.

Before the 1960s concern about the preservation of our architectural heritage had been confined to a tiny elitist movement that aimed at saving a few "significant" structures, such as colonial churches, public buildings, and the homes of historic figures. It is ironic to recall that the prevalent attitudes of the late nineteenth and early twentieth century—that period whose buildings preservationists now seek to protect—were hostile to the idea of preservation. At that time to be modern, or, as they then phrased it, to be "up-to-date," was the most desirable of conditions. Metaphors from Darwin's theory of evolution ruled cities as well as the animal kingdom. The old had to give way to the new; it was the law of life. A city filled with old buildings was to be pitied; it was in the doldrums. Take, for example, local attitudes toward the disposition of Wilmington's Old Town Hall in 1916 when the City-County Building was nearing completion. Old Town Hall was a classic federal-period building with the elegant windows, brickwork, and proportions commonly found in the public buildings of the 1790s. The structure had been the seat of Wilmington's government for over a century. A great deal of the city's history had been enacted within its walls. And yet in 1916 many voices called for the demolition of the building. The *Every Evening* favored preserving the Town Hall as a historic monument, but the *Sunday Star*'s editor admonished city council not to indulge in such "sentiment."[52] A Market Street merchant wrote to the *Star* in the same vein. Just because the building was old and had received famous men did not make it "historic." "If all the halls, hotels, meeting rooms or barracks in the United States are called historical . . . we would have nothing but old shacks in the heart of cities." "Where are the men who believe in a beautiful Wilmington, in a modern city?" he asked. "Everything old shall go and make room for newer ideas. According to the rule of nature the old must make way for the young . . . it is time that Wilmington awakens from its old fashioned, dreamy ways, and becomes a wide-awake city with up-to-date ideas."[53] A similar view was expressed by another writer who said that "history is alright in its place, but graveyards and old city halls are certainly out of place on the main business street."[54] Ultimately, the Historical Society of Delaware purchased the Old Town Hall, and the building is currently in far better condition than are the stores owned by its former opponents, but clearly the spirit of preservation did not run deep in the Wilmington of 1916.

If the popular attitude toward a city landmark was so negative, how much less were early twentieth-century people inclined toward sentimental feelings regarding mere houses. No matter how old, intricately decorated, or unusual a house might be, those who could afford to, preferred a new one instead. Then, in the 1960s, perceptions underwent a transition, largely because of the example of successful restoration in Washington's Georgetown and Philadelphia's Society Hill, both of which became attractive residential enclaves preserving a historical flavor. Historical restoration became a chic do-it-yourself hobby for professional people who wished to recreate the urban environment of the remote past. The Society Hill restoration was particularly pertinent to Wilmington because of the proximity of Philadelphia and because the Society Hill landscape bore a striking resemblance to what was left of Wilmington's oldest residential neighborhoods.[55]

In the years following World War II, while Wilmington's leaders had been struggling to reverse their city's decline, Philadelphia was experiencing a similar deterioration, yet one modified by the signs of a significant renaissance. During the 1950s Philadelphia's reform mayors Joseph Clark and Richardson Dilworth undertook a large-scale renewal of their city's central business district, but government-initiated renewal efforts failed to stem the decline of the principal downtown retail district along Market Street. In Wilmington downtown merchants responded to similar problems by establishing branch stores in suburban malls. Philadelphia's merchants did the same, but their investments in center city real estate were more substantial than were those of Wilmington's merchants. Furthermore, the big city's major retailers and owners of retailing real estate had more clout in their city than did their counterparts in Wilmington. One such real-estate financier, Albert M. Greenfield, a self-made multimillionaire, made the restoration of his boyhood neighborhood in the Society Hill section near Independence Hall and the Market Street retailing district his personal crusade. With his skills, knowledge, and money, Greenfield convinced public and private powers that the health of Philadelphia's center core depended on the salvation of Society Hill as a residential neighborhood, and by the mid-1960s this once deteriorated section was well on its way to becoming a national showplace of successful renewal.[56] The entire area was declared a historic site, and private home owners, thus assured of the area's upward direction, poured millions of dollars into restoring and remodeling old houses. Buildings too far decayed to be saved were razed and replaced with rows of townhouses with modern facades designed to blend with the traditional architecture around them. Owners decorated the exteriors of their houses with elements that became the symbols of the back to the city movement: gas lights, brass door knockers, and molded iron insurance plates.

The dramatic success of Society Hill was bound to have some effect on Wilmington, but the smaller city had no one comparable to Greenfield to spark such a movement there. In fact, Wilmington's bankers and real-estate brokers had far less reason to preserve downtown real-estate values than did those in Philadelphia, because there were no large, costly department stores in the smaller city's business district. Furthermore GWDC, the major force behind renewal in Wilmington, was interested in modernizing the city's downtown with new office buildings not in preserving or restoring its past architecture. In Wilmington the back to the city movement initially had to depend on the scattered actions of a few individual house buyers. In 1964 the local press picked up on the story of the Gunther family, who had left the suburbs to buy a rowhouse on Wawaset Street fronting on Brandywine Park. Their investment spearheaded the restoration of other houses in the row, where, as Mr. Gunther told the reporter, his view of the Brandywine "would cost a fortune in any other city. . . ."[57] Two years later another couple attracted similar attention when they moved into a house built in 1885 on Trenton Place, in the northern part of west center city. "Romance Returns to Dying Street" the headlines read, while the story went on to describe how Charles B. Reeder, a Du Pont Company economist, and his wife, a real-estate broker, had abandoned the suburbs in order to convert a city house into a "Georgetown-style townhouse."[58] The Gunthers and the Reeders were successful trend setters and soon both the Wawaset Street area and nearby "Happy Valley," also facing the Brandywine, and the region around Trenton Place, called "Trinity Vicinity," experienced real-estate booms. Gas lights and brass knockers were not slow to follow.

The back to the city movement signaled a new aesthetic spirit in America that looked at cities in a very different way from that of the preceding years. In the 1950s it was commonly believed that cities had to be remade by introducing downtown freeways, parking buildings, and massive urban renewal efforts if they were to become competitive with the attractions of cheap, uncluttered land in the rapidly growing suburbs. In Wilmington, as elsewhere in the nation, the results of this policy had been disappointing. By 1970 critics were demanding that urban leaders stop trying to compete with the suburbs and get back to doing those things that cities could do best.

Cities had unique features that were not being appreciated or utilized. Originally built for pedestrians, their densely packed space offered varied architecture, activities, and types of people, and they were the traditional center for culture and entertainment. Society Hill and similar residential showcases were only part of a new urban ambiance that also included such restorations as San Francisco's Giardelli Square, where nineteenth-century industrial buildings were transformed into eye-catching shops and restaurants.

The restoration spirit first affected Wilmington's policy-makers during the mayoralty of Harry Haskell, when preservationists frustrated the mayor's efforts to construct a large interior shopping mall building on King Street immediately south of the new Civic Center. The shopping mall would have completed the urban renewal plan begun with the Civic Center which was intended to link the renewed Poplar Street residential area with the city's downtown by means of a corridor of modern construction. For various reasons the mall was never built. First, preservationists succeeded in preventing the demolition of Wilmington's 1841 Customs

House, one of the buildings that stood on the land to be redeveloped. Then other serious problems interfered with the plan. Developers made clear that they would not invest in the mall unless the city provided a large parking building and the state constructed a spur linking the mall with I-95. Since these improvements required federal funds and could be neither promised nor supplied quickly, would-be mall builders shied away from the downtown mall, and the developer who had shown the most interest eventually built a regional mall on vacant land southwest of the city on I-95, which precluded the construction of another in the city. In the meantime the city had gone ahead with the demolition of the entire six-block area, save the old Customs House.

Wilmington's plans for a downtown shopping mall coincided with the appearance of a new trend in urban planning that discarded the concept of recreating suburban-style structures in the city in favor of the adaptive use of existing structures to create a peculiarly urban environment. In light of the successful restorations of old shopping areas during the 1970s in other cities, such as Savannah's waterfront, Boston's Quincy Market, and Baltimore's Inner Harbor, one is tempted to condemn as shortsighted the decision made in the 1960s to tear down blocks of old buildings, many in good condition, along the east side of King Street to accommodate the Civic Center and the shopping mall project. Destruction for the latter project, since it was never built, is particularly difficult to justify in retrospect. Caught between two eras in urban development, Wilmington managed to lose out on both.

The lingering demise of the mall project provided the opportunity for a plan more in keeping with the preservationists' approach to urban renewal to come to the fore in the form of another Haskell administration project, the conversion of Market Street into a pedestrian mall. Pedestrian malls have been a common means used to rejuvenate downtown shopping streets, particularly in middle-sized American cities. They are attractive to city planners and politicians, because they create a shopping environment designed for pedestrians at relatively little cost. The city merely closes off its primary shopping street to automotive traffic and installs some plantings, park benches, attractive lighting and perhaps areas of plexiglass-covered archways to shield walkers from the rain. In 1972 when Allentown, Pennsylvania, was building its Main Street Mall, Wilmington's planners paid close attention. In the fall election of that year, Thomas Maloney, a young city councilman who was running against Haskell in the mayoralty election, visited Allentown. Inspired by what he saw there, Maloney adopted the Market Street Mall in mid-planning and made it his own. In November Maloney defeated Haskell, or, more accurately, the city returned to its normal Democratic allegiance. But no matter which candidate had won, the Market Street Mall would have gone forward.

Only eight years out of college when he ran for mayor, Tom Maloney had already demonstrated a flair for dramatic public-relations exercises that was uncommon in the usually mundane world of Wilmington politics. Maloney first made local headlines in 1968, when his party tried to revoke a promise to run him for city council. So many Maloney supporters called the city government that they broke the telephone switchboard, while a group of girls paraded in front of City Hall bearing signs that read "Whatever Happened to Tom Maloney?"[59] The Democrats quickly restored Maloney to the ticket, and he went on to become the most articulate critic of the Haskell administration on the Democratic-controlled council.

Actually, Maloney and Haskell had much in common. They associated with the liberal wings of their respective parties and were committed to the creation of a professionally competent city administration. But where Haskell, the well-to-do gentleman politician, had emphasized large-scale, costly projects such as the enclosed mall on King Street, Maloney was more inhibited, because of the city's declining resources. Consequently he tried to get the maximum effect from the minimum expenditure. This change in approach was by no means entirely attributable to background or political style, for by 1973, when Maloney took office, it was obvious as it had not been before, that the city's income, even with the wage tax and the county's assumption of some former city functions, was still barely adequate to maintain existing services.[60] Haskell had installed the professional personnel who first perceived the financial plight that the Maloney administration faced. Thus, the trend of the times, the necessities of public finance, and the new mayor's talent for clever public relations all pointed to a more preservationist approach to solving urban problems.

In planning the Market Street Mall, the Maloney administration was fortunate in finding that two private restoration projects were already underway that could lend distinction and glamour to Market Street's drab storefronts. In 1972 a group called the Delaware Ethnic Studies and Cultural Center was organized by George Whiteside III, a local architect. Whiteside hoped to save several eighteenth-century houses located in parts of the city where the urban renewal bulldozers were then at work and convert them to new uses as the headquarters for his organization's activities. These houses, including two duplexes, had once been the homes of artisans and wage earners. In the days when preservationists cared only for important landmarks these houses would have been ignored, because they had neither high style features nor famous inhabitants, but according to the new canons of the preservationist movement, their very commonness

Thomas C. Maloney in conversation with a citizen on Market Street Mall during his mayoralty, 1973–1977. *(Courtesy of the Mayor's Office, City of Wilmington)*

made them all the more historically significant. With Whiteside's help the Ethnic Studies and Cultural Center laid plans to move several of these buildings from their original locations to form a historical enclave in the oldest part of the east side, near the Christina River adjacent to Old Swedes Church. Envisioned as a center where various ethnic groups could hold activities such as fairs, demonstrations, exhibits, and meetings, the enclave would also radiate stability and progress throughout the recently deci- mated east side. The concept attracted support from several ethnic orga- nizations, and the Wilmington Housing Authority agreed to underwrite some of the costs involved in relocating the houses, but the project re- mained far short of the funds necessary to get started. When the Ethnic Studies and Cultural Center approached the Maloney administration for help, plans for the mall were well underway. The mayor and his city planner, Patricia Schramm, recognized the potential in such a plan, but their price for helping was changing the location of the historic enclave from Old Swedes Church to Market Street and associating it with a more long-standing and financially sound institution, the Historical Society of Delaware.[61]

As remade by Maloney, the enclave, named Willingtown Square to honor a Wilmington founder, was located across Market Street from the Historical Society's headquarters at Old Town Hall between 5th and 6th streets. As part of the Market Street revitalization the project received substantial federal urban renewal funds and became a special feature of Wilmington's bicentennial celebration.

In Willingtown Square Maloney had found an anchor for the lower end of the mall, but the city's most noteworthy preservation coup had been completed several years earlier in the more significant retail block of Market Street between 8th and 9th streets. There, buried behind commercial false fronts and a gaudy movie marquee, stood the Victorian cast-iron facade of the Grand Opera House, built by the Masonic Order in 1871. The Grand had been Wilmington's premier theater in the late nineteenth century, when many famous troupes played there. But with the rise of vaudeville and motion pictures, the Grand fell behind and slumped into being a third-rate movie house. Over the years the old theater had become a battered remnant of its initial grandeur, its painted ceiling lost to view behind a false dropped ceiling, its stage obscured by a movie screen, its walls covered by faded red velvet curtains. Together with other downtown movie houses, the Grand steadily lost customers and finally closed its doors in the late 1960s. Meanwhile, however, the Greater Wilmington Development Corporation, having abandoned their plan to include a city auditorium in the new civic center as too costly, was casting about for an alternative way to provide the city with a cultural center. At the same time, the Wilmington Opera Society was searching for a new stage for their biannual productions.[62] Both groups fastened their gaze upon the Grand, and the derelict theater suddenly became the object of attention by the press and by other groups and individuals eager to improve Wilmington's anemic cultural life and to restore the city's most important surviving late-nineteenth-century building.

On 22 December 1971, less than three years after National Guard patrols had been withdrawn from the streets of Wilmington, the Grand was the scene of a remarkable event. Exactly one hundred years to the day after the concert and ball that had inaugurated the old theater, the city celebrated its proposed restoration with a gala show. The packed house included members of the local chapter of the Victorian Society, a preservation group, some of whom came attired in the evening dress of a century before. Horse-drawn carriages brought Mayor Haskell, Governor Peterson and other dignitaries to the front of the opera house. The city's social

leaders, arrayed in black ties and ball gowns, sat in the old theater alongside less formally dressed Wilmingtonians to watch a succession of per-
formers representing every ethnic group, theatrical company, and musical
ensemble in the community. At the end everyone stood and toasted the
restoration of the Grand. Never had any local enterprise begun with such
high hopes and widespread support.

The restoration of the Grand Opera House was a Cinderella story, the
most spectacularly successful preservation effort in Wilmington's history.
There were over 3,600 contributors, including major local foundations,
while the state, in addition to providing monetary support, declared the
building to be Delaware's Center for the Performing Arts.[63] The Grand was
the major focal point for Wilmington's bicentennial celebration; it was also
a key element in Mayor Maloney's mall project. The restoration revealed a
remarkably beautiful building both inside and out, and its restoration has
attracted a great variety of top flight talent to Wilmington. Leontyne Price
was the performer on 20 November 1974, when the completed facade was
lit for the first time, and Eugene Ormandy and the Philadelphia Orchestra
inaugurated an important stage of the interior restoration.

For all these successes, however, the Grand, Willingtown Square,
and the mall have had a modest impact on Market Street. The mall has
brought a certain amount of excitement and urbanity to the city's principal
shopping street, but, in spite of the new outdoor cafes, boarded-up storefronts are still common, and in 1979 the street's largest retailer, Wilmington Dry Goods, closed its doors and shifted its operations to the suburbs.
Nearly a decade after the pedestrian mall was completed, Market Street
was still dependent on the lunchtime trade of office workers to stay alive as
a retail center.

The search for cheaper solutions to urban problems resulted from a
reduction in federal aid. In the Great Society days of the Johnson administration, the federal government had committed great sums toward improving the lives of city dwellers, especially the poor. But as the 1970s opened,
the Nixon administration was determined to cut back on the Great Society
programs, because they were both costly and politically unpalatable. Most
particularly, the failure of the Johnson administration's highly touted experimental Model Cities Program to bring rapid, dramatic improvements
in city life prompted Nixon's HUD administrators to phase out such costly
experiments. Wilmington's Mayor Haskell was among the most vocal
advocates of the Nixon era panacea, revenue sharing, a policy of returning
money and decision making to the local communities. The hostility of local
governments to programs controlled from Washington was partly attributable to frustrations and disappointments growing out of Model Cities, a
program whose broad ambitions had masked many ambiguities. Conceived

in 1966 to coordinate and improve public services for low-income neighborhoods, Model Cities was designed to blend participation by local residents with control by city governments. In retrospect it has become clear that the notion that the federal bureaucracy could impose a new local power structure on city governments was ill conceived. The poor, heretofore excluded from community power, had neither the skills nor the means to influence city governments.[64]

Wilmington's unsatisfying experience with Model Cities was typical. The program concentrated on the city's troubled west center city, site of the rioting of 1968, an area that was already being served by a social program funded by GWDC called the West Center City Neighborhood Association. In 1969, the year in which the Model Cities program was established in west Wilmington, a team from the University of Delaware's Division of Urban Affairs had evaluated the effectiveness of GWDC's neighborhood program. Their report previewed the types of problems that later plagued Model Cities. C. Harold Brown, the demographer who wrote the study, admitted at the outset that dealing with poor people in a blighted neighborhood was fraught with difficulty. The people were discouraged, hard to reach, and very mobile. The GWDC program attempted to reach these people and to give them opportunities to discuss and define their own needs. According to Brown this policy had led to two problems: it encouraged the false belief that to discuss the complex problems afflicting the poor was in itself somehow to solve these problems, and it clouded over the real lines of authority in decision making. The demographer concluded that "there is no question but that Wilmington still has a great many social pathologies and people with problems. The neighborhood service centers hold great promise as part of a total delivery system, but the author is just not sure whether the people of Greater Wilmington are willing to make the commitment necessary to honestly deal with these problems."[65] GWDC had intended its neighborhood program as an experiment, a demonstration of what could be done to improve life in blighted areas of the city. No one except the federal government had the wealth to follow upon on such demonstrations with long-term assistance. But Model Cities proved to be just as short-lived as the GWDC program, and just as subject to ambiguities in its leadership and goals.

One of Harry Haskell's first acts as mayor was the appointment of staff members to administer Wilmington's Model Cities planning grant. Haskell sensibly made the program an extension of the work already done by GWDC. As director of Model Cities he chose William Myers, a black native Wilmingtonian and graduate of Lincoln University, who was director of GWDC's West Center City Neighborhood Association. In announcing his choice to a neighborhood group gathered in West Presbyterian

Church, the mayor remarked "You folks have the ball and I'm giving it to you. There is no substitute for local leadership."[66] But Haskell was unable to fulfill this promise, for as his chief aide Allan Rusten recalls, "the federal government was publicly saying 'this will be a partnership between city government and the neighborhood.' Then privately they said, 'the mayor is responsible, if any money is misspent it's your fault.'"[67]

In Wilmington, as elsewhere, Model Cities developed into a bureaucratic muddle. Wilmington got $1.7 million a year, roughly one-half of which went to salaries to its largely ill-prepared, poorly supervised, uncoordinated staff. Constant disagreements between the mayor and the neighborhood council led to a revolving door of directors and council presidents. After an initial period marked by what Rusten perceived as a "hodgepodge of ideas without any kind of overall plan," Model Cities did focus on a few specific programs, such as the creation of a new bus route to serve the area, housing rehabilitation, and a motivational center for high-school dropouts. That some of these were mismanaged and wasteful was hardly surprising in the prevailing atmosphere of poor organization and bad faith.[68] By early 1972 the Nixon administration was phasing out Model Cities and placing its more successful components under other jurisdictions. HUD officials told Mayor Haskell that Wilmington's had been "one of the more successful" Model Cities programs, and the mayor grandly declared that it had been "a gamble I would take again."[69] But the fact was that federal funding for urban programs was being cut, and government-sponsored efforts to include residents of the target neighborhoods in the planning and implementation of such programs were being phased out also. As the mayor saw it, however, the council had not been a truly democratic body but was instead misused by a few aggressive residents for their own ends. Throughout the United States, mayors and city administrators were relieved to be free of federal bureaucracy coupled with the demands made by the neighborhood councils that Model Cities had spawned. From the viewpoint of residents of Wilmington's west center city, Model Cities had offered hope, a means to climb back from the devastation of the 1968 riots. Their hope went largely unfulfilled. The difficulties that demographer Brown had found in GWDC's neighborhood program had proved to be even more pronounced when subject to administration from Washington.

When Tom Maloney became mayor he faced the problem of keeping up the momentum of urban progress in an era of reduced resources for social programs. There was no federal program to replace Model Cities. Locally, GWDC had lost its desire to fund social programs after the WYEAC debacle. Mayor Maloney found it much easier to maintain prog-

The Grand Opera House built in 1871 and restored a century later, an anchor of the Market Street Mall. *(Courtesy of the City of Wilmington, Department of Planning)*

ress in construction projects than in social projects. The Market Street Mall was one example of Maloney's policy. Urban homesteading was another.

In 1973, in the face of cutbacks in HUD's financing of Wilmington's housing rehabilitation program, the mayor announced a new homesteading plan under which the city would virtually give away vacant houses to people who could promise to rehabilitate them within a reasonable period of time. It was estimated that there were 1,500 vacant houses in Wilmington; some were owned by the federal government because of FHA mortgage foreclosures, but most had become the city's property when slumlords forfeited them for failure to pay property taxes.[70] Homesteading was an appealing idea that generated a great deal of publicity. Wilmington was only one of a number of cities that tried it, but because the Wilmington program was the first in the nation to be implemented, it brought special attention to the city and to its mayor.

The program was often misunderstood. It was not a substitute for federal housing subsidies. Federally funded rehabilitation turned substandard and derelict buildings into acceptable properties that the Wilmington Housing Authority could rent to low-income tenants. Homesteading, by contrast, was aimed at making people home owners. The house they bought might cost only one dollar, but to make it livable would cost them approximately $9,000. Homesteading, then, was not for the desperately poor but for people who could qualify for a rather hefty bank loan. As such, homesteading could play a useful role in a comprehensive effort aimed at revitalizing Wilmington, but by itself it could never restore the city's hundreds of abandoned houses.[71] The homesteading program typified the general strategy of the Maloney administration, which was to preserve the semblance of momentum in the city in spite of sharply declining resources.

From the mid-1960s to the mid-1970s, thanks to the leadership of three very different but capable mayors, Wilmington fought back against decline. In spite of the declining tax base, the wage tax helped the city to maintain services. Beyond everyday services, however, Wilmington had to depend upon the federal government for money. The creation of the new county government unburdened the city of some expenses, and the back to the city movement slowly reversed the powerful trends of the 1950s and 1960s toward urban decay and racial and income segregation within city and suburbs. Had these been the only influences upon events, one could be justified in concluding that the city and its suburbs had reached a *modus vivendi* and were approaching a state of equilibrium and might achieve even greater cooperation in the future, but two other major influences intruded during the 1970s that made it impossible to end the distrust and competition that have marked the urban-suburban relationship since the 1950s. The decision of the Wilmington Medical Center to relocate its major hospital outside the city caused much disruption. The most serious and pervasive issue dividing city and suburbs, however, was that of busing to desegregate city and suburban schools.

The issue of interdistrict desegregation has a long and complex history that grows out of many of the themes already examined in this book. In 1954, when the U.S. Supreme Court heard *Brown* v. *the Board of Education of Topeka, Kansas, et. al.*, a case that included several suits in New Castle County, the court declared that racially separate school systems were inherently unequal. In much of Delaware, as throughout the South, the reaction of whites to the Brown decision was publicly hostile. In the rural area of Delaware, south of the Chesapeake and Delaware Canal, the black population was spread out roughly equally in tiny back-street enclaves within each town and farm region. There, whites stubbornly resisted efforts to integrate the schools for more than a decade, but when integration was finally achieved each school district had similar proportions of black and white students: roughly 20 percent black to 80 percent white in each district.

In the Wilmington area, by contrast, suburbanization had already modified population patterns so that most black people lived not only in the city or immediately south of it, but within segregated enclaves within the city. As we have seen, in 1954 the Wilmington Board of Education led the state in declaring its abandonment of its segregated school system. After the Brown decision, children were assigned to schools on the basis of their residence, not their race. This change was significant, but not radical, however, because of neighborhood racial segregation. The city's school board also adopted a voluntary transfer policy that permitted students to enroll in a school other than the one to which they were assigned if the school of their choice had extra seats. This policy, in effect, softened desegregation for white families living in areas that were predominantly black.

In 1954, when Wilmington abandoned its dual school system, the total number of students in the city's public schools was declining in comparison to the period immediately before World War II, while the percentage of black students was increasing. In 1937 over seventeen thousand youngsters were enrolled, 16 percent of them black, compared to an enrollment of fewer than thirteen thousand in 1953, 26 percent of whom were black.[72] The suburban boom of the 1950s rapidly increased the minority composition of the city school system. A former Wilmington school administrator estimated that the city lost five thousand white middle-income school-age children to the suburbs in the years from 1954 to 1959.[73]

Simultaneous with the integration of the city schools was the expansion of suburban school districts. With the development of high-quality, twelve-year public school programs in the suburbs during the 1950s, suburban children no longer sought admission to city high schools. In modern American society, the middle-class worker depends upon educational skills for his or her livelihood. Education is his capital. Racial issues aside, middle-class people demand public schools that can prepare their children for the collegiate training on which their careers will depend. The intrusion of large numbers of lower-class children into a school threatens educational excellence as perceived by middle-class parents. Catholic parents could remain in the city and send their children to parochial schools, upper-income groups, likewise, could send their offspring to private schools, but middle-income Protestants and Jews dependent on the public schools often chose to relocate in suburban areas, where their educational values remained dominant. By the mid-1960s, Dr. Gene Geisert, superintendent of the Wilmington public schools, faced with a dramatic change in the constituency served by his schools, reinforced the trend toward a lower-class-oriented school system when he chose to emphasize programs aimed at educationally disadvantaged children at the expense of maintaining advanced college preparatory courses and other "enrichment" programs in subjects such as music and art.

In the 1960s Wilmington's schools underwent severe trauma. Teachers and administrators in formerly placid schools were ill-equipped to handle youngsters who brought their often violent, poverty-filled world to school with them. Extortion became common, even in elementary schools. One black student murdered another in a corridor at P.S.du Pont High School, and Wilmington High School was disrupted by interracial fights. Many frustrated white teachers resigned or found jobs in suburban schools. All of these ills were noted in the news media and were a frequent subject of conversation and concern in the Wilmington area.

1968, the year of the riots, National Guard patrols, and the apogee of interracial tensions and fears in Wilmington, was also the year in which the state legislature adopted a comprehensive revision of school district lines throughout the state. The Education Advancement Act of 1968 was a carefully prepared measure, based upon a 1966 study by an ad hoc gubernatorial committee and on studies by the State Department of Public Instruction. The act's main purposes were to reduce the total number of school districts in the state and to set policy under which future redivision of districts would occur. The new law treated the Wilmington school district differently from other districts through a combination of two of its declarations: one that made the boundaries of the Wilmington district coterminous with the city boundaries, and another that set a ceiling of 12,000 students per district. By contrast, the boundaries of the Newark School District or the New Castle-Gunning Bedford District went far beyond their municipal boundary lines, but, of course, these small cities contained far fewer children than Wilmington did. Nothing in the Educational Advancement Act pointed to racial motiviations for these provisions, and at the time it was adopted the act was not perceived as being unfair to Wilmington. In fact, the city's legislators, blacks included, voted for the act.

A significant factor in the black politicians' acquiescence in the 1968 school law was the growing power that blacks wielded over the city's school board. Contrary to the view commonly held among middle-class whites, black parents cared very much about their children's education and were intent upon improving the city's troubled schools. Blacks had little say in city government, but the dominance of black children in the city school system, coupled with growing black militancy in school-related issues, made them a force to be reckoned with in school politics. In 1970 new appointments by Mayor Haskell and Governor Peterson gave the board its first black majority.

Flushed with victory, the black board members, led by the Rev. Lloyd Casson, a Wilmington-born Episcopal clergyman, faced a daunting battle to improve the educational climate in an environment sputtering with friction. It was the style of the period to resist compromise, to couch requests for reform in the language of nonnegotiable demands. It was not an easy time to wield authority, especially for the leaders of a highly self-conscious emerging minority. In that climate the teachers, taking their cue from their counterparts in New York City, unionized and demanded salaries higher than those available in the suburban schools. A militant parents' organization, the Home and School Council, also demanded a voice in setting school policy. In 1972 the board underwent a humiliating experience when followers of a local black principal forced them to rescind their offer of the superintendency to a black woman from New York City. With these immediate problems requiring its attention, the board was not involved in the early stages of the desegregation case that was to completely recast nearly the entire school system of the county.[74]

Contrary to what one might assume, the first steps toward city-county desegregation came not from blacks but from white parents who had chosen to remain in the city. When Mayor Haskell took office in 1969, he established a number of neighborhood groups, called task forces, that were intended to provide two-way communication between the mayor's office and the citizens. The task force in the vicinity of P.S. du Pont High School included home owners who were experienced soldiers in the battle to retain the top-quality education and high property values that had once characterized their area. They had only recently won a victory over real-estate brokers' blockbusting techniques in their neighborhood, when they convinced city council to agree to an ordinance banning the display of "for sale" signs.[75] These people had witnessed the rising turmoil in the schools with great alarm. They also knew that as recently as a decade before, some suburban children had attended city public schools, because the city schools were then perceived to be superior to the schools in the suburbs. Now that the situation was reversed and the suburban schools were better equipped and had fuller programs, especially for college preparatory students, city people were prohibited from enrolling their children in public schools outside the city limits. In 1970, for example, the suburban districts had turned down a voluntary transfer plan proposed by the city superintendent. The mostly white, middle-class residents in the vicinity of P. S. du Pont High School, which had once been acclaimed the best high school in the state, were acutely aware of the reversal in the fortunes of their neighborhood schools. They resented the fact that the new law precluded them from transferring their children into the more orderly and academically enriched schools in the nearby Mt. Pleasant and Alfred I. du Pont Districts. Their neighborhood task force was searching for some legal means to reinstate the interdistrict transfer policy. According to a study of the origins of the desegregation suit, "the idea of bringing a lawsuit to alter the Wilmington district boundaries originated in this task force."[76] To reverse transfer policy, members of the task force saw no option but legal redress.

When task force leaders contacted the American Civil Liberties Union about their problem, they precipitated an eight-year court battle over racial segregation in New Castle County. Initially begun on behalf of white children, not black children, the cause at first attracted support neither from civil rights groups nor from black school board members and politicians. The Wilmington chapter of the NAACP declined to support the suit, and the black-controlled city school board was, as already noted, immersed in its own set of issues. Furthermore, many blacks were reluctant to expose their children to the emotional shock of desegregation and were fearful of losing federal funds for catch-up educational programs, which were available only to schools with a preponderance of disadvantaged youngsters.[77] In keeping with the concerns expressed by the suit's initiators, their first important allies, aside from ACLU, were Mayor Haskell and his city solicitor—men who, like the task force parents, were seeking ways to reverse the process of white flight from the city. If the city could not hold its remaining middle-class residents, white or black, it could not survive, and a major way to encourage middle-class residence was to provide desirable public schools. Given the preponderant number of poor, educationally disadvantaged children already in the city school system, and the city system's recently enacted policy of emphasizing catch-up programs for the educationally deprived at the expense of college preparatory courses, there could be no reversal in middle-class flight from the city unless the walls erected against cross-district transfers by the 1968 Education Act were broken down.[78]

The suit was called *Evans* v. *Buchanan*, but neither Evans nor Buchanan had anything to do with the problems afflicting Wilmington's schools. This rather peculiar fact underlines a much more important and ill-undersood feature of the case. Those who brought the suit were concerned about a limited problem: the legal barriers preventing the transfer of students from city to suburban schools. Legal redress, however, required a much broader approach, because it had to address constitutional issues and the only way to do so was through the racial issues originally raised in *Brown* v. *the Board* in 1954. By 1971 the Supreme Court's seemingly simple dictum that segregated schools were inherently unequal had been subjected to an immense amount of interpretation and reinterpretation to determine what constituted segregation. In most of Delaware, as in many other states that had maintained legally segregated school systems before 1954, the court's plea for "all deliberate speed" resulted only in deliberate delay. In 1956, two years after the Brown ruling, Mrs. Brenda Evans, a black parent who lived in the rural town of Clayton, Delaware, filed a suit in federal court against the Delaware State Board of Education, whose president was Madelyn Buchanan, because the state board had not eliminated its dual system.[79] It took ten years of litigation before the state complied. During that same decade, Wilmington and its suburbs, the first parts of the state to begin desegregation, had become, in fact, resegregated. By 1970, 70 percent of Wilmington's public school population was black, while only one suburban district—De La Warr, immediately south of the city—had more than a tiny handful of black students. Some suburban districts were totally white. Because these facts fit the situation that had been originally addressed in Brenda Evans's suit, the 1970 law suit was subsumed under that earlier case.

Evans v. *Buchanan* proved to be enormously complicated. Before the courts could resolve its major issue, virtually every party who might be conceivably involved had entered the suit, including not only the ACLU, the City of Wilmington, the NAACP, and the State Board of Education, but all eleven of the Wilmington area's school boards. Nearly every law firm in a city noted for its many lawyers was employed by some participant in this mammoth legal battle. To further complicate matters, the case was heard in two different federal courts. In its early stages, a panel of three federal judges, two, Caleb Wright and Caleb Layton, from Delaware, and the other, John J. Gibbons, from New Jersey, heard the case and made the fundamental judgments on its remedy. Then the suit was transferred to

another U.S. District Judge from Delaware, Murray Schwartz, for implementation. If this were not enough to ensure public confusion, the case was
intimately bound up with the ongoing opinions of the U.S. Supreme Court
regarding cases from other states that were tantalizingly similar to the
Delaware case yet not so exactly parallel as to resolve the legal tangles of
Evans v. *Buchanan.*

The District Court was asked to address two issues: were New Castle
County's schools segregated, and, if so, what change in the school system
would constitute desegregation. In 1974 the three-judge panel found that
the schools in Wilmington and its suburbs were segregated;[80] but the force
of this ruling was defused one month later, when the U.S. Supreme Court
ruled in a comparable case in Detroit, Michigan, that courts could not
require the integration of city and suburban school districts, unless it could
be shown that "there has been a constitutional violation within one district
that produces a significant segregative effect in another district," that is,
that acts of government had assisted racial segregation.[81] In the spring of
1975, lawyers for the plaintiffs convinced a majority of the judges that in
Delaware, unlike Michigan, various governmental actions had assisted
segregation. The plaintiffs' attorneys successfully argued that the failure of
the state to pass open-housing legislation, the failure of the county to build
low-income housing, and the special treatment accorded to the Wilmington School District in the Educational Advancement Act of 1968 all pointed
to a consistent policy by both state and local government to segregate white
people from black people.[82] The significance of the judges' decision on this
point was that the court demanded an interdistrict remedy, the first
imposed in the United States.

When the Evans case moved into the remedy stage, the court attempted to remove itself from the action. The judges hoped that the state
legislature would act to replace its earlier Educational Advancement Act
with legislation that would desegregate New Castle County's schools.
When the legislature refused to pick up this political bombshell, the court
reluctantly established an interim board of education to draw up desegregation plans. To the mass of suburban dwellers, *Evans* v. *Buchanan* was
like a dark cloud that from a distance had seemed small and unworthy of
concern but that suddenly had become large and ominous. It was especially incomprehensible because New Castle County had officially ended
its dual school system years before. This remedy was not, therefore,
perceived by suburbanites to be an equitable, constitutional thing called
desegregation, but was seen rather as an unfair infringement on people's
rights that would lead to the destruction of neighborhood schools. Opponents did not talk about desegregation but about forced busing. Busing was
universally loathed in the suburbs and was none too popular among city

View of Market Street Mall from the roof of the Grand Opera, Summer, 1982. *(Photograph by Ruth Anne Clarke. Courtesy of the Historical Society of Delaware)*

people either. The power of this sentiment demolished any possibility that the politically sensitive legislature could create a new school law acceptable to the court. Fear of busing also encouraged people to move out of New Castle County or to enroll their children in private schools, thus reducing the public school population, and it divided the interests of hitherto united suburban districts.

One such divisive issue was whether the sprawling Newark District, the largest in the suburbs, should be included within the scope of desegregation. Unlike most other suburban districts, Newark's included a substantial municipality of 21,000 people, but fewer than five percent of its public school students were black.[53] As the home of the University of Delaware and of the Du Pont Company's Engineering Department, Newark's population included many people who prized education to an ususual degree. Newark people argued that since they had integrated their schools and since their district included a city comparable to, though smaller than, Wilmington they should be excluded from the case. The Mount Pleasant District in Brandywine Hundred argued the contrary.

Residents of Mount Pleasant, the oldest, most settled suburban region, feared that if Newark were excluded, suburban settlement patterns would shift, causing property values in Brandywine Hundred to plummet. The Mount Pleasant District's lawyers, therefore, insisted that Newark be included in a desegregation plan. The tug-of-war between these two districts demonstrated the immense impact that desegregation was expected to have upon property values and school quality, the most sacred concerns of suburban residents, and thereby pointed to the necessity of including all Wilmington suburbs in plans for its implementation.

The De La Warr District raised another significant conceptual issue. De La Warr was unique among the suburban districts because the majority of its students were black and because its tax base was by far the lowest in the county. The district's tax problems stemmed in part from the comparative poverty of the people who lived there, but De La Warr also contained a more than typical share of tax-free property, including the extensive grounds of the state hospital at Farnhurst and the complex highway approaches to the Delaware Memorial Bridge. Lawyers for De La Warr argued that equity required a remedy that would pool the taxes of the various districts. To some degree De La Warr's concerns ran counter to the interests of Wilmington, the other predominantly black district. Whereas De La Warr wanted consolidation of districts to equalize available revenues, Wilmington hoped to achieve desegregation without relinquishing the autonomy of its black-controlled board.

Even under the best of circumstances, the opposition of these and similar forces was certain to prevent a quick and painless solution; but the circumstances in New Castle County were hardly the best. Throughout the long legal process, many people believed that some sudden reprieve would alter the situation. The Supreme Court would overrule the local district judges, Congress or the state legislature would pass a statute against busing, or the United States would adopt an anti-busing amendment. Leaders of the most popular anti-busing group in the county, the Positive Action Committee, continually reminded their constituents that such hopes could be fulfilled if only people would demonstrate their opposition to busing more vigorously. Meanwhile, behind the scenes and out of the headlines, the egos of superintendents from various districts collided as each maneuvered to benefit his own career.[84] In this hostile atmosphere it is hardly surprising that neither the legislature nor the state or local school boards could provide the judges with an acceptable plan. In May 1976 a majority of the three judges rejected the plans presented to them by the various litigants and created an interim school board charged with providing an acceptable interdistrict plan.[85]

Evans v. *Buchanan* now passed into a new phase. The panel of judges had made clear that unless some responsible state agency could produce an acceptable alternative they would require the dissolution of the existing school districts in favor of one unified district. With this ruling the panel bowed out, leaving the difficult task of implementing their rulings to District Judge Murray M. Schwartz of Wilmington. Like his colleagues before him, Judge Schwartz found that the state legislature, the new board that succeeded the interim board, and the State Board of Education were unwilling to take upon themselves the onus of desegregation. Taking the plan submitted by the court-appointed board as his base, the judge reluctantly but skillfully fashioned a plan designed to satisfy the constitutional requirement for equality while minimizing the disruption of students' lives. The keys to the plan that emerged from Judge Schwartz's court were the creation of a single school district that placed 80,000 children from eleven previous districts under one school board with one superintendent and one tax rate and the establishment of what was known as the 9–3 plan. Under this plan, students from predominantly white areas would attend school for three years in Wilmington or De La Warr, while students from these formerly majority black districts would attend school in the suburbs for nine years.[86]

On 11 September 1978, the long-feared, court-ordered desegregation plan went into operation without incident. With the glare of the national media focused upon them, thousands of children boarded buses to go to their new schools. Another barrier separating the city from its suburbs had fallen. Suburban children who had never been into the city and city children who had no experience of the suburbs met on one another's home ground. Serious problems still remained to be solved, especially the difficult matter of equalizing teachers' salaries. But the whole community could take some satisfaction in the fact that, regardless of the nearly universal abhorrence of busing and the high feelings that it engendered, there were no ugly scenes of mass protest, no violence, no serious threats to close the schools.

In *The Politics of School Desegregation*, Jeffrey Raffel of the University of Delaware's College of Urban Affairs describes in detail how various groups and individuals contributed to the implementation of the desegregation order. Raffel, who was on special assignment to the governor's office to assist in desegregation, viewed the entire process from the inside. He identifies several factors that influenced the peaceful outcome. One of the most significant was the Breakfast Group, organized in 1976, which met regularly to provide a forum where officials from city, county, and state government, the schools, parents groups, and other community organizations could discuss the issues away from the glare of publicity. The Break-fast Group was a communications device, a means to develop new ideas, an advisory group, and a testing ground for emerging leaders.[57] Both Mayor William McLaughlin of Wilmington and County Executive Mary Jornlin offered responsible leadership that also helped to maintain the peace. Most indicative of the mood that prevailed among the state's political leaders was a statement made by Governor Pierre S. du Pont IV to an audience of blacks in Dover in 1977. "Continued rhetoric denying the existence of the Court's action is counterproductive," the governor declared.[58] No less significantly, desegregation's most vociferous foe, James Venema, a politi-cally ambitious former salesman who presided over the Positive Action Committee, was a social conservative who shrank from the brink of violence.[59] In addition, the very ponderousness of the legal process served finally to prepare people for the inevitable.

By the early 1980s, desegregation has produced a mixture of effects that cannot be made to disclose the future. During the 1970s public school enrollments declined in many parts of New Castle County. In large part this decline resulted from a combination of the falling birthrate and the maturation of the county's population. The fact that public school enroll-ments have fallen while nonpublic enrollments have risen during the 1970s is very significant, but cannot be attributed solely to busing, because the same phenomenon has occurred in Kent and Sussex counties, where integration is no longer an issue. It appears that people are dissatisfied with the public schools for a variety of reasons, of which desegregation is but one. During the years 1975 through 1979, nine new independent schools were created in New Castle County and nonpublic enrollments rose from 15,052 to 18,996, while public school enrollments declined precipitously from 83,079 to 63,593.[90] Falling public school enrollments due to demo-graphic factors as well as to dissatisfaction have led to many school closings that have served to perpetuate the feelings of uncertainty and the decline in loyalty in a particular school that have been among the most disruptive elements accompanying desegregation.

Despite these serious ongoing problems, desegregation has had a positive effect on Wilmington. The order brought to a close a long-standing historic tax advantage for county residents over city residents. Before the 1978 order, tax rates varied a great deal from district to district, depending upon property values and the willingness of residents to be taxed. The lowest property values were in Wilmington and the De La Warr district. In order to maintain its schools and pay its debts and the salaries demanded by urban teachers, the city set its tax rate at $2.940. Meanwhile, in the older working-class suburbs around Richardson Park and Elsmere, an area long devoted to low taxes, residents were paying a rate of $1.040 on houses valued at only a few thousand dollars more than those in the city. By contrast, in the wealthy Alexis I. du Pont District, where the average property was in excess of quadruple the value of the average city property, the tax rate of $1.239 was adequate to maintain a high-quality school system.[91] Since 1978 the rate has been the same regardless of whether one lives in the city or its suburbs. Desegregation thus has been the single most effective step toward restoring the city's ability to compete successfully with its own suburbs. The city is no longer the victim of the high tax rate coupled with poor schools that once drove its residents to the suburbs.

In the context of the history of the 1970s, desegregation can be seen as a great tug-of-war that pitted the suburbs against the city for high stakes. A victory for one could only be perceived as a loss for the other. In the midst of this battle it became nearly impossible to discern any ways in which the whole community, city and suburbs together, could benefit. The hostile, suspicious environment created by *Evans* v. *Buchanan* increased the antagonism inherent in other city-county issues quite unrelated to desegregation. The most striking example of this phenomenon was the ferocious battle over Plan Omega, the proposal to remove the area's major hospital facility from the city to the suburbs.

To understand this issue, one must go back to the years immediately after World War II. At that time Wilmington had several hospitals, including Saint Francis Hospital, a Catholic institution, and Riverside, an osteopathic hospital. The three largest hospitals in the city, the Memorial, the Delaware, and the Wilmington General, were nonprofit, nonsectarian, privately endowed institutions. Each had its own board of directors, its own policies, its own major donors, and its own personality. The Memorial, founded in 1888, was the oldest. Originally it attracted homeopathic doctors, while the allopaths practiced at the Delaware. The R. R. M. Carpenter family were major benefactors of the Memorial, while the Lammot du Ponts, the Harringtons, and H. Fletcher Brown were major donors to the Delaware. These two hospitals were located along the Brandywine near the heart of the city. The Delaware faced onto heavily traveled Washington Street at the intersection of the commercial and residential portions of the city, while the Memorial stood only a few blocks away. The Wilmington General was located in the midst of the white ethnic neighborhoods in the western part of the city. Its chief benefactor, Irénée du Pont, helped found the institution in part to assist Jewish doctors, who were formerly excluded from practice in the other two.

Over the years, as medical practice became more standardized, the differences that had once marked the hospitals faded, but old loyalties died hard. During the 1950s some doctors and board members began to question the policy of complete autonomy as inefficient and costly. In 1961, in

Wilmington's central business district in the late 1970s, showing the collection of mid-rise office buildings in close proximity to the Du Pont Building. This area remains the heart of New Castle County's economy. *(Photograph by Action Photo. Courtesy of the Greater Wilmington Development Council)*

response to these concerns, the hospitals agreed to create a hospital board of review, but they gave it only advisory powers. Chaired by the president of the News-Journal papers, Charles L. Reese, Jr., the board of review included other top executives whose opinions were sure to be respected by the wealthy men who dominated the individual hospital boards. Despite its lack of authority, the board of review successfully consolidated the three hospitals' nursing schools in 1962. This accomplishment proved to be the first step toward a complete merger of the hospitals. In 1963 leaders from the board of review and from the three hospital boards formed the Joint Committee on Hospital Merger. The eleven members of the joint committee represented the most powerful, the most wealthy, and the most prestigious men in Wilmington. It was characteristic of such a group that they held their meetings at the highly exclusive Wilmington Club where the city's leaders of business and the law have traditionally met for lunch. A study by a nationally known hospital consulting firm convinced the committee that a merger was imperative in order to keep Wilmington abreast of advances in health care. The study showed that the existing 300- to 400-bed hospitals could not attract the interns and residents necessary to maintain hospital services and to instruct hospital staffs in the latest techniques. Furthermore, with hospital costs rising rapidly, expensive duplications were likely to bankrupt the individual units. In 1965, in light of these strong arguments, the three hospital boards agreed to merge into one corporate entity to be called the Wilmington Medical Center.[92]

Although the merger was controversial among local physicians, hospital board members, and others directly involved with day-to-day hospital operations, it was never a public issue. From the point of view of hospital patients, the main result of merger was the consolidation of certain types of care in one or another of the existing hospitals. But from the first the merger implied broader goals that did excite the interest and concerns of people outside the medical establishment. In the study commissioned earlier by the joint committee, the consultants went beyond their recommendation for corporate merger to point out that the existing hospital facilities should be viewed as a mere stopgap until the medical center could construct a new hospital or hospitals. Drawing on census figures from 1950 and 1960, they anticipated continued growth for New Castle County, especially between Wilmington and Newark along the route where I-95 was then nearing completion. The consultants noted two potential ways that the hospital might meet this need. One way, replacing the three existing hospitals with one large facility, would be the best course for optimum patient care. On the other hand, this plan would leave either the city or the burgeoning county without a hospital. Therefore, the consultants recommended "the establishment of two major general care institutions, one in the center of the city and one to the southwest along the Wilmington-Newark axis."[93] The controversy that emerged from these recommendations remained unresolved for nearly twenty years.

In 1968 the Medical Center hired another nationally known consulting firm to provide them with more specific long-range plans. These consultants presented the board with three options, all predicated on the eventual phasing out of the Memorial and Wilmington General divisions. Option one, the twin plan, called for two 800-bed hospitals, one an extension of the old Delaware Hospital, the other a new hospital to be located between Wilmington and Newark. This plan, the consultants noted, emphasized fairness to population groupings but required the continued duplication of programs. Option two proposed the construction of a 1,400-

bed hospital between Wilmington and Newark and the reduction of the Delaware Division to an emergency and routine care facility. Option three followed the opposite course: the expansion of the Delaware Division into a 1,500-bed hospital center augmented by small emergency and routine care facilities scattered throughout the suburbs. The consultants recommended the third option as the most advantageous, because it would produce the maximum consolidation, make the best use of existing facilities, and keep the hospital in the midst of the most populous area.[94]

Upon receipt of this report, the Medical Center's board formed a site selection committee chaired by a retired Hercules Company executive, John J. B. Fulenwider. The subcommittee quickly eliminated the twin hospital concept because of the duplication argument and concentrated on options two and three. Although they originally considered over forty potential sites for a big hospital, they soon reduced that number to a handful. The committee lost enthusiasm for the Delaware Division site recommended by the consultants upon discovering that the Brandywine Cemetery Association, which occupied a large property adjacent to the hospital, would not sell. In contrast to this refusal was the tempting donation of a large parcel of land adjacent to I-95 midway between Wilmington and Newark.[95]

In July 1969 the Medical Center announced that H. B. du Pont's Welfare Foundation had offered the hospital board 200 acres of its 600-acre tract on I-95 near Stanton, Delaware. H. B. du Pont had acquired the tract some five years before, anticipating that the newly constructed superhighway would place this tract at the center of future development. Rather than see such a large parcel of prime real estate be developed commercially, du Pont wished it to be put to some public use. A hospital fulfilled the benefactor's intentions admirably, and suited the hospital site committee as well. A spokesman for the Medical Center board told the press that the gift "ends a long search . . . for a site suitable for the construction of a major health complex."[96] The news failed to delight everyone. Mayor Haskell, for one, declared that although there was "undoubtedly a need to have a medical facility somewhere midway between Wilmington and Newark . . . moving the majority of the services would have tremendous negative social impact. . . ." He urged instead that the hospital board apply more pressure to the Brandywine Cemetary Association to sell its land, noting that he recommended this course in spite of the fact that his own parents were buried there.[97] The county planning department also opposed the proposed use of the Stanton site, because the area lacked adequate sewers and roads and because the county planners anticipated that the relocation would have a damaging effect on Wilmington. Unfortunately, at this juncture H. B. du Pont, the one disinterested yet powerful and involved person who might have adjudicated the dispute, died. The newspapers reported Mayor Haskell's eulogy that "when history is written, I believe he will go down as the first person of great wealth in our area who began to understand the depth and critical nature of the urban problem in America."[98] It was ironic, therefore, that the mayor perceived H. B. du Pont's final public legacy to not be in the city's best interests.

Confronted by opposition from city leaders and fearful that a wrong decision might attract a profit-making hospital to the area, the Wilmington Medical Center Board reexamined the idea of building twin hospitals of roughly 500 beds each. Their shift in plans provoked a counterproposal from Wilmington's new mayor, Thomas Maloney, to expand the Delaware Division into an 800-bed hospital and build a 200-bed unit on the Stanton site. The effect of the Maloney plan on the board was directly contrary to what the mayor had intended. It rekindled the board's interest in an uneven split, but in favor of the county rather than the city. The Medical Board's chairman, Joseph Dallas, a Du Pont Company vice-president, later testified in court that the board members "were intrigued with the thought that, if we concentrated our construction in terms of new construction rather than in terms of dismantling and rearranging, we could perhaps build a bigger hospital in the suburbs and a smaller hospital in the city that would give us more bang for a buck."[99] In the fall of 1975 the board voted to construct a major general hospital at Stanton and to reduce the Delaware Division to emergency and routine care. They named this proposal Plan Omega.

In reaching this decision, the board had been guided by comprehensive plans for several different-sized hospitals submitted to them by the architectural firm of Metcalf and Associates. Metcalf's plan to increase the Delaware Division from 440 beds to 800 beds would have required construction of three additional buildings at a total estimated cost of $88,218,000. The limitations of space and the existing street pattern confined the architects to rather pedestrian, rectangular mid-rise buildings in their design for an enlarged Delaware Division, but they presented a far more imaginative futuristic plan for a hospital at the undeveloped Stanton site. The Plan Omega hospital was conceived as a series of interconnected octagons attached to a large rectangular block. The idea was to free different functions architecturally, so that change or growth in one part would not adversely affect any other. The novelty and flexibility of this design was no doubt alluring to the board and was a factor in their decision to adopt the Stanton plan if construction costs could be kept to $73 million. Assured that this was possible the board chose Plan Omega.[100]

By 1975, when the board made its decision, the matter of hospital relocation had become the subject of political debate between residents of the city and those who lived southwest of the city. In part, this controversy was the inevitable result of the board's earlier hesitancy in deciding on a plan. The board's ambivalence reflected the changed atmosphere in which such institutions must act. By the 1970s philanthropists with huge fortunes were a dying breed even in Wilmington. Industrial executives had taken the places of millionaire philanthropists on the hospital board. Less paternalistic than their predecessors, these men were conditioned to depend on outside expert advice and were more attuned to public opinion. Where once big donors had been able to dictate hospital policies, in the 1970s the federal government, through its Medicare program, and medical insurance companies such as Blue Cross were the biggest source of hospital funds. These changes, together with such factors as rapidly rising medical and construction costs, and the stabilization of New Castle County's formerly expanding population revealed in the 1970 census, all acted to confuse and inhibit action.

By the mid-1970s, city and county residents were sharply at odds over both the school busing issue and the location of the proposed hospital. In the fall of 1974, a group in the Newark area formed the Suburban County Hospital Task Force to campaign for construction of a major hospital in the Newark area. When Mayor Maloney suggested his 800–200 plan, Mrs. Shirley M. Tarrant, president of the task force, was quoted as saying that the mayor had thrown Newark a "doggey-bone."[101] Mrs. Tarrant's boisterous tactics attracted nearly 3,000 people to her organization. On the opposite side stood the NAACP, which campaigned to keep the major hospital in Wilmington. While Mrs. Tarrant's group focused on public relations, the NAACP went to court. Arguing that Plan Omega violated the civil rights of Wilmington residents, the NAACP urged HEW to intervene and block the hospital project. This case, called "bitterly contested" by the federal judge who heard it, was in the courts from 1976 until 1980, when Judge James L. Latchum ruled that as Plan Omega involved no "discriminatory intent" the Wilmington Medical Center could go forward with its building plans. The judge reached this decision only after the Medical Center agreed to provide frequent free shuttle service from the city to the Stanton hospital and to prevent the Delaware Division from becoming a racially identifiable "ghetto" facility.[102]

At the time of writing, the court battle over Plan Omega has finally ended with a victory for the hospital board, and ground is finally broken for the new hospital building. Meanwhile the state legislature has recently put an end to the three-year-old single school district by redividing it into four pie-shaped districts, each to include a part of the city of Wilmington. These events, the result of long controversy, when perceived against the entire background of community development covered in this book, suggest that the 1970s marked an important watershed in interrelationships within the greater Wilmington area. Sociologist Morris Janowitz, in discussing present-day America's advanced industrial society, points to the significance of the public school system, especially the high school, in preparing young people to participate in the larger social systems. The high school is the mediator between the family and neighborhood and the world of work. Thus it provides "a sense of collective identity loosely linked to residential locality."[103] The effect of suburbanization has been to isolate socioeconomic groups so that, in a region as populous as Wilmington, before desegregation individual public high schools had become quite homogeneous, racially, economically, and socially. Each school district had provided its own sense of community. This identification with one's school district, which was the most serious obstacle to desegregation, explains the recently enacted move back to more local districts. Part of the reason why identification with school districts was so powerful was that there was so little else in suburbia to give residents a sense of community. Other elements that once provided cohesion for local society have largely disappeared. A shopping mall along an interstate highway fails to generate the feeling of identification that earlier urbanites could feel with Market Street as a central place in their community.

Students of suburbanization have emphasized the political and social fragmentation that this spatial phenomenon has produced. Some scholars have called this pattern a "crazy quilt" that leads to governmental inefficiency and deprives individual families of a sense of belonging to a larger whole. To the extent that the old school districts helped to overcome feelings of fragmentation, their disappearance is unfortunate. But perhaps it is even more important in a county whose total population is still not quite 400,000 to emphasize the importance of the total community that lies beyond the comfortable level of one's own homogeneous locality.

Jon C. Teaford, in a recently published book about city-suburban relationships, has analyzed the political forces that have led to the metropolitanization of government in some cities in the United States. He concludes that the group that most vigorously supports the metro concept consists of elite businessmen who live in the suburbs but whose office buildings are located downtown, and whose business names are associated with the city in question.[104] By contrast, those most opposed to metro government are blue-collar workers living in inner suburbs, who fear higher taxes and black incursion into their neighborhoods. This national pattern applies well to the Wilmington area, where the local business elite tried unsuccessfully in 1970 to convince the community at large that metro government was in the best interests of all.

The failure of metro government here demonstrates a significant, but often-ignored, point about power dynamics in the Wilmington area. Many commentators have portrayed Delaware, and especially its major city, as a virtual fiefdom of the du Ponts and their industrial complex. In the early 1970s, two of Ralph Nader's associates produced the best-known study in this vein. Entitled *The Company State*, the Nader book was an attempt to define the proper role for corporate power in America.[105] After a lengthy description of the impact of Du Pont influence, Nader's associates proclaimed that "a large corporation should act so as to provide the community with a maximum of benefits and a minimum of domination."[106] Although the means by which giant enterprises might achieve this delicate balancing act were left obscure, the indictment of Du Pont was clearly intended as a guidebook of how not to do it.

While no one would deny the dominance of the chemical industry in Wilmington's economy, it is important to note that the power of the city's corporate elite to work their will on the community has declined very significantly since the 1920s. This trend is primarily attributable to the interconnection of three factors: the change of generations within the du Pont and related families, the success of the chemical industry in transforming the community, and the growth of the federal government's involvement in local affairs. The first of these points has been dealt with throughout this book and requires no further elaboration. As for the second, the large suburban middle-class population surrounding Wilmington is largely a result of the chemical industry's presence, and the Du Pont Company and its major stockholders must attempt to keep these people contented. It is by no means clear which side is in the driver's seat, and on an issue such as metropolitanization, the middle-income majority can overrule the upper-income minority.

The final factor, federal involvement, is at once the most pervasive and the most difficult to summarize. Its influence can be seen in everything from FHA home financing in the 1930s, through slum clearance and low-income housing in the 1940s and 1950s, to interstate highway construction in the 1960s and desegregation in the 1970s. One dramatic index of federal influence was the recent stalemate surrounding Plan Omega. Prior to the 1960s, Wilmington's major hospitals were the creatures of their wealthy donors, and no one could have blocked the hospital boards had they decided to relocate their facilities, nor would it have seemed appropriate to try. Federal health subsidies such as Medicare and Medicaid and declining private gifts and endowments have subsequently changed the power structure within the hospitals, even though their board membership lists remain much as before. These changes, in turn, provided the rationale for opponents of Plan Omega to block the implementation of the hospital board's relocation decision.

In retrospect one can argue that federal policy has been at least as arbitrary as the elite whose money and power it has now largely replaced. The laws affecting city life that have been passed by Congress and implemented by the federal bureaucracy have usually been designed to relieve a current crisis. Since one of the hallmarks of modern American society is rapid change, it has been impossible for even the best-intentioned legislators or bureaucrats to imagine policy goals that will outlive a single decade. In the 1930s the FHA was created to stimulate the housing industry and relieve urban crowding. No one foresaw that suburban sprawl would be its chief result. Similarly, slum clearance, the location of interstate highways through cities, and other federally funded programs produced powerful but unanticipated results. Communities that were well organized to channel federal spending toward coherent goals, such as New Haven, Connecticut, under Mayor Richard Lee, prospered in this environment. Wilmington, for the complex series of reasons outlined in this study, was not so fortunate. If history is any guide to the future, it would seem prudent for residents of greater Wilmington to recognize that city and suburbs are interdependent and that neither can prosper without the other. Only with this realization can the mistakes of the past become the lessons for tomorrow.

APPENDIX

Comparative Growth Patterns

of Cities in the

Philadelphia Region

Table 1 shows the population within the corporate boundaries of eight regional cities from 1900 through 1980, together with the percentage of change from the previous census year.

Table 2 extracts from that data the percentage of change in those cities from the census year when each reached its greatest growth to 1980. The cities are arranged in order from Allentown, which has lost the least, to Wilmington, which has lost the most.

Table 3 presents the change in the size of the total standard metropolitan areas of the five cities which have their own suburbs from 1950 to 1980. The cities are arranged beginning with Lancaster, which has experienced the greatest overall growth, through Philadelphia, which has had the least.

Table 4 represents the numbers and percentage of inhabitants living outside of the urban corporate limits in the metropolitan areas of each of the five cities in 1950 and 1980, in descending order of suburban dominance. The figures for suburban population were obtained by subtracting the city populations from those of their SMA's. The arbitrary nature of SMA determination by the Bureau of the Census makes these numbers less reliable than those for city populations. Together these data show that while all of the area cities have lost population while experiencing suburban growth not all have experienced these trends to the same degree. Wilmington has been the most extreme example in both categories, having lost 38 percent of its maximum urban population, while in 1950 and again in 1980 the percentage of its metropolitan population living outside its corporate limits has been the largest in the area.

TABLE 1
Population in Eight Cities of the Philadelphia Region

City	1900	1910	1920	1930	1940	1950	1960	1970	1980
Camden									
Population	75,935	94,538	116,309	118,700	117,536	*124,555	117,159	102,551	84,910
Percent Change		+24.5	+23.0	+2.1	−1.0	+6.0	−5.9	−12.5	−17.2
Trenton									
Population	73,307	96,815	119,289	123,356	124,697	*128,009	114,167	104,638	92,124
Percent Change		+32.1	+23.2	+3.4	+1.1	+2.7	−10.8	−8.3	−12.1
Chester									
Population	33,988	38,537	58,030	59,164	59,285	*66,039	63,658	56,331	45,794
Percent Change		+13.0	+51.0	+.2	+.1	+11.0	−4.0	−13.0	−18.7
Wilmington									
Population	76,508	87,411	110,168	106,597	*112,504	110,356	95,827	80,386	70,195
Percent Change		+14.3	+26.0	−3.2	+5.5	−1.9	−13.2	−16.1	−12.7
Reading									
Population	78,961	96,071	107,784	*111,171	110,568	109,320	98,177	87,643	78,686
Percent Change		+21.7	+12.2	+3.1	−.5	−1.1	−10.2	−10.7	−10.2
Lancaster									
Population	41,459	47,227	53,150	59,949	61,345	*63,774	61,055	57,690	54,725
Percent Change		+13.9	+12.5	+12.8	+2.3	+4.0	−4.3	−5.5	−5.1
Allentown									
Population	35,416	51,913	73,502	92,563	96,904	106,756	108,347	*109,527	103,758
Percent Change		+46.6	+41.6	+25.9	+4.7	+10.2	+1.5	+1.1	−5.6
Philadelphia									
Population	1,293,697	1,549,008	1,823,779	1,950,961	1,931,334	*2,071,605	2,002,512	1,948,609	1,688,210
Percent Change		+19.7	+17.7	+7.0	−1.0	+7.3	−3.3	−2.7	−13.4

*Year of highest population.

TABLE 2

Population Change from Highest Census Year to 1980

City	Change (percent)
Allentown	− 5.6
Lancaster	− 14.0
Philadelphia	− 19.0
Trenton	− 28.0
Reading	− 29.0
Chester	− 31.0
Camden	− 32.0
Wilmington	− 38.0

TABLE 3

Change in Standard Metropolitan Areas
of Five Regional Cities, 1950–1980

City	1950	1980	Percent Change
Lancaster	76,280	362,346	+ 375
Reading	154,931	312,509	+ 102
Wilmington	268,387	524,108	+ 95
Trenton	189,321	307,863	+ 63
Philadelphia	2,922,470	4,716,818	+ 61

TABLE 4

Change in Suburban Population of Five Regional Cities,
1950–1980

City	1950		1980	
	Suburban population	Percent of total SMA	Suburban population	Percent of total SMA
Wilmington	158,031	59	453,913	87
Lancaster	12,506	16	307,621	85
Reading	45,611	29	233,823	75
Trenton	61,312	32	215,739	70
Philadelphia	850,865	29	3,028,608	64

NOTES

Introduction

1. See Appendix for the ranking of regional cities according to various criteria.
2. Alfred D. Chandler, *The Visible Hand: The Managerial Revolution in American Business* (Cambridge, Mass.: Belknap Press, Harvard University Press, 1977), p. 417.
3. Robert S. and Helen M. Lynd, *Middletown in Transition* (New York: Harcourt, Brace and Company, 1937), p. 76.
4. Robert O. Schulze, "The Bifurcation of Power in a Satellite City," in Morris Janowitz, ed., *Community Power Systems* (Glencoe, Ill.: Free Press, 1961), p. 22.
5. Floyd Hunter, *Community Power Structure* (Chapel Hill: University of North Carolina Press, 1953), pp. 109–10.
6. Robert A. Dahl, *Who Governs?* (New Haven, Conn.: Yale University Press, 1961), p. 98.
7. J. Rogers Hollingsworth and Ellen Jane Hollingsworth, *Dimensions in Urban History* (Madison: University of Wisconsin Press, 1971).
8. Terry N. Clark, *Community Power and Policy Outputs, A Review of Urban Research* (Beverly Hills: Sage Publications, 1973), p. 51.

Chapter 1

1. *Sunday Morning Star* [Wilmington], 6 October 1912.
2. *Old Home Week Official Souvenir Program*, Wilmington, Delaware, 6–12 October 1912, Eleutherian Mills Historical Society (Hereafter cited as EMHL).
3. Ibid.
4. *U.S. Census of Manufacturers* (Washington: 1914), I:228–29.
5. For a more complete exposition of this argument see James T. Lemon, "Urbanization and the Development of Eighteenth Century Southeastern Pennsylvania and Adjacent Delaware," *William and Mary Quarterly*, 3rd ser. 24: 501–42 (1967).
6. Carol E. Hoffecker, *Brandywine Village: The Story of a Milling Community* (Wilmington: Old Brandywine Village, Inc., 1974), passim.
7. Louis McLane, *Documents Relative to the Manufactures in the United States* (Washington: 1833), p. 655.
8. Industrialization in nineteenth-century Wilmington is discussed in Carol E. Hoffecker, *Wilmington, Delaware: Portrait of an Industrial City* (Charlottesville: University of Virginia Press, 1974), chapter 1.

9. Henry Seidel Canby, *The Age of Confidence* (New York: Farrar & Rinehart, 1934), pp. 8–10.

10. U.S. Census, 1890, *Population* (Washington: 1895), I:526; 1920, *Population* (Washington: 1922), III:175.

11 *Wilmington Board of Trade Journal*, July 1902.

12. *Wilmington Board of Trade Journal*, January-February 1903 and March-April 1903.

13. *Every Evening* [Wilmington], 8 May 1903.

14. *Wilmington Board of Trade Journal*, March 1902.

15. *Every Evening*, 26 March 1903.

16. *Every Evening*, 28 March 1874. This change in the grid pattern dates from the time when Washington Street Bridge was built.

17. *Sunday Star*, 18 June 1911; 26 May 1912.

18. Frank R. Zebley, *The Churches of Delaware* (Wilmington: 1947), p. 48.

19. *Sunday Star*, 18 March 1906; 5 May 1907. The City Beautiful Movement grew out of the Chicago World's Fair of 1893, where city planners and architects had demonstrated the grand effects that could be achieved by carefully placing ornamental buildings, fountains, and statues along broad boulevards.

20. Ibid., 28 February 1897.

21. These statements can be confirmed by perusing the real-estate advertisements that appeared in the *Every Evening* during the first decade of the twentieth century. Banks are then for the first time advertising heavily as rental agents and offering mortgages.

22. *Sunday Star*, 22 February 1914.

23. Ibid., 15 February 1914.

24. U.S. Census, 1910, *Population*, I, pp. 85, 179, 860, 861, 1163.

25. Carol E. Hoffecker, "Four Generations of Jewish Life in Delaware," Toni Young, ed., *Delaware and the Jews* (Wilmington: Jewish Historical Society of Delaware, 1979), p. 40.

26. Caroline Golab, *Immigrant Destinations* (Philadelphia: Temple University Press, 1977), see chapter 6, "The Geography of Neighborhood," passim. Golab argues on the basis of housing patterns in Philadelphia that Jews assimilated the values of the predominant WASP culture more heavily than did groups like the Italians and Poles, who tended to remain clustered together in their original areas of settlement.

27. Bureau of Jewish Social Research, "Wilmington Jewish Communal Survey: Community Organization" (New York: 1929), Harry Bluestone Collection, Jewish Historical Society of Delaware Collection, Historical Society of Delaware, Wilmington, Del. (Hereafter cited as HSD).

28. *Sunday Star*, 20 August 1911.

29. Vincent J. Kowalewski, "A History of the Polish Colony in Delaware," H. Clay Reed, ed., *Delaware: A History of the First State* (New York: Lewis Historical Publishing Co., 1947), II, pp. 633–38.

30. U.S. Census, 1910, *Population*, II:756.

31. Ibid., II:283.

32. Ellen Calomiris, "Conflict, Cooperation, Acceptance: The Italian

Experience in Delaware," unpublished research paper, University of Delaware, 1981, pp. 4–5.

33. Samuel Bird speech on William P. Bancroft, 21 Oct. 1965, Bancroft-Bird Collection, HSD.
34. Calomiris, pp. 6–9.
35. Ibid., p. 12.
36. Joseph Errigo, *History of St. Anthony's Church, Wilmington, Delaware* (Wilmington: Hambleton Press, 1949).
37. Christopher Ward, *One Little Man* (New York: 1926). A novel set in turn of the century Wilmington includes this passage on page 294: "There was life . . . in the trolley parks or in an evening's parade up and down Market Street, blazing with lights, crowded with people."
38. *Delaware Life Magazine*, 6 September 1902.
39. Ibid., 12 April 1902.
40. The most successful history of the company to date is Alfred D. Chandler and Stephen M. Salsbury, *Pierre S. du Pont and the Making of the Modern Corporation* (New York: Harper & Row, 1971).
41. Ibid., p. 93.
42. Ibid., p. 125.
43. E. I. du Pont de Nemours and Company, series 2, p. 2, file 16, Pierre S. du Pont to Executive Committee, 31 October 1905, EMHL.
44. Ibid., Alfred I. du Pont to T. Coleman du Pont, 12 January, 1907, EMHL.
45. *Sunday Star*, 1 December 1912.
46. Wilmington *Morning News*, 6 November 1912.
47. For a discussion of the City

Beautiful Movement and the impact of the Chicago Fair see Mel Scott, *American City Planning* (Berkeley: University of California Press, 1971), chapters 1 and 2.
48. A. O. H. Grier, *This Was Wilmington* (Wilmington: 1945), pp. 37–38.
49. *Every Evening*, 20 February 1913.
50. J. J. Raskob Papers, File 398, EMHL.
51. Hoffecker, *Wilmington, Delaware: Portrait of an Industrial City*, p. 64.
52. *Sunday Star*, 25 February 1912; 26 May 1912.
53. *Sunday Star*, 2 June 1912.
54. *Morning News*, 1 and 2 June 1912.
55. Samuel P. Hays, "The Politics of Reform in Municipal Government in the Progressive Era," *Pacific Northwest Quarterly* 55 (October 1964): 157–69.
56. Blake McKelvey, *The Urbanization of America* (New Brunswick, New Jersey: Rutgers University Press, 1963), pp. 254–57.
57. William George Johnson, "The Life and Political Career of Henry Algernon du Pont," Master's thesis, University of Delaware, 1967, p. 47.
58. *Every Evening*, 4 April 1912.
59. Henry George, *Progress and Poverty* (New York: 1879).
60. John W. Donaldson, *Caveat Venditor: A Profile of Coleman du Pont* (N.P.: Private printing, 1964), p. 2.
61. Delaware State Highway Department, *Annual Report* (Dover, 1917).

62. John Rae, "Coleman du Pont and His Road," *Delaware History* XVI, 3, pp. 171–83.
63. *Sunday Star*, 9 April 1911.
64. *Every Evening*, 5 April 1912.
65. *Sunday Star*, 10 December 1911.
66. T. Coleman du Pont, *The Attainment of Good Roads Everywhere* (New York: National Highways Association, 1913).
67. *Every Evening*, 7 December 1911.
68. Delaware State Highway Department, *Annual Report* (Dover: 1917), pp. 19–33.
69. Rae, "Coleman du Pont and His Road," p. 179.
70. *Every Evening*, 5 April 1912.
71. Pierre S. du Pont Papers, File 472, EMHL.
72. Ibid.
73. Ibid.
74. *Charter, Laws and Ordinances of the City of Wilmington, Delaware* (Wilmington: 1910), pp. 554–62.
75. *Levy Court Minute Book*, 1 March 1910, Delaware State Archives.
76. *Every Evening*, 13 February 1893.
77. Ibid., 9 March 1898.
78. Ibid., 4 December 1906. The lines included the Wilmington and Chester Traction Company, Wilkes-Barre Traction Company, Trenton Railway Company, and the Schuylkill and Norristown Railway Company.
79. P. T. Reilly, "Local Mass Transportation in Wilmington and Vicinity," H. C. Reed, ed., *Delaware: A History of the First State*, II:530.
80. *Sunday Star*, 27 June 1909.
81. Pierre S. du Pont Papers, File 497, Wilmington and Philadelphia Traction Company prospectus, 1906. EMHL.
82. Ibid., Oscar T. Crosby to Pierre S. du Pont, 12 July 1911, EMHL.
83. Ibid., 4 January 1912, EMHL.
84. *Every Evening*, 13, 27, 29 March 1907.
85. Pierre S. du Pont Papers, File 497, Pierre S. du Pont to Henry Scott, Esq., 9 January 1913 and 16 January 1913, EMHL.
86. For contrasting strategies see Sam B. Warner, Jr., *Streetcar Suburbs* (Cambridge: Harvard University Press and The M.I.T. Press 1962), and Robert M. Fogelson, *The Fragmented Metropolis: Los Angeles, 1850–1930* (Cambridge: Harvard University Press, 1967).
87. *Sunday Star*, 12 July 1891.
88. *Every Evening*, 4 April 1902; 1 August 1903.
89. Ibid., 18 August 1905.
90. Ibid., 13 July 1906.
91. U.S. Census, 1910, *Agriculture* (Washington: 1913), VI:266–267.
92. U.S. Census, 1910, *Population by Counties* (Washington: 1912), p. 61.

Chapter 2

1. E. I. du Pont de Nemours & Company, *Annual Report*, 1914.
2. Alfred D. Chandler and Stephen M. Salsbury, *Pierre S. du Pont and the Making of the Modern Corporation* (New York: Harper & Row, 1971), p. 289.
3. Atlas Powder Company, *Annual Report*, 1913; Hercules Powder

Company, *Annual Report*, 1913;
Du Pont Company, *Annual Report*, 1913.

4. Du Pont Company, *Annual Report*, 1915, p. 3; 1916, p. 2.
5. Ibid., 1916.
6. Marquis James, *Alfred I. du Pont, The Family Rebel* (Indianapolis: The Bobbs-Merrill Company, 1941), pp. 254–96.
7. *Every Evening*, 19 July 1916.
8. *Sunday Star*, 7 January 1917.
9. U.S. Census, 1920, *Manufacturers*, IX, pp. 218–19.
10. *Sunday Star*, 16 July 1916.
11. *Every Evening*, 18 February 1918.
12. *Sunday Star*, 18 March 1917.
13. Ibid., 27 May 1923.
14. Ibid., 29 October 1916.
15. E. I. du Pont de Nemours & Company, *Du Pont Magazine*, 5, 9:1 (July 1918): 16–17.
16. Frank P. Gentieu, *The First Fifty Years at Carney's Point* (from series of articles published in the *Carney's Pointer*, May 1951-October 1952), photocopy at EMHL.
17. *Sunday Star*, 8 July 1916.
18. Ibid., 15 July 1917.
19. William C. Groben, "Union Park Gardens—A Model Suburb for Ship Workers at Wilmington, Delaware," *Architectural Record* 45 (January 1919): 12–19.
20. *Sunday Star*, July 15, 1934.
21. E. I. du Pont de Nemours & Company, "Wawaset, A Residential Community for the E. I. du Pont de Nemours & Company," pamphlet, 1918, EMHL.
22. *Sunday Star*, 16 January 1916.
23. Ibid., 23 January 1916.

24. Ibid., 7 January 1917.
25. Ibid.
26. Ibid., 8 August 1920.
27. Ibid., 13 June 1920.
28. Ibid., 12 November 1922.
29. Arthur H. Blanchard, et al., *Report on New Castle County Highways, 1916*; *Sunday Star*, 23 April 1916.
30. Frederick L. Paxson, "The Highway Movement," *American Historical Review*, 50, 1:2 (January 1946): 239–40.
31. Delaware State Highway Department, *Annual Report*, 1917.
32. Longwood Manuscripts. Group 10, File 661, J. P. Nields to H. R. Sharp, 2 October 1916, EMHL. Hereafter cited as LMSS.
33. LMSS, 10, 661, Pierre S. du Pont to Mrs. W. E. Hawkins, 29 July 1918, EMHL.
34. The State Highway Department also agreed to P. S. du Pont's request that they preserve an ancient pear tree along the Kennett Pike believed to have shaded General George Washington on his march to Chadds Ford in September 1777. Pierre S. du Pont Papers, File 699, Indenture between Pierre S. du Pont and Delaware State Highway Department, 25 September 1920, EMHL.
35. LMSS, 10, 687, Pierre S. du Pont to Andrew C. Gray, Esq., 6 December 1915, EMHL.
36. Ibid., J. P. Nields to P. S. du Pont, 8 December 1915, EMHL.
37. Ibid., P. S. du Pont to J. P. Nields, 1 December 1915, EMHL.

38. Ibid., Wilmington Institute Free Library, brochure, EMHL.
39. Ibid., J. P. Nields to P. S. du Pont, 27 October 1915, EMHL.
40. Ibid., P. S. du Pont to J. P. Nields, 21 March 1916, EMHL.
41. Ibid., J. P. Nields to P. S. du Pont, 5 February 1916; P. S. du Pont to J. P. Nields, 7 February 1916 and 14 February 1916, EMHL.
42. Ibid., J. P. Nields to P. S. du Pont, 7 April 1921, EMHL.
43. Ibid., P. S. du Pont to J. P. Nields, 9 April 1921, EMHL.
44. Ibid., J. P. Nields to P. S. du Pont, 11 April 1921, and 13 May 1921, EMHL.
45. Wilmington Institute Free Library, "Exercises at the Opening of the New Building of the Wilmington Institute Free Library, May 5, 1923," pamphlet, EMHL.
46. LMSS,10, 241, Pierre S. du Pont to Zara du Pont, 22 August 1912, EMHL.
47. LMSS, 10, 688, Group 10, Addresses of J. J. Raskob and P. S. du Pont, 9 July 1918, EMHL.
48. Ibid., Pierre du Pont to Mrs. Henry Ridgley, 12 August 1918, EMHL.
49. Ibid., typewritten manuscript by the Reverend Mr. Joseph H. Odell "Giving Away Another Man's Money in the War Zone" included this model letter: "You may never know the [benefactor] . . . by name but you are looking . . . into the mind and soul of a man who is at once a philanthropist and a seer. Yet, if I gave his name you would instantly recognize it as that of

one who has been vituperated and vilified as a leader in 'Big Business.' Personally, I think he is one of God's gentlemen."
50. Service Citizens of Delaware, *Service Bulletin* 4,3 (September 1922), HSD.
51. Robert S. Taggert, "Pierre S. du Pont and the Great School Fight in 1919–1921," *Delaware History* 17 (1976–77): 155.
52. Service Citizens of Delaware, "Shall Wilmington Stop Growing? The Importance of Immediate Home Building," pamphlet, November 1919, HSD.
53. LMSS, 10, 688, group 10, J. H. Odell to Jeanette Eckman, 29 July 1919; Jeanette Eckman to J. H. Odell, 5 August 1919, EMHL.
54. Ibid., Helen C. Shaw to P. S. du Pont, 27 October 1919, EMHL.
55. Ibid., William H. Kilpatrick to Joseph H. Odell, February 27, 1922, EMHL.
56. Ibid., P. S. du Pont to William H. Kilpatrick, March 13, 1922, EMHL.
57. Ibid., William H. Kilpatrick to P. S. du Pont, 10 April 1922, EMHL.
58. Ibid., P. S. du Pont to J. H. Odell, 14 April 1922, EMHL.
59. Joint Citizens Committee on Education in Cooperation with the General Service Board of Delaware, "Proposed Changes in the Wilmington School System," pamphlet, 1917, Morris Library, Univ. of Delaware.
60. Superintendent, Wilmington Public Schools, *Annual Report*, 1921–22, p. 19.
61. Ibid., 1925, p. 39.

62. Ibid., p. 43.
63. *Sunday Star*, 25 March 1928.
64. Ibid., 13 May 1928; 27 September 1931.
65. S. M. Stouffer, "The Pierre S. du Pont High School in Wilmington," *American School Board Journal* 92 (1936): 35.
66. LMSS, 10, 712–29, P. S. du Pont to S. M. Stouffer, 21 October 1935.
67. LMSS, 10, 241, P. S. du Pont to Zara du Pont, 22 August 1912, EMHL.
68. Chandler and Salsbury, *Pierre S. du Pont*, p. 582.
69. Chamber of Commerce of Wilmington, Delaware, *Wilmington*, January, 1927.
70. *Sunday Star*, 18 September 1921.
71. Ibid., 13 January 1929.
72. The Chamber of Commerce published a monthly magazine, *Wilmington*, beginning in May 1926 through April 1927. The brief life of this publication even during the high tide of 20s business optimism suggests the continuing troubles of the city's retail and wholesale trade and manufactures.
73. Ibid., 8 March 1936.
74. U.S.Census, 1930, *Population*, I:185.
75. *Every Evening*, 5 November 1929.
76. *Sunday Star*, 9 November 1924, advertisement for Brown and Whiteside, architects.
77. Regional Planning Federation of the Philadelphia Tri-State District, *The Regional Plan of the Philadelphia Tri-State District* (Philadelphia: William F. Fell Co., 1932), p. 32.

78. *Sunday Star*, 9 January 1921.
79. Ibid., 5 February 1928; 15 March 1925.
80. Ibid., 8 February 1925.
81. Ibid., 14 March 1926.
82. Ibid., 13 February 1927.
83. Ibid., 6 August 1930.
84. *State Board of Education Reports*, 1927.
85. Superintendent, Wilmington Public Schools, *Annual Report*, 1925, p. 56.
86. Ibid., p. 53.
87. Gloria T. Hull, "Alice Dunbar-Nelson: Delaware Writer and Woman of Affairs," *Delaware History* 17: 87–103.
88. *Sunday Star*, 3 October 1926.
89. Ibid., 3 October 1926; 10 October 1926; 24 October 1926.
90. Ibid., 21 November 1926.
91. *Every Evening*, 19 February 1918.
92. *Sunday Star*, 4 July 1920.
93. Ibid., 8 August 1920.
94. Ibid., 22 October 1922.
95. *Every Evening*, 1 July 1930.
96. Chief Engineer, Delaware State Highway Department, *Annual Report*, 1925.
97. Regional Planning Federation *Regional Plan*.
98. Ibid., p. 43.
99. *Sunday Star*, 21 October 1934.
100. Regional Planning Federation, *Regional Plan*, p. 398.
101. *Sunday Star*, 20 October 1929.
102. *Every Evening*, 30 October 1929.
103. Ibid., 2 November 1929.
104. E. I. du Pont de Nemours & Company, *Annual Report*, 1930, 1931, 1932.
105. Associated Charities, *Associated Charities Progress* 4, no. 2 (5 November 1929).

106. The Family Society, *Family Society Progress* 5, no. 4, (28 October 1930), 6, no. 2 (27 October 1931).

107. American Public Welfare Association, Fred K. Hoehler, Director, "Public Welfare Survey of the State of Delaware," June 1938. Morris Library, University of Delaware.

108. LMSS, 10, 1171, Alfred I. du Pont to Pierre S. du Pont, 29 August 1939, EMHL.

109. James, *Alfred du Pont*, p. 464.

110. American Public Welfare Association, "Public Welfare Survey," p. 9.

111. *Sunday Star*, 29 October 1933.

112. Mayor's Employment and Relief Committee, "Work and Relief in Wilmington, Delaware, 1931–32," pamphlet, Morris Library, University of Delaware.

113. *Sunday Star*, 31 May 1931.

114. Ibid., 20 November 1932.

115. Mayor's Committee, "Work Relief in Wilmington."

116. The Family Society, *Family Society Progress* 8, no. 4 (24 October 1933).

117. *Sunday Star*, 20 November 1932.

118. The priorities of Wilmington's elite are strikingly reflected in the predictions of sociological theory. Eugene Lewis, *The Urban Political System* (Hinsdale, Ill.: The Dryden Press, 1973), p. 117, writes concerning elitist goals: "Economic growth and measured socio-economic upward mobility with concomitant suburbanization and human homogenization might also be inferred from a description of an elite-dominated urban political system. An elite-dominated urban system might also be expected deliberately to ignore those who could safely be ignored, including blacks and the poor."

Chapter 3

1. *Sunday Star*, 4 November 1934.

2. Delaware State Highway Department, *Annual Report*, 1936.

3. W. E. Leuchtenburg, *Franklin D. Roosevelt and the New Deal, 1932–1940* (New York: Harper & Row, 1963), pp. 134–35.

4. *Sunday Star*, 7 May 1939.

5. Ibid., 26 November 1939.

6. Ibid., 14 January 1940.

7. Ibid., 17 September 1933.

8. Ibid., 23 September 1934.

9. Mrs. Gerald B. Street, chairman, et al., "Report on the Housing Commission of the State of Delaware," 1932, pamphlet, Morris Library.

10. *Sunday Star*, 17 September 1933.

11. Ibid., 17 August 1941.

12. William F. Groben, "Union Park Gardens—A Model Garden Suburb for Shipworkers at Wilmington, Delaware," *Architectural Record*, 1919, p. 14.

13. *Journal-Every Evening*, 18 November 1942.

14. *Sunday Star*, 28 September 1941.

15. Ibid., 28 December 1941.

16. E. I. du Pont de Nemours & Company, *Annual Report*, 1944,

p. 12, Hercules Corporation, *Annual Report*, 1944, pp. 12–13.

17. *Sunday Star*, 3 January 1943 and 2 January 1944.
18. Ibid., 9, 16, 30 May 1943; 4 February 1945.
19. Delaware State Highway Department, *Annual Report*, 1941–42.
20. Ibid., 1945; 1947; 1948.
21. Ibid., 1949.
22. U.S.Census, 1950, *Population* 5, 2, pt. 8, pp. 8–11; *Housing* 5, 1, pt. 2, pp. 81-21.
23. *Sunday Star*, 20 May 1948.
24. Ibid., 1 February 1948.
25. Ibid., 3 October 1948 and 17 October 1948.
26. Paul Dolan, *The Government and Administration of Delaware* (New York: Crowell Publishing Company, 1956), p. 326.
27. Interview with B. Gary Scott, Realtor, 5 June 1980. Each area of the suburbs produced its own dominant builders. In Brandywine Hundred Gray Magness, a descendent of a local farming family related by marriage to a leading plumber, was the giant of the industry. Magness introduced the split level to Delaware in Graylyn Crest, his first major development. Signs proclaiming "Built and Backed by Magness" became a common sight along roads that only recently had been flanked by rolling farmlands. Southwest of Wilmington was the territory of Frank Robino, whose split-level communities with evocative names like Sherwood Park and Heritage Park lined the corridor

west of the Kirkwood Highway. South of the city, Gordy Builders were most active, constructing blue-collar communities like Wilmington Manor and Collins Park.

28. Muriel Crosby, *An Adventure in Human Relations* (Chicago: Follett Publishing Company, 1965), p. 3.
29. Interview with Dr. Muriel Crosby, 4 June 1980.
30. *Sunday Star*, 14 September and 5 October 1952.
31. Ibid., 12 October 1952.
32. *Journal-Every Evening*, 2 January 1957.
33. Ibid., 8 January 1954.
34. Charles Abrams, *The City is the Frontier* (New York: Harper & Row, 1965), p. 82.
35. Ibid., p. 87.
36. Roy Lubove, *Twentieth-Century Pittsburgh: Government, Business and Environmental Change* (New York: John Wiley & Sons, 1969).
37. Harold Kaplan, *Urban Renewal Politics, Slum Clearance in Newark* (New York: Columbia University Press, 1963).
38. *Journal-Every Evening*, 14 August 1958.
39. *Sunday Star*, 14 October 1951.
40. Ibid., 16 December 1951.
41. Ibid., 15 October 1950.
42. Ibid., 11 March 1951.
43. Ibid., 25 March 1951.
44. Philip G. Rhoads, "Operations and Purpose of Woodlawn," 1972, typewritten ms. On page 20 Rhoads notes that the Citizens Housing Corporation was created to buy houses, rehabilitate them and rent them to

black tenants. Modestly financed, its profits have been invested in buying more properties, in 1960 the Citizens Housing Corporation owned 60 units, all on the East Side.

45. *Sunday Star*, 6 May 1951.
46. Ibid., 12 August 1951.
47. *Journal-Every Evening*, 12 June 1953.
48. Ibid., 10 December 1953.
49. Interview with Dudley Finch, 25 August 1978.
50. Finch had excellent instincts for combining the needs of tenants with maintenance of goals. He favored keeping the design and components of public housing simple. People who had never used a kitchen sink before, he pointed out, should be supplied with free-standing models so that they can see the cockroaches that climb along the waterpipes rather than with the cabinet models that became popular during the 1950s.
51. Wilmington Housing Authority, "The Redevelopment Plan for Poplar Street Project A," June 1956.
52. *Journal-Every Evening*, 15 April 1954.
53. Wilmington Housing Authority, "Poplar Street A Proposal, July 10, 1963," Revised, 1 March 1970. The problem of rehousing those displaced by slum clearance was by no means limited to Wilmington, nor was the misconception advanced by Carolyn Weaver that the slum dwellers would be able to move back to new houses in their old neighborhoods. Charles Abrams, *The City Is the Frontier* (New York:

Harper & Row, 1965), pp. 82–85.
54. Interview with Dudley Finch, 25 August 1978.
55. *Journal-Every Evening*, 17 February 1956.
56. Ibid., 15 April 1955.
57. Ibid., 8 June 1955.
58. *Randolph* v. *Wilmington Housing Authority, Delaware Chancery Reports*, 37, p. 203.
59. Ibid., p. 226.
60. Ibid., p. 229.
61. Delaware State Highway Department, "Report on the Transportation Study: Wilmington Metropolitan Area," 1948.
62. Ibid.
63. Parsons, Brinckerhoff, Hall, and MacDonald, "General Plan: Wilmington Metropolitan Area Arterial Route Analysis," December 1950.
64. *Sunday Star*, 22 July 1951.
65. Mark Rose, "Express Highway Politics, 1929–1956," Ph.D. diss., Ohio State University, 1973, p. 184.
66. Ibid., p. 229.
67. Ibid., pp. 198–99.
68. Interview with Hugh Rodney Sharp, Jr., 20 September 1978.
69. The Union Street route was to pass along the eastern edge of Elsmere paralleling Union Street through the city. North of Wilmington it was to parallel the B&O Railroad's right of way.
70. *Journal-Every Evening*, 14 February 1957.
71. Ibid., 20 February 1957.
72. Ibid., 25 February 1957.
73. Ibid., 5 March 1957.
74. Ibid., 7 March 1957.
75. Ibid., 25 March 1957.

76. Transcript of Delaware State Senate Hearing on the Wilmington Expressway, 18 March 1957.

77. *Journal-Every Evening*, 13 April 1957.

78. Maurice du Pont Lee Papers, Acc. 1452, Box 38, undated circular opposing passage of HB 548, EMHL.

79. *Journal-Every Evening*, 11 April 1957.

80. Ibid., 27 February 1957.

81. Interview with James D. Wilson, 27 July 1978.

82. Interview with William Miller, 1 August 1978.

83. *Journal-Every Evening*, 1 May 1957.

84. *Morning News*, 14 May 1957.

85. *Journal-Every Evening*, 14 June 1957.

86. *Morning News*, 21 June 1957.

87. Thomas Herlihy's Brief for *Piekarski, et al., v. Delaware State Highway Department*. Private papers in possession of Mrs. Charles Daniels.

88. *Journal-Every Evening*, 28 June 1957.

89. Helen Leavitt, *Superhighway–Superhoax* (Garden City, New York: Doubleday & Company, 1970), p. 31.

90. Frank J. Obara to Thomas Herlihy, Jr., 23 May 1958, Daniels papers.

91. These remarks made by Commissioner Benjamin F. Shaw II were reported in the *Journal-Every Evening*, 17 May 1957.

92. Interview with H. R. Sharp, Jr., 20 September 1978.

93. Interview with Richard Haber, 7 August 1978.

94. *Morning News*, 27 June 1957.

95. Irving Warner to Bertram Tal-lamy, 1 February 1958, Daniels papers.

96. Irving Warner, typed statement dated 26 August 1957, Daniels papers.

97. Irving Warner to U.S. Congressman Harry G. Haskell, 27 September 1957, copy in Daniels papers.

98. *Journal-Every Evening*, 6 May 1957.

99. Wilbur Smith Associates, "Traffic and Parking, Wilmington, Delaware," 1959.

100. *Journal-Every Evening*, 17 May 1957.

101. Charles Abrams, *The City Is the Frontier*, and Jane Jacobs, *The Death and Life of Great American Cities* (New York: Random House, 1961) provide an introduction into this literature.

102. See Jeanne R. Lowe, *Cities in a Race with Time* (New York: Random House, 1967), for examples of other cities' more successful efforts to use federal programs to achieve local redevelopment goals.

103. *Journal-Every Evening*, 3 July 1962.

104. Robert and Helen Lynd predicted a similar pattern in the relationship of the X family to Middletown in their famous studies of American city life. Of the second generation among the X family, they wrote, "the supporting power of their wealth will remain, but one suspects that the intensity of devotion to local causes will eventually be somewhat less among these younger families that have not fought shoulder to shoulder with the city's business pioneers.

. . ." Robert S. Lynd and Helen M. Lynd, *Middletown in Transition* (New York: Harcourt, Brace and Company, 1937), p. 100.

105. Unsigned copy of a letter sent to Irénée du Pont, Spring, 1957, Daniels papers.

106. M. du Pont Lee Papers, Acc. 1452, Irénée du Pont to Maurice du Pont Lee, 5 April 1957, Wm. du Pont Lee Papers, EMHL.

107. Ibid., 6 June 1957.

Chapter 4

1. *Journal-Every Evening*, 13 April 1960.

2. New Castle County Regional Planning Commission, *Planning/ Population: A Background Study* (March 1966), p. 17.

3. Charles Tilly, *Race and Residence in Wilmington, Delaware* (New York: Teachers College, Columbia University, 1965), p. 17.

4. *Journal-Every Evening*, 25 November 1960.

5. Ibid., 30 November 1960.

6. Ibid., 18 May 1961.

7. The club featured a portrait of José F. Pilsudski overlooking its horse-collar-shaped bar. When it was torn down in 1964 the building still bore marks from a police attack on a group of Communists to whom the club had given shelter in 1932. *Journal-Every Evening*. 28 January 1964.

8. Ibid., 30 January 1964.

9. Ibid., 6 March 1963.

10. Ibid., 30 July 1957.

11. Interview with Louis L. Redding, 26 March 1980.

12. *Journal-Every Evening*, 25 February 1959.

13. Ibid., 27 February 1959.

14. Ibid., 8 April 1959.

15. Ibid., 7 August 1959 and 8 August 1959.

16. Ibid., 27 March 1959 and 18 April 1959.

17. Muriel Crosby, *An Adventure in Human Relations* (Chicago: Follett Publishing Company, 1965), pp. 24–25.

18. Ibid., p. 65.

19. Jackson-Cross Company Realtors, "Potential Uses of Poplar Street Project A," April 1960.

20. Ibid.

21. *Journal-Every Evening*, 1 July 1960.

22. Interview with Richard P. Sanger, 23 May 1980.

23. *Journal-Every Evening*, 26 September 1960.

24. Ibid., 26 September 1960.

25. Interview with Irénée du Pont, Jr., 3 June 1980.

26. Raymond A. Bauer, Ithiel de Sola Pool, and Lewis A. Dexter, *American Business and Public Policy* (New York: Atherton Press, 1963), p. 265.

27. H. B. du Pont shared his relatives' and business acquaintances' view that more heavy industry was unwelcome near Du Pont's corporate-research headquarters, but, putting his hometown's future ahead of other considerations, he approved the idea of attracting other corporations to the area as an important way of rescuing Wilmington from the doldrums. Interview

with Richard P. Sanger, 23 May 1980, and *Journal-Every Evening*, 12 January 1959.

28. Interview with the Hon. John E. Babiarz, 5 August 1980.

29. *Journal-Every Evening*, 10 February 1964 and 4 November 1964.

30. Ibid., 3 July 1962.

31. Interview with Peter Larson, 11 June 1980.

32. *Journal-Every Evening*, 15 September 1960.

33. Ibid., 6 October 1961.

34. Ibid., 13 November 1961.

35. Ibid., 28 October 1961.

36. Ibid., 17 January 1963.

37. Ibid., 13 April 1962.

38. Ibid., 17 December 1962.

39. Project B was a small renewal project at 5th and Du Pont streets that replaced an old brewery with row houses.

40. *Journal-Every Evening*, 6 August 1964.

41. Lawrence Schein, *The People of Metropolitan Delaware: A Population Profile of New Castle County* (Wilmington: Community Services Council of Delaware, 1964), p. 82.

42. Ibid., pp. 28 and 87.

43. Ibid., p. 100.

44. Ibid., p. 113.

45. C. Harold Brown and Robert A. Wilson, "Evaluation, Neighborhood Improvement Program," University of Delaware Division of Urban Affairs, 1969, vol. 2, p. 3.

46. Ibid., p. 22.

47. Interview with Patricia Schramm, 3 June 1980.

48. Brown and Wilson, vol. 1, p. 2.

49. Ibid., p. 15.

50. Letter from Edward J. Goett, Chairman, WYEAC Advisory Committee, to Hon. John L. McClellan, Wilmington, Delaware, 22 October 1968, published in "Riots, Civil and Criminal Disorders," Hearings Before the Permanent Subcommittee of the Committee on Government Operations, 90th Congress, 2nd session, pt. 14, p. 2944.

51. Testimony of Captain John T. McCool, Wilmington Police Department before the Permanent Subcommittee on Investigations of the Committee on Government Operations, United States Senate, 90th Congress, 2nd session, 8–11 October 1968, pt. 14, entitled "Riots, Civil and Criminal Disorders," p. 2827.

52. Edward J. Butler, "The Role of the Change Agent in Community Development," Master's thesis, University of Delaware, 1968, p. 62.

53. Interview with Richard Pryor, 11 June 1980.

54. *Delmarva Dialog*, 23 June 1967.

55. Joseph Cepuran, "CAP Expenditures in The Fifty States: A Comparison," *Urban Affairs Quarterly* 4, 3 (March 1969): 325.

56. *Journal-Every Evening*, 1 February 1957, 20 September 1960, and 5 October 1965, and interview with Mrs. Pearl Herlihy Daniels, June 1980.

57. *Morning News*, 28 June 1967.

58. Interview with City Councilman James Baker, 12 June 1980.

59. *Journal-Every Evening*, 29 July, 31 June, and 1 August 1967.

60. Joseph A. Bradshaw, Chairman, Investigating Committee on the Cause of Civil Unrest; report to Governor Charles L. Terry, September 1967, Pearl Herlihy Daniels' papers. Governor Terry's investigative committee was a miniature version of the Commission on Civil Disorders appointed by President Lyndon B. Johnson in July 1967. The commission, chaired by Governor Otto Kerner of Illinois, produced a massive, widely circulated study entitled *Report of the National Advisory Commission on Civil Disorders* (New York: E. P. Dutton and Co. and Bantam, 1968). The Kerner Commission identified 164 separate racial disorders during the first nine months of 1967 only five of which they classified as major riots. They urged a much intensified war on poverty to counteract the poverty, joblessness, lack of education and alienation in urban ghettos.

61. Butler, "The Role of the Change Agent," p. 64.

62. *Delmarva Dialog*, 23 June 1967.

63. Hubert H. Humphrey to Charles L. Reese, Jr., 31 August 1967. Pearl Herlihy Daniels Papers.

64. Edward J. Goett, Chairman Report of the Ad Hoc Committee to Study the Program and Financing of WYEAC, April 1968. Other committeemen were Irénée du Pont, Jr., Rodney Layton, Henry Russel, and W. Spencer Thompson.

65. Permanent Subcommittee, Committee on Government Operations Hearings, U.S. Senate,

"Riots, Civil and Criminal Disorders," p. 2796.

66. *Journal-Every Evening*, 18 May 1968.

67. Ibid., 29 December 1967.

68. Ibid., 15 November 1967.

69. Ibid., 7 February 1968.

70. Ibid., 5 June 1968.

71. Ibid., 5 November 1968.

72. Ibid., 4 October 1967.

73. Ibid., 7 December 1967.

74. Ibid., 5 April 1968.

75. Ibid., 19 March, 16, 19, 20 May 1964.

76. The policy also allowed the realty board and its individual members the right to oppose open housing legislation and permitted individual realtors to refuse open housing listings. *Journal-Every Evening*, 31 March 1965.

77. Ibid., 3, 5, 23 June 1965.

78. Ibid., 7, 9 December 1965.

79. Ibid., 5 April; 18, 22 May; 2 June 1967.

80. Ibid., 12 December 1967.

81. Ibid., 2 December 1967.

82. Ibid., 4 and 5 August 1967.

83. Ibid., 6 September 1967.

84. Ibid., 12 September 1967.

85. Ibid., 10 September 1967.

86. Ibid., 21 December 1967.

87. Ibid., 1 April 1968.

88. *New York Times*, 5–11 April 1968.

89. *Journal-Every Evening*, 8 April 1968.

90. Ibid., 9 April 1968.

91. Interview with the Rev. Mr. Lloyd Casson, 19 August 1980.

92. *Journal-Every Evening*, 10 April 1968.

93. Long before the riot occurred, Governor Terry, Mayor Babiarz, and the commander of the Delaware National Guard had met

and agreed to a three-stage contingency plan. In case of disorder the mayor was to specify whether he wanted a small, medium, or large guard presence in the city. On 9 April 1968, Mayor Babiarz requested the lowest level guard support, or plan A; but Governor Terry instead put into effect plan C, total mobilization. The entire Delaware National Guard Troop, 2,800 strong, was sent to Wilmington. Interview with the Hon. John E. Babiarz, 5 August 1980.

94. *Journal-Every Evening*, 24 April 1968.
95. Ibid., 18 May 1968.
96. Ibid., 23 May 1968.
97. *Morning News*, 16 July 1968.
98. Arthur W. Grimes, Inspector, Report of the Department of Public Safety, Wilmington, Delaware, 4 September 1968.
99. *Journal-Every Evening*, 7 April; 13 May; 11, 14 June 1969.
100. Permanent Subcommittee, Committee on Government Operations Hearing, U.S. Senate, "Riots, Civil and Criminal Disorders," p. 2381.
101. *Journal-Every Evening*, 3 September 1968.
102. Ibid.
103. Ibid., 4 September 1968.
104. Permanent Subcommittee on Government Operations Hearings, U.S. Senate, "Riots, Civil and Criminal Disorders," p. 2822.
105. Ibid., p. 2815.
106. Ibid., p. 2914.
107. Ibid., pp. 2943–44.
108. Copy of a memorandum from James Grady to the Greater

Wilmington Development Council Executive Committee, 2 August 1967, Pearl Herlihy Daniels Papers.
109. Calvin Trillin, untitled article, *New Yorker*, 7 December 1968, p. 190.
110. *Journal-Every Evening*, 17 January 1969.
111. Ibid., 23 January 1969.

Chapter 5

1. Interview with B. Gary Scott, realtor, 5 June 1980.
2. 1933 Report of County Planning Commission.
3. New Castle County Regional Planning Commission, "Rules and Regulations: Guide for Real Estate Development and Land Subdivisions Filing of Plats," March 1944.
4. *Sunday Star*, 9 May 1948.
5. Memorandum from GWDC subcommittee on county planning, Mrs. W. W. Heckert, chairman, to Russell W. Peterson, chairman, Comprehensive Planning committee, undated, in Box 1, "County Reorganization," HSD.
6. *Evening Journal*, 25 April 1963.
7. Ibid., 14 December 1963 and 3 January 1964.
8. The other members included chairman Samuel R. Russell, Mrs. Thomas Herlihy, Jr., Frank O'Donnell, F. Earl McGinnes, Harry Lambert, and Sherman W. Tribbitt.
9. *Evening Journal*, 21 February; 25 June; 27 June; and 10 July 1963.
10. Governor's Committee on Reorganization of the Government of

New Castle County, "Report and Proposed Legislation," May 1964, in Box 1, "County Reorganization," HSD.

11. *Evening Journal*, 9 November 1966.

12. During the same years that her husband was head of county government, Louise Conner was in the forefront of a small band of state legislators who favored open housing, a position that cost her reelection in 1972. In 1971 when someone burned a cross on the front lawn of the Conners' house in Delaire, the Conners were at a loss to know for which of them it was intended. Interview with William and Louise Conner, 26 September 1980.

13. Interview with Allan Rusten, administrative assistant to Mayor Harry Haskell, 4 September 1980.

14. Interview with the Hon. Harry Haskell, 29 October 1980.

15. *Evening Journal*, 12, 22 December 1969, and 4 February 1970.

16. Delaware Government Research Foundation, New Castle County Governmental Management Study, Committee Report, February 1980.

17. *Evening Journal*, 16 February 1970.

18. Ibid., 8, 30 April 1970.

19. Ibid., 9 June 1970.

20. Ibid., 7 January 1971.

21. New Castle County Government Management Study, 1970.

22. New Castle County Regional Planning Commission, "Planning/Economic Characteristics: A Background Study," 1967.

23. U.S. Bureau of the Census, 1970, *Census of Population and Housing, Delaware, Preliminary Pamphlet*.

24. Special Committee on Housing in New Castle County, Delaware, Mrs. Richard J. Both, Chairman, Report, 1 February 1971.

25. Interview with Mrs. Richard J. Both, 28 August 1980.

26. Both committee report.

27. *First Annual Report of The Council on Environmental Quality together with the President's Message to Congress*, August 1970, Washington: U.S. Government Printing Office, 1970.

28. *Evening Journal*, 22 January 1965.

29. Ibid., 10 November 1962.

30. Ibid., 25, 27 June 1964.

31. Ibid., 18 September 1963.

32. Ibid., 15 February 1964.

33. Ibid., 13 February 1964.

34. Ibid., 8 December 1964.

35. Ibid., 16 December 1969.

36. Ibid., 4, 8 April 1970.

37. Interview with William Conner, 26 September 1980.

38. *Evening Journal*, 3 September 1970.

39. Ibid., 27 March, 22 June 1970.

40. Ibid., 22 June 1970.

41. Ibid., 9 March 1972.

42. Interview with William Conner, 26 September 1980.

43. *Evening Journal*, 11 June 1971.

44. Interview with Stephen Clark and Philip G. Rhoads, president and past president of Woodlawn Trustees, 22 September 1980.

45. Philip G. Rhoads, "The Operations and Purpose of Woodlawn," 1972, unpublished ms.

46. Interview with Stephen Clark

and Philip G. Rhoads, 22 September 1980.

47. *Evening Journal*, 29 November 1965.

48. Ibid., 17 February 1969.

49. Ibid., 29 November 1965.

50. Interview with Mrs. Henry E. I. du Pont, 8 August 1980, and *Evening Journal*, 18 January, 2 March 1973.

51. For one example of many, see *Journal-Every Evening*, 3 August 1960.

52. *Sunday Star*, 21 May 1916.

53. Ibid., 30 July 1916.

54. Ibid., 3 December 1916.

55. The resemblances between Wilmington and Philadelphia are so evident that one is inclined to ignore their equally significant differences, of which size is the most obvious. From colonial times the economic activities carried on in the two cities were remarkably parallel. But in the course of the twentieth century, Wilmington's conversion to a one-industry town marked a significant separation from the experience of its larger neighbor. In addition, proximity to Philadelphia has always hurt Wilmington's retail buisiness, and the smaller city never attracted full-scale department stores to its retail center.

56. Jeanne R. Lowe, *Cities in a Race with Time* (New York: Random House, 1967), pp. 344–45.

57. *Evening Journal*, 19 March 1964.

58. Ibid., 31 October 1966.

59. Interview with the Hon. Thomas Maloney, 24 September 1980.

60. Ibid.

61. Minutes of the Executive Committee, Delaware Ethnic Studies and Cultural Center, 26 November 1974, HSD.

62. Toni Young, *The Grand Experience: A History of the Grand Opera House* (Watkins Glen, New York: The American Life Foundation, 1976), p. 142.

63. Ibid., pp. 142–79, passim.

64. The full title of the Model Cities legislation was the Demonstration Cities and Metropolitan Development Act of 1966. A summary of the act's provisions may be found in *United States Code and Administrative News*, 5, 1, 89th Congress, 1966, pp. 1467–514. On the inherent weakness of the federal plan to include the poor in decision making see Eugene Lewis, *The Urban Political System* (Hinsdale, Illinois: The Dryden Press, 1973), pp. 262–65.

65. C. Harold Brown, "Evaluation: Neighborhood Improvement Program" (University of Delaware Division of Urban Affairs, 1969), pt. 1, pp. 15, 26, and 27.

66. *Evening Journal*, 29 January 1969.

67. Interview with Allan Rusten, 5 September 1980.

68. *Evening Journal*, 6, 7 January 1972.

69. Ibid., 10 January 1972.

70. Ibid., 17 May 1973.

71. According to city housing officials, between 1973 and 1981 homesteaders have applied to restore 123 houses.

72. Department of Public Instruction, State of Delaware, *Annual Report*, 1954, pt. 2, p. 67.

73. Interview with Dr. Muriel Crosby, 4 June 1980.
74. Interview with the Rev. Lloyd Casson, former president of the Wilmington Board of Education, 19 August 1980; also see the *Evening Journal*, 26, 27 August 1972.
75. Julie A. Schmidt, "School Desegregation in Wilmington, Delaware: A Case Study in Non-Decision-Making," M.A. thesis, University of Delaware, 1979, p. 164.
76. Ibid., p. 162.
77. *Evening Journal*, 22 October 1970.
78. Interview with the Hon. Harry Haskell, 29 October 1980.
79. *Evans v. Buchanan*, 152 F. Supp. 886 (1957).
80. Ibid., 379 F. Supp. 1218 (1974).
81. *Millikin v. Bradley*.
82. *Evans v. Buchanan*, 393 F. Supp. 428 (1975).
83. Jeffrey A. Raffel, *The Politics of School Desegregation: The Metropolitan Remedy in Delaware* (Philadelphia: Temple University Press, 1980), p. 20.
84. Ibid., p. 70.
85. *Evans v. Buchanan*, 416 F. Supp. 328 (1976).
86. Ibid., 447 F. Supp. 982 (1978).
87. Raffel, *Politics of School Desegregation*, pp. 146–47.
88. Ibid., p. 106.
89. Ibid., p. 170.
90. Robert F. Boozer, "Non-Public Schools in Delaware, 1979–80." Delaware Department of Public Instruction, 1979.
91. Raffel, *Politics of School Desegregation*, p. 91.
92. Charles L. Reese, Jr., "Merger: A Brief History of the Developments which Led to the Creation of the Wilmington Medical Center on November 1, 1965," typewritten ms., 1972, Wilmington Medical Center file, HSD.
93. Booz, Allen, and Hamilton, "Community Hospital Planning Study," September 1962, WMC file, HSD.
94. Cresap, McCormick, and Paget, "Wilmington Medical Center: Alternative Long-Range Plans for Future Development," August 1968.
95. Testimony of John J. B. Fulenwider, Chairman of the WMC Inc. Site Committee, before Federal District Court, 30 October 1979 in *NAACP v. MWC, Inc.*, Civil Action 76-298, pp. 1550–74, transcript in possession of WMC, Inc.
96. *Evening Journal*, 3 July 1969.
97. Ibid., 11 August 1970.
98. Ibid., 14 April 1970.
99. Testimony of Joseph Dallas, chairman of the W.M.C. Inc. board of trustees, *NAACP v. WMC, Inc.*, 30 October 1979, p. 1495–96, transcript in possession of WMC, Inc.
100. Testimony of Oliver Deehan, Director of Planning, W.M.C. Inc., *NAACP v. WMC, Inc.*, 31 October 1979, p. 1710, transcript in possession of WMC, Inc.
101. Testimony of Shirley M. Tarrant, *NAACP v. WMC, Inc.*, 31 October 1979, p. 1774, transcript in possession of WMC, Inc.
102. *NAACP v. WMC, Inc.*, Civil Action 76-298, 13 May 1980.
103. Morris Janowitz, *The Last Half-Century: Societal Change and*

Politics in America (Chicago: University of Chicago Press, 1978), p. 297.

104. Jon C. Teaford, *City and Suburb, the Political Fragmentation of Metropolitan America, 1850–1970* (Baltimore: The Johns Hopkins Press, 1979), pp. 150–51.

105. James Phelan and Robert Pozen, *The Company State* (New York: Grossman Publishers, 1973), p. 4.

106. Ibid., p. 409.

INDEX

Adas Kodesh Synagogue, 29, 178
Addicks, John Edward O'Sullivan, 47–48
Advocate, 95
Age of Confidence, 18
Alapocas, 110, 227
Alfred I. du Pont School District, 223
American Car and Foundry Company, 39
American Civil Liberties Union, 246
Apartment buildings, 121
Artesian Water Company, 93
Associated Charities, 101
Atlas Chemical, 202
Atlas Powder Company, 61, 65, 88, 195
Augustine Cut-Off, 108
Automobiles: effect of, on Wilmington, 53, 70–71, 89, 99, 116–17, 124–25

Babiarz, John E., 173–74, 176, 179, 186–87, 192, 198, 200–201, 215
Baker, F. Raymond, 127
Ballinger and Perrot, 68
Bancroft, Joseph, 33
Bancroft, William Poole, 33, 226–27
Bancroft flats, 33
Bancroft textile mill, 15, 33
Bank of Delaware, 193
Banks, 35; and real estate market, 26
Bayard, Thomas F., 45
Baynard, Samuel H., 24–26
Baynard Boulevard, 24
Bellefonte, 57–58, 90
Belleview Manor, 110

Bethlehem Steel (Harlan plant), 65
Biondi, Frank, 174
Blacks: education of, 83, 94–95, 123–24, 245; employment of, 101; housing for, 28, 91, 94–96, 112, 126, 131, 163–64, 167–68, 180, 195; migration to city, 9; neighborhoods, 160, 188, 190; segregation of, 95, 169; status in Wilmington, 28, 94, 179; youth gangs, 184–85, 190, 192, 200–203
Blumenthal's morocco factory, 31
Board of Health, 127
Board of Trade, 21
Both, Mrs. Richard J., 220–21
Brandywine Hills, 110
Brandywine Hundred, 227
Brandywine Park, 24
Brandywine Springs Park, 20
Breakfast Group, 251
Brown, C. Harold, 182, 239
Brown, George N., 190
Brown, H. Fletcher, 253
Brown v. *Board of Education of Topeka, Kansas*, 123
Buchanan, Madelyn, 247
Buck, C. Douglass, 102, 215, 221, 225
Burckel, W. Garrett, 147
Bureau of Municipal Research, 79
Burton, William ("Dutch"), 177
Butler, Edward J. ("Ned"), 184, 187, 203

Canby, Henry Seidel, 17–18
Carpenter, R. R. M., 65; family, 253

Carvel, Elbert, 213, 215
Casson, Lloyd, 245
Catholic Interracial Council, 129
Catholic Social Services, 184
Central Labor Union, 104
Chamber of Commerce, 21, 66, 87, 97, 101
Chandler, Alfred D., 4, 39
Chemical Industry, 88
Cherry Island, 20–21, 201
Christina Securities Company, 65, 172
Christina Bridge, 138–39
Christina River, 13, 17
Chrysler Corporation Parts Division, 118
Citizens Housing Alliance of Delaware, 221
Citizens Housing Association, 127, 129
City Beautiful movement, 43
City charter reform, 44, 46, 91, 155, 174, 207, 213, 215
City Club, 44
City Council, 129, 146, 148–51, 194
City-County Building, 44
Civic Center, 176, 178–79, 192, 233
Clark, Terry N., 7
Claymont School, 106
Clayton House, 35
Coleman du Pont Road, Inc., 51
Collins Park, 166–67
Community Action of Greater Wilmington (CAGW), 186–87
Community Power Structure, 6
Community Services Council of Delaware, 179
The Company State, 260
Concerned People of Riverside-Eastlake Extension, 185
Concerned Youth of the Northeast, 185
Concord Pike, 13, 72
Coner, Louise, 215
Conner, William J., 215, 218, 225
Copeland, Charles, 65

Council of Civic Associations of Brandywine Hundred, 223
Council on Youth, 116
Courthouse, 41, 43
Customs House, 178, 233–34

Dahl, Robert A., 6
Dallas, Joseph, 257
Delaware Automobile Association, 53
Delaware Avenue, 72
Delaware Citizens for Freeways, 148
Delaware Ethnic Studies and Cultural Center, 235–36
Delaware Expressways Committee, 150
Delaware Government Research Foundation, Inc., 218
Delaware Hospital, 253
Delaware Malleable Iron Company, 21
Delaware Memorial Bridge, 136–40, 142
Delaware Realty and Improvement Company, 65
Delaware Trust Company, 35, 88
De La Warr School District, 250
Democratic Party, 9, 148, 156, 173, 213, 215
Depression, 101–5
Dewey, John, 83
Dimensions in Urban History, 7
Di Sabatino, Ernest and Sons, 176
Downtown Wilmington, Incorporated, 194
Dravo Corporation, 115
Drew Elementary School, 168
Dunbar, Paul Lawrence, 95
du Pont family: influence on Wilmington, 8, 57, 156
du Pont, Alfred I., 38, 55, 63, 102
du Pont, Eugene, 38
du Pont, Frank 140–41, 143
du Pont, Henry Algernon, 48–49
du Pont, Henry Belin, 9, 172, 174, 179, 181, 194, 213, 215–16, 256–57
du Pont, Irénée, 65, 85, 157, 253

du Pont, Irénée, Jr., 203
du Pont, Lammot, 38, 65, 101, 253
du Pont, Pierre S.: and City Beautiful movement, 43; and Delaware Automobile Association, 53; and Depression relief, 103–4; and Du Pont Company, 4, 38, 40, 63–64, 85; and highway reform, 72–73; philanthropies of, 73–74, 76–77, 103–4; and regional planning, 99; and school reform, 74, 77, 79, 83; and Service Citizens of Delaware, 80; and Wilmington Institute Library, 75–76; and Wilmington Light, Power and Telephone Company, 55
du Pont, Pierre S., IV, 252
du Pont, T. Coleman, 38–39, 47, 49–51, 57, 63–64, 71
du Pont, Mrs. William Henry, 228
Du Pont Building, 40–41
Du Pont Company, 4, 60, 65, 88; Anti-Trust Suit (1914), 60–61; Chestnut Run facility, 120; and Depression, 101; diversification of, 84–85, 110, 119; and General Motors, 85; headquarters in Wilmington, 40, 193; housing, 69–70; and housing integration, 195, 204; influence on Wilmington, 4–5, 8–9, 87, 157, 169, 172–73, 260; powder mills, 15; reorganization (1902), 35, 38–40; reorganization (1915), 64–65; and World War I, 63, 66–67; and World War II, 8, 115–16
Du Pont Construction Company, 66
Du Pont Engineering Company, 73
Du Pont Experimental Station, 85, 119–20
Du Pont Highway, 52, 98

Eastlake, 113–14, 116, 129
East Side Home Owners Association, 133
Eden Park, 68
Edgemoor Gardens, 114

Edgemoor Terrace, 110–11
Edgewood Hills, 110
Elderly, the, 102
Electric service, 54, 56, 90
Elsmere, 57, 90, 93
Emalea P. Warner Junior High School, 83
Equitable Trust Company, 35
Evans, Brenda, 247
Evans v. Buchanan, 206, 247–48, 251
Ezion Methodist Church, 177–78

Fabrikoid, 85
Fairfax, 121
Family Society, 101–4
Farmers' market (King Street), 125
Farnhurst State Hospital, 106
Federal Building, 106
Federal Housing Administration, 108, 110
Fidanza, Nicholas, 33
Finch, Dudley, 129, 132, 135, 155, 225
Flowers, Leonard, 192, 200
Follin, James W., 131
Ford's Morocco Factory, 30
Foulkwoods, 223
Frank, William P., 48
Fulenwider, John J. B., 256
Furness, Frank, 34

Geisert, Dr. Gene, 244
General Motors Corporation, 85; Boxwood Plant, 118, 120
General Services Administration, 175
George Gray Elementary School, 83, 164
George, Henry, 49
Gibbons, John J., 206, 247
Githens, A. M., 76
Goett, Edward J., 158, 191, 202
Gottmann, Jean, 219
Governor's Housing Commission, 126
Grady, James, 202
Grand Opera House, 237–38

Greater Wilmington Development Council (GWDC), 9, 171–74, 179, 181–82, 191–92, 194, 201–3, 215, 232, 237, 239–40
Greenfield, Albert M., 232
Gun Powder Trade Association, 60
Gunther family, 232–33

Haber, Richard, 142, 146
Happy Valley, 233
Harlan and Hollingsworth Company, 21, 39, 85
Harrington family, 253
Harvey, LeRoy, 76
Haskell, Harry G., 153, 204–5, 215–17, 233, 235, 237–40, 245–46, 256
Hays, Samuel, 47
Heald, Joshua T., 18, 57
Hearn, James F., 139
Hercules Powder Company, 61, 65, 88, 110, 115, 195
Herlihy, Thomas, Jr., 129, 143, 146, 149–50
Herlihy, Mrs. Thomas, 186–87, 202
Highlands, 165
Highway Department: and Depression, 107; and highway construction, 98, 138; and interstate highways, 139, 142, 144, 148, 150, 153, 162; organization of, 51–52, 71; and regional planning, 100, 120; and suburbanization, 8, 117, 210; and urban renewal, 155
Highways: conditions of, 53; construction of, 13, 49–52, 71–73, 98–99, 107–8, 138–55; interstate, 9, 136, 142–54, 162
Historic preservation, 230–34
Historical Society of Delaware, 231, 237
Hollingsworth, Ellen J., 7
Hollingsworth, J. Rogers, 7
Holloway, Herman, Sr., 195–96
Home Builders Association of Delaware, 195
Hospitals, 253–58

Hotel Du Pont, 41
Housing: conditions of, 79; construction, 21–22, 24–26, 33, 89–90, 110–11, 119–20, 220–25; fair housing bill, 195; industrial, 66–70, 195–96; integration of, 166–70; planning, 100; residential patterns, 17–18, 90–91; public (low-income), 94, 128, 162, 171, 225–26; reform, 228–29; segregation of, 128–29; urban homesteading, 242
Howard High School, 83, 94–96
Hunter, Floyd, 6

Immigrants, 28–29; Americanization of, 78
Interstate and Defense Highway Act of 1956, 152
Interstate 95. See Highways
Interstate Railway Company, 54
Italians: community, 30, 33–34; employment of, 33

Jackson and Sharp Company, 39
Jackson-Cross Real Estate, 168
Janowitz, Morris, 259
Jews, 29
Johnson, Thomas, 49
Joint Committee on Hospital Merger, 254
Juvenile delinquency, 116

Keller, Beverly J. ("B.J."), 184
Kendree, Jack M., Planners, 168
Kennett Pike, 15, 73
Kirkwood Highway, 118, 120
Kilpatrick, William H., 80
King, Martin Luther, Jr.: assassination of, 194, 197–98
Kruse, Edwina, 95
Kurtz, Charles C., 56

Lammot, Eugene, 148–49, 156
Lancaster Pike, 15, 72
Larson, Peter A., 174–75, 193–94
Latchum, James L., 258

Layton, Caleb, 247
Layton, Rodney M., 202
Lea Boulevard, 108
League of Women Voters, 132, 171
Lee, Maurice du Pont, 147, 150, 157
Levy Court, 97, 210, 212–13, 215
Lewis, Archie, 205
Lindamere, 110
Lippincott's department store, 35, 50
Lynd, Helen M., 5
Lynd, Robert S., 5
Lyons, Garrett, 148

McClafferty, William J., Jr. ("Woody"), 218
McClellan, John L., 201
McHugh, Frank A., 103–4
McLaughlin, William, 252
Maloney, Thomas, 234–36, 240, 257–58
Market Street, 34–35, 124, 159, 232, 237; Mall, 234–35, 238
Marshall, Leo, 174, 215
Maynard, Clark, 106
Mayor's Employment and Relief Committee, 103–4, 107
Megalopolis, 219
Memorial Hospital, 253
Merchandise Mart, 124
Merritt Hotel, 34
Metcalf and Associates, 257
Middletown, 5, 7
Mill Creek Hundred, 223
Miller, Charles ("Chezzie"), 185, 190
Miller, William, 143, 148–49
Mills, 15
Mills, C. Wright, 11
Model Cities Program, 239–40
Montrose, 57–58
Mother Church of the African Union Methodists, 178
Mount Pleasant Special School District, 121
Movie theaters, 35
Moyed, Ralph, 192
Mullen, Ethelda, 101

Myers, William, 239

Nader, Ralph, 260
National Association for the Advancement of Colored People (NAACP), 196, 258
National Guard, 198, 200, 204
Neighborhood House, 34
Neilan, Edwin P., 172
Nelson, Alice Dunbar, 95
Nelson, Robert J., 95
Newark School District, 249
New Castle County government: reorganization, 207, 210, 212–15, 218–19
New Castle County Housing Authority, 226
New Castle County Planning Department, 219
New Castle Road, 72
New Haven (Connecticut): as industrial city, 6
Newport Pike, 72
Newport to Gap Pike, 15
New York-Delaware Realty Construction Company, 68
Nields, John P., 74, 76
Nolen, John, 68
North Side Improvement Company, 24

Oakmont, 167
Obara, Frank J., 149–51
Odell, Joseph H., 78, 80
Office for Inner City Development, 184
Operation Breakthrough, 224
Operation Free Streets, 204
Opportunities and Industrialization Center, 182–83

Parking authority, 125
Parks, 33, 106, 147, 218
Penn, William, 12
Pennsylvania Avenue, 72

Pennsylvania Railroad, 65; car shops, 20–21; passenger station, 21, 34
Peoples Railway Company, 20, 54
Peoples Settlement, 177
Peterson, Russell, 181, 204–5, 215, 224–25, 237
Philadelphia: compared to Wilmington, 16
Philadelphia Pike, 13, 72
Philadelphia, Wilmington and Baltimore Railroad, 16
Philanthropy, 104–5
Pierre S. du Pont High School, 83–84, 106, 164, 244
Pike Creek Valley, 223
Plan Omega, 257–58, 260
Poles: community, 30–32, 165; Turn Hall, 32
Politics, 9, 47–49, 57
The Politics of School Desegregation, 251
Polly Drummond Civic Association, 224
"Poplar Street Project A," 131
Poppiti, Michael, 177
Port of Wilmington, 65–66, 106
Positive Action Committee, 250
Preston, W. Ellis, 176
Price's Run Service Center, 181
Progress and Poverty, 49–50
Progressive movement, 41, 43, 45
Pryor, Richard, 158, 185
Public schools: Board of Education and, 80, 82, 247, 251; and busing, 9, 207, 248; desegregation of, 123, 243–53; Pierre S. du Pont and school reform, 79–80, 82–84; and school districts, 8–9, 121; segregation of, 123, 248; suburbanization and, 93, 121–23
Public Works Administration, 84, 106
Pusey and Jones Company, 65
Pyrites Company, 65

Quaker Hill, 203
Queen Theater, 35

Raffel, Jeffrey, 251
Randolph, Mary, 133
Randolph v. Wilmington Housing Authority, 133–35
Raskob, John J., 41, 43–44, 74, 77, 99–101
Rayfield, George, 166
Reed, James H., 49
Reeder, Charles B., 233
Reese, Charles L., Jr., 254
Reese, Monsignor Thomas, 184–85
Referendum League, 46
Regional planning, 99–100, 120
Regional Planning Commission of New Castle County, 120
Regional Planning Federation of the Philadelphia Tri-State District, 99
Reilly, John E., 145–46
Republican Party, 8–9, 48, 57, 102, 210, 215
Rhoads, Philip G., 228
Richards, Robert H., 45
Richardson Park, 58, 90, 93
Riots, 9, 198
Riverside project, 162
Rodney Square, 41, 43, 74
Romney, George, 226
Rusten, Allen, 216, 240

Sacred Heart Catholic Church, 149, 163
Saint Anthony's Church, 34
Saint Hedwigs Church, 32
Saint Paul's Roman Catholic Church, 149–50, 163
Saint Stanislaus Kostka Church, 31
Salsbury, Stephen, 39
Salvation Army, 103
Sanger, Richard, 162–63, 171
School Code of 1919, 79–80
Schramm, Patricia, 216, 236
Schulze, Robert O., 5
Schwartz, Murray M., 248, 251
Sears, Roebuck & Company, 124
Service Citizens of Delaware, 77–80
Sharp, Hugh Rodney, 65

Sharp, Hugh Rodney, Jr., 141, 149, 151
Sharpley, 228
Shaw, Benjamin F., 154
Shellpot Park, 20
Shipbuilding, 85
Shipley, William, 13
Slums, 111–12, 163–64; clearance of, 112, 125–35, 155, 168–70, 203–4; and urban renewal, 133, 160–61, 176–78, 181, 192–94, 230–32, 235–37, 239–42
Society Hill (Philadelphia), 232
South Wilmington, 111
Sparks, Frank C., 103
Splane, Francis X. ("Pat"), 171
State Human Relations Council, 195–96
Stock-market crash, 1929, 100–101
Stoeckle Hotel, 34
Strawbridge and Clothier, 124
Street and Sewer Department, 21
Suburban County Hospital Task Force, 258
Suburbanization, 8, 57–58, 88–90, 108, 116–21, 123–24, 212, 259
Suburban Road Act of 1945, 117
Suburban Water Company, 93
Suburbs: annexation of, 91, 93

Taft, Robert A., 125
Tanneries, 30–31, 85
Tarrant, Shirley M., 258
Taxation, 216–17
Taxpayers' Revolt, the, 225
Teaford, Jon C., 259
Terry, Charles L., 188, 195–98, 200–201, 215
Thomas F. Bayard School, 83
Tilton, E. L., 76
Town Hall, 43, 231
Townsend, John G., Jr., 52
Traffic control, 98, 125
Trillin, Calvin, 204
Trinity Vicinity, 233

Trolley lines, 18–21, 53–57; electric, 19
Tucker, John Francis, 34

Union Park Gardens, 68–69, 100, 114
United Neighbors for Progress, 181
United States Shipbuilding Company, 21, 39
Upham, Charles M., 72
Utility companies, 55–56, 91, 210

Vandever Avenue, 21
Venema, James, 252

Wagner, Robert, 108
Wagner-Steagall Housing Act of 1937, 108, 110, 112
Wagstaff, Roy, 196
Walnut Street Bridge, 154
Walz, August F., 156
John Wanamaker department store, 124
Warner, Irving, 153
Warner Company, 153
Washington Heights, 24
Washington Heights Methodist Church, 25
Washington Street Extension, 108
Water Department, 93
Water supply, 93
Wawaset, 69–70
Weaver, Carolyn, 132–33
Weaver, Jennie, 34
Weiner, Leon, 148, 167, 176–77, 225
Welfare agencies, 101–2, 182, 186–91, 197; and unemployment relief, 103–4, 106–7
Welfare Foundation, 256
West Center City Neighborhood Association, 239
Westover Hills, 89–90, 100
West Side Conservation Association, 181
White Coalition for Justice Without Repression, 204
Whiteside, George, III, 235

Wilhelm, Paul A., 193
William P. Bancroft School, 83
Willing, Thomas, 13
Willingtown Square, 237
Wilmington: business district, 35,
    124, 175–76; and city planning, 16,
    91, 96, 98, 117, 174, 210–12, 219;
    colonial background of, 12–13;
    comparison with other industrial
    cities, 3–7; economy of, 15, 87,
    101, 114–16; ethnic neighborhoods
    in, 27–34, 165; geography of, 13,
    20; government of, 45, 155–56,
    216–18; growth of, 17; industries
    of, 11–12, 16, 21, 39, 65, 85, 87–
    88, 110; population of, 20, 160,
    220; 7th ward, 20; 9th ward, 20,
    24, 26, 29, 89, 124, 163–64
Wilmington and Great Valley Turn-
    pike, 13
Wilmington and Northern Railroad,
    49
Wilmington and Philadelphia Trac-
    tion Company, 54, 56–57
Wilmington and City Railway Com-
    pany, 18–20, 53–54, 56
Wilmington Construction Company,
    110
Wilmington Gas and Electric Com-
    pany, 55
Wilmington General Hospital, 253
Wilmington High School, 82–83, 93,
    244
Wilmington Housing Authority: pub-
    lic housing projects, 113, 128–29;
    and slum clearance, 112, 131, 133–

35, 203; and urban renewal, 168–
    69, 176–77, 194, 242; and Willing-
    town Square, 236
Wilmington Institute Free Library,
    33, 74–76, 218
Wilmington Light, Power and Tele-
    phone Company, 55
Wilmington Marine Terminal, 66
Wilmington Medical Center, 9, 207,
    242–43, 255–58
Wilmington Opera Society, 237
Wilmington Renewal Associates, 176
Wilmington Savings Fund Society, 35
Wilmington Trust Company, 40, 88
Wilmington Youth Emergency Action
    Council (WYEAC), 185–91, 201–4
Wilson, Charles E., 118
Wilson, Horace, 57
Wilson, James, 147
Wilson, Robert A., 182
Wolcott, Daniel J., 135
Women: wartime occupations of, 115
Woodlawn Trustees, 33, 128, 226–28
World War I, 65–66; housing, 66–70
World War II, 8, 112, 114–15; hous-
    ing, 68–70, 113–14; V-J Day, 116
Worth Brothers steel plant, 65
Wright, Caleb, 206, 247

Young Mens' Christian Association
    (YMCA), 179, 184
Ypsilanti (Michigan): comparison with
    Wilmington, 5–6

Zion Lutheran Church, 163